Everyone's

Everyone's Democracy

Confronting Political Inequality in America

Elliott Fullmer

McFarland & Company, Inc., Publishers
Jefferson, North Carolina

ISBN (print) 978-1-4766-8857-2
ISBN (ebook) 978-1-4766-4704-3

LIBRARY OF CONGRESS AND BRITISH LIBRARY
CATALOGUING DATA ARE AVAILABLE

Library of Congress Control Number 2022033309

Front cover image © Andrii Yalanskyi/Shutterstock

Printed in the United States of America

*McFarland & Company, Inc., Publishers
Box 611, Jefferson, North Carolina 28640
www.mcfarlandpub.com*

To my little cupcake, Lily

Contents

Acknowledgments

No person is an island, and I am in debt to many people and organizations who have aided both this project and my professional development over the years.

Though this book is ostensibly a commentary on American politics, it draws heavily on history to trace the development and evolution of U.S. institutions. My love of history began early with the help of several outstanding teachers, including Sister Marie Fenton, Anthony Iaconelli, and Joseph Carmichael. My parents, Helene and Keith Fullmer, also deserve thanks for allowing me to follow my interests and passions from a young age.

The arguments in this book were strengthened by various organizations that routinely publish helpful commentary and analysis pertaining to American democracy, including the Annenberg Public Policy Center, the Brennan Center for Justice, Equal Citizens, New America, and the Pew Research Center. Academic research by Robert M. Alexander, Robert Dahl, Lee Drutman, Charlotte Hill, Alex Keena, Michael Latner, Doug Mack, Lilliana Mason, Anthony McGann, Amy Melissa McKay, and Charles Anthony Smith was also particularly helpful.

I am grateful to family, friends, colleagues, and students who have sharpened my insights through rich conversations. While this list is surely incomplete, I wish to thank Michael Bailey, Richard Banach, Lauren Bell, J. Furman Daniel, III, Sean Gordon, Ben and Jessica Lazarus, Jim Lengle, Richard Meagher, Yu-Ming Liou, Paul Musgrave, Fouad Pervez, Zacchary Ritter, Kirby Struhar, Taylor Williams, Gary Wasserman, Clyde Wilcox, and John Yannelli.

More generally, my students at Randolph-Macon College are a constant source of motivation. Their keen insights and questions inspire my own work. I am also grateful to my college's Rashkind Family Foundation Endowment, which provided generous funding throughout my 2020–21 sabbatical.

Being married to a savvy, assiduous, and brilliant political consultant has numerous advantages. Conversations with my wife, Jenna, always bring new insights, ideas, and perspectives regarding the political world. Our frequent discussions have undoubtedly made me a stronger teacher and researcher.

Finally, our young daughter Lily deserves special thanks. While the pandemic brought so much pain and loss, I am eternally grateful that we had so much quality time together. (And thanks for listening when I sometimes outlined arguments for the book out loud!)

Preface

In May 2020, I submitted my grades and began my first academic sabbatical. With the Covid-19 pandemic raging, it would surely not be the sabbatical I had planned. There would be less "recharging," traveling, and recreational reading. And there would be more childcare, masking, and social isolation. While unconventional, my sabbatical did afford me the opportunity to think broadly about American politics and its current predicament. Following years of researching electoral reforms using large datasets and complicated statistical models, I appreciated the opportunity to set aside the *trees* and spend some time examining the *forest*. After more than a decade of teaching and exploring, what did I ultimately have to say about American politics in the twenty-first century?

While I have perspectives on presidential power, federal spending, federalism, systemic racism and sexism, and more, I felt most driven (and qualified) to comment on the state of political equality in the United States. Simply put, I was troubled by the extent to which many U.S. political institutions treat citizens unequally. While new amendments and judicial interpretations have made the U.S. Constitution more democratic since 1787, there is considerably more work to do. Furthermore, I was frustrated that debates on the status of American democracy are so often driven by partisan political motives rather than basic principles of fairness. So in between feeding, changing, and chasing a quarantined toddler, I ventured to complete a readable, objective, and research-driven evaluation of political (in)equality in the U.S. While I hoped to offer some specific prescriptions for the ills facing American institutions, my more modest goal was simply to advance the conversation on these important topics. The pages that follow represent my best effort to do that. Any mistakes or imperfections are mine alone.

Introduction

On October 26, 2020, the U.S. Senate confirmed Amy Coney Barrett as the newest justice on the U.S. Supreme Court. Just 48 years old, Barrett had served as a judge on the U.S. Court of Appeals for the Seventh Circuit for three years. Now, with a lifetime appointment on the Supreme Court secured by a narrow 52–48 Senate vote, Barrett seemed poised to anchor the High Court's conservative wing for decades to come.

Some objected to Barrett's confirmation due to her well-known socially conservative views. Barrett had opposed legal abortion and gun control, ruled in favor of strict immigration enforcement, and refused to broadly apply anti-discrimination statutes. But Barrett's views were not the only reason her confirmation was controversial. Her appointment—following the death of Justice Ruth Bader Ginsburg—came just weeks before the 2020 presidential election. Many believed that with the election so soon (in fact, tens of millions of Americans had *already* voted early), Ginsburg's replacement should be made during the following presidential term. Critics felt that Senate Republicans were being hypocritical by advancing Barrett's nomination after they had refused to allow President Obama to fill a Supreme Court vacancy for 11 months at the end of his second term.

While it received far less attention than the above criticisms, Barrett's nomination also served as an unfortunate reminder of the democratic deficiencies plaguing American politics. Barrett was appointed by a president, Donald Trump, who had lost the popular vote by nearly three million votes in 2016. In fact, Barrett became the fifth sitting Supreme Court justice (the third selected by Trump) appointed by a president who received fewer votes than his opponent.[1] Meanwhile, the 52 senators who voted to confirm Barrett represented 13.5 million *fewer* Americans than the 48 senators who opposed her nomination. By winning the support of senators representing lightly populated states, Barrett was able to secure sufficient backing despite the fact that senators representing a majority of the country opposed her. Setting aside her views or the timing of her confirmation,

3

it was difficult to argue that Barrett had earned a mandate to rule on constitutional matters ranging from LGBTQ+ rights to healthcare policy for generations to come.

Political Equality in America

The principle of political equality is not complicated. It simply posits that all adult citizens are entitled to equal influence over their government. In a democratic republic, where citizens choose representatives to govern on their behalf, political equality is present when all citizens (1) are easily able to vote and (2) have their votes count equally. When this is the case, candidates securing majority (or at least plurality) support in elections can credibly claim to best represent the collective "will of the people."[2] Subsequently, the government's decisions are legitimate because "the people" selected the officeholders who made them. In upholding political equality, a democratic government may still wish to erect protections against majority tyranny. It may, for example, require supermajorities for certain actions or divide power between institutions and allow them to "check and balance" one another. Such barriers to action do not violate the principle of political equality so long as they do not empower some individuals more than others. The aforementioned appointment and confirmation of Supreme Court Justice Amy Coney Barrett, however, *does* highlight clear violations of this principle. The president who appointed her was not preferred by a majority or plurality of voters. Donald Trump earned just 46.1 percent of the popular vote in 2016, but won a majority in the Electoral College nonetheless. Those senators choosing to confirm Barrett did not represent a majority of Americans. To make matters worse (from a political equality perspective), Barrett was the third Supreme Court justice successfully appointed by Trump during his single four-year term. His three predecessors—Presidents Bill Clinton, George W. Bush, and Barack Obama—each appointed just two justices during their respective eight-year stays in the White House. Trump's imprint on the High Court was therefore disproportionate to the confidence placed in him by the American people.

Political inequality has always been part of the American system. The Constitution crafted by the Framers in 1787 had clear democratic defects. Most glaring was the Framers' approval of slavery, which denied millions of Black Americans *any* rights of citizenship. In addition, the Constitution failed to guarantee voting rights, allowing states to deny participation as they desired. The result was widespread disenfranchisement for free Blacks, women, and (for a more limited time) non-landowning white males. Furthermore, there were limited opportunities for *any* citizens to vote in national elections. U.S. senators would be chosen by state legislatures, while states could decide if eligible citizens would play a role in presidential elections.

The Constitution also advanced political inequities through malapportioned institutional designs. Institutions are malapportioned when they weigh the votes of some citizens more than others. For example, imagine that a city has five wards. One ward has 100,000 residents, two have 50,000 residents, and two have 10,000 residents. Despite the population discrepancies, each ward is given one vote on the city council. In this example, residents of the most populated ward are the victims of malapportionment, as they will be served by one representative (comprising 20 percent of the council) despite having over 45 percent of the city's residents. The Connecticut Compromise, which created the bicameral U.S. Congress (consisting of the House and the Senate), left the country with a deeply malapportioned national legislature. Each state was granted two senators regardless of its population. At the time the Constitution was ratified, this meant that residents of Delaware (the smallest state) enjoyed over 12 times as much Senate representation as those living in Virginia (the largest state).

The U.S. House of Representatives, with seat allocation based on state population, was designed to be more representative. But malapportionment would not be entirely absent from the House. Until the Supreme Court ended the practice in 1963, many states routinely created House districts with huge population discrepancies. In the early 1960s, for example, both Michigan and Texas had House districts with more than four times as many residents as their respective smallest districts.

The malapportioned Senate would also create inequities in the presidential election process. Rather than allow citizens to directly choose the president, the Framers instead created the Electoral College. Each state was given a number of electors equivalent to its House and Senate delegations. Because the Senate is badly malapportioned, electoral vote allocations to states were destined to be as well (though not as severely). Lightly populated states would have more electoral votes per person than larger states, giving them disproportionate say over the nation's chief executive.

While the Constitution came with major democratic flaws, it has nonetheless managed to maintain its legitimacy for over 200 years. The reasons are arguably twofold. First, while the document's particulars hardly advanced political equality, its preamble did set a bold standard for egalitarianism. It famously declared:

> We the People of the United States, in Order to form a more perfect Union, establish Justice, insure domestic Tranquility, provide for the common

defence, promote the general Welfare, and secure the Blessings of Liberty to ourselves and our Posterity, do ordain and establish this Constitution for the United States of America.

The Preamble is clear that "the people" are charged with forming and directing their own government. It does not declare that only certain types of people (e.g., those with money, those of a particular race) shall be privileged to do so. The term "the people" most logically means all people, much like "the workers," "the troops," or "the bankers" refers to all members of these respective groups unless otherwise noted. Because the Preamble expresses such a lofty, inclusive vision, reformers—both citizens and politicians alike—have repeatedly been able to cite the Constitution when calling for political and social reforms. Consider the Declaration of Sentiments drafted at the Seneca Falls Convention in 1848. In formally demanding new rights for women, attendees simply added the words "and women" to the Constitution's Preamble. To a majority of activists present, the Constitution was fundamentally correct in calling for "the people" to "ordain and establish" any government that holds power over them. It simply needed to clarify that "the people" indeed includes women.

The Constitution has also proven resilient because of its capacity for change. Amending the Constitution is difficult, which explains why it has only happened 27 times (and just 17 since 1791). But many of the Constitution's aforementioned defects *have* been corrected through amendments. The Thirteenth Amendment banned slavery, while the Fourteenth Amendment guaranteed "equal protection" under the law. The Fifteenth, Nineteenth, and Twenty-Sixth Amendments barred voting rights from being denied on the basis of race, sex, or age (for those at least 18 years of age), respectively. The Seventeenth Amendment provided for the direct election of senators, while the Twenty-Third Amendment gave the District of Columbia voting rights in presidential elections. In some cases, most notably the Voting Rights Act of 1965, additional congressional action has been needed to properly enforce constitutional rights.

The Constitution has also relied on evolving interpretations of its words to become truer to its creed. In the 1950s and 1960s, for example, the Supreme Court led by Chief Justice Earl Warren expanded the scope of the Fourteenth Amendment's Equal Protection Clause to ban racially segregated (and unequal) public schools, end anti-miscegenation laws, and prohibit malapportioned House districts. Later courts would expand "equal protection" guarantees by restricting gender and LGBTQ+ discrimination.

Through constitutional amendments, legislative acts, and court interpretations, the U.S. has gradually—if too slowly—moved towards political equality.

In this book, I argue that while progress has indeed been made, there is much more work to do. Political inequities in the Constitution remain unaddressed, while new challenges are emerging. Malapportionment in the Senate now gives some Americans nearly 70 times as much influence in the upper chamber as others, making it nearly six times less representative today than in 1790.[3] Owing mostly to Senate malapportionment, the Electoral College weighs small state residents almost four times as much as large state residents; as a result, the country occasionally gets presidents that most voters do not want. While House districts are now required to have roughly equal population in all states, partisan gerrymandering—currently allowed by the federal courts—is worsening. State legislative majorities are finding it easier to draw House seats in a manner that makes it more likely that their party will secure more seats. When one party is more easily able to convert votes to seats (and therefore power in the national legislature), political equality is compromised.

While various constitutional amendments and laws now protect voting rights for most Americans, citizens remain burdened by unnecessary photo identification requirements, insufficient polling sites, long lines, voter purges, and confusing procedures. In some states, problems are growing due to politically motivated voter suppression efforts. Disenfranchisement is even worse in the District of Columbia and the U.S. territories, where millions of Americans have no congressional representation or (in the case of the territories) say in choosing the president.

Other institutional designs are at odds with egalitarianism. The chance nature of federal court appointments and the exceptionally long tenure of judges means that some presidents (and Senates) have disproportionate capacity to shape courts. Given the enormous role that the federal courts now play in setting public policy, this is problematic. Regarding campaign finance, the Supreme Court's current interpretation of the First Amendment allows wealthy citizens, businesses, and interest groups to dump millions into political campaigns. Research suggests that this spending is a wise investment, as donors gain disproportionate access to elected officials and increased agenda-setting power in Congress. Finally, American democracy is threatened by the rise of disinformation and bias in both traditional and new forms of media. Too many Americans lack the resources or skills to navigate a political environment riddled by fake news, sensationalism, and conspiracy theories. Without the ability to obtain and digest accurate information about political developments, citizens simply cannot hold elected leaders accountable.

Why Care About Political Equality?

"Life is unfair!"

Nearly all of us hear this line fairly early in our lives, generally from a caretaker, a relative, a teacher, or a friend. And then, sure enough, we are continuously reminded that it is true. As a young child, it may rain on your birthday, but not on your friend's. Your buddy may have newer toys, better shoes, or a bigger room. You may get stuck with the worse algebra teacher, the more abrasive coach, or the less sympathetic admissions officer. Some of your classmates may have more success dating, less acne, or more timely growth spurts. As we get older, we experience and observe far more consequential embodiments of unfairness. Fate claims the lives of thousands of young, law-abiding, kind people each year, robbing them of the joys of life. Physical and mental health problems, fatal or not, surely do not burden all of us equally. Finally, economic inequality means that Jeff Bezos and Elon Musk are worth more than $100 billion, while several million Americans sleep in cars, on public benches, and under bridges each year.

Indeed, inequality is everywhere. It is a basic fact of life on this planet. So why should we care about political equality? We cannot make life entirely fair, so why gripe over some imperfections with the political system? After all, the U.S. has surely functioned *well enough*, given that the nation is one of the world's most prosperous. Right?

It is reasonable to ask why political equality should demand our attention. And while this book is not fundamentally about political philosophy, it is important to briefly highlight some central assumptions that motivate calls (including mine) for political equality. First, unlike some of the aforementioned forms of unfairness, political equality is something that we (people) can reasonably control. We cannot prevent all natural disasters, fatal illnesses, and freak accidents, but as democratic citizens, we do have a measure of control over the structure of our governments. Much like the scourges of tax evasion, sexual assault, and pollution, there are actions that we can take to reduce unfairness in government. After all, it was the tireless activism of abolitionists, suffragists, and civil rights marchers that made the United States a more inclusive democratic society in previous generations.

Given that political equality is something that we *can* affect, it is worth examining whether it is indeed something that we *should* pursue. Arguably, the fact that humans are generally bothered by perceived injustice is a pretty good indication that advancing fairness is consistent with human nature. As children, we get angry when our sibling gets a nicer gift than us. As teenagers, we get annoyed when our curfew is earlier than that of our friends. And as adults, it bothers us when a colleague with the same experience and skills earns more money. As political scientist Robert Dahl writes in *On Political Equality*, "Human beings are naturally endowed with a sensitivity to the unequal distribution of rewards to others whom they view as comparable to themselves in relevant ways."[4] Dahl notes that humans are not alone in having a preference for fairness. He cites a study of capuchin monkeys who were each given granite pebbles and taught to exchange them with experimenters for cucumbers and grapes. Previous experiments had demonstrated that the monkeys overwhelmingly preferred grapes to cucumbers. In the study, those monkeys who were (1) given a cucumber in exchange for their pebble and (2) could see that other monkeys were given a grape for completing the same task became upset.[5] Because it was unfair!

In his 1971 book, *A Theory of Justice*, political philosopher John Rawls employs a thought experiment to demonstrate that fairness and equality are inherently just. Rawls imagines how people would determine principles of justice from behind a hypothetical "veil of ignorance." He describes an "original position," whereby

> no one knows his place in society, his class position or social status, nor does anyone know his fortune in the distribution of assets and abilities, his intelligence, strength, and the like. [We can] ... even assume that the parties do not know their conceptions of the good or their special psychological propensities.[6]

Behind this veil of ignorance, people would have no sense of privilege or marginalization. They would be wholly unaware of whether inequality would ultimately benefit or hurt them. Under this condition, Rawls argues that people would reason that "each person is to have an equal right to the most extensive liberty compatible with a similar liberty for others." In other words, all persons would be granted the same basic rights and powers in a society (i.e., political equality). In the real world, of course, political actors and citizens often *do* wish to retain unequal power structures. Why? In many cases, those already enjoying an advantage are reluctant to forfeit it. As a result, they may develop or defend arguments to rationalize why unfair institutions are actually prudent and necessary. For Rawls, however, if such advantages never existed, people would embrace equality when forming institutions.

In addition to being just, political equality is also prudent. As philosophers Thomas Hobbes, John Locke, Jean-Jacques Rousseau, and Rawls have all suggested, government can be viewed as a social contract. In democratic societies, people concede personal liberties in the interest of empowering a collective unit (a government) to pool resources and address problems that they cannot reasonably solve themselves. People need a variety of services—security, water treatment, highway repairs, etc.—that they cannot practically perform alone. In modern times, societies have often determined that other collective services, including safety net programs, serve the public interest as well. So, people form governments, choose representatives who will lead them, and maintain the power to remove officials if they do not prudently wield their authority.

There is a longstanding debate regarding how a representative should approach decisions in office. Are representatives merely *delegates* who should follow their constituents' wishes? Or are they—as Edmund Burke famously argued in the late eighteenth century[7]—*trustees* who are charged with acting according to their conscience, even when doing so is at odds with those they represent? In her 1967 book, *The Concept of Representation*, political theorist Hanna Pitkin argues that representatives must serve both roles. Elected officials are charged with "making present" those who cannot be present themselves (citizens). But in "acting for" one's constituents, representatives cannot realistically be "mere instrument(s)," as governing inevitably requires discretion.[8] A House member forced to vote on 30 amendments to a bill in a late-night session cannot accurately poll her constituents on each particular measure. Furthermore, even if this were possible, representatives have a responsibility to convert constituents' views into coherent and workable public policy. Nevertheless, there are strong indications that citizens generally expect their elected officials to dutifully advance their own preferences. Researchers have observed that citizens are more likely to see their governments as legitimate if they believe that they accurately represent the popular will.[9] On an individual level, others have reported that citizens are more supportive of governments that give them what they want (shocking!).[10] And logic dictates that *more* citizens will generally be pleased with a government's decisions when that government has been chosen by a majority. It is when minority coalitions gain power of governing coalitions—due to political inequality—that a mismatch between society's collective will and those in power is more likely to occur. Such a mismatch only breeds despair and disillusionment with government and those who run it. No one benefits from that.

Plan for the Book

Growing up in New Jersey, I am naturally a Bruce Springsteen fan. I have attended 15 live shows since 2006, including one in Oslo, Norway! My office walls at Randolph-Macon College feature multiple Bruce posters, a sad attempt to convert my Generation Z students to his music. When asked about his inspiration as a songwriter, Bruce often comments, "I have spent my life judging the distance between American reality and the American dream."[11] While I lack Bruce's poetic and musical talents, this quotation largely encapsulates my goals for this book. The United States has certainly set high democratic ideals for itself. In its founding years, it deemed that "all men are created equal" and that "we the people" are entitled to form a government. Just years later, it enshrined protections for religious freedom, political speech, due process, and more into its Constitution. Following a bloody civil war, it would not only (finally) end human bondage, but also guarantee "equal protection" under the law for all citizens. But while the United States has set high standards for its democracy, it has often struggled to achieve them. Today, while great strides have surely been made, political equality remains elusive.

In the chapters that follow, I highlight the democratic deficiencies that continue to plague American politics. While I do not submit that my efforts capture *all* such inequities, I do venture to tackle a broad range of them. Chapter 1 explores Senate malapportionment and its effects, while Chapter 2 details the many undemocratic features of the Electoral College. Chapter 3 focuses on political inequality in the House, paying close attention to the troubling rise of partisan gerrymandering. Chapter 4 lends much-needed attention to the shameful disenfranchisement of Americans living in Washington, D.C., and the territories, while Chapter 5 highlights flaws regarding the appointment and confirmation of federal judges. Chapter 6 examines recent voter suppression efforts, while Chapter 7 chronicles the troubling influence of wealthy donors on elected officials. Finally, Chapter 8 confronts developments in the political information environment, including the rise of polarized media sources and the proliferation of misinformation (and disinformation) on the internet.

In addition to describing these various democratic deficits, I take great care to document the historical processes that have shaped institutions. Each of the topics covered in this book owes its current predicament to laws, court cases, social movements, and norms from past years. Only through an understanding of history can we fully appreciate why systems operate as they do. Furthermore, examining the dynamics that have inspired change in the past offers important lessons regarding the possibilities of (and barriers to) future reforms.

In each chapter, I discuss specific changes that could improve political equality in the institution in question. In some cases, recommended changes involve legislation that has already been considered by Congress in recent years. In others, reform ideas are admittedly more ambitious. While I am candid about their obstacles, I do not shy away from bold reform proposals; history reveals that many ideas initially seen as radical and unachievable can eventually gain broad support. Abolition and women's suffrage once seemed like hopeless fringe efforts, but thankfully reformers persisted. Just a few decades ago, the idea that same-sex marriage would be a constitutionally protected right seemed unfathomable. More recently, Black Lives Matter has gone from a highly unpopular movement in the mid–2010s to one supported by a majority of Americans less than a decade later. When courageous citizens help bring awareness to injustice and demand change, society's consciousness can change. And when people gain new perspectives or become impassioned by new concerns, reforms that once seemed far-reaching become possible.

Even bold reforms, however, are nearly always bound to be imperfect. When considering changes to any system, including a government, it is essential to understand the power of path dependence. Society is always constrained by decisions made in the past. Any future changes will need to consider existing structures in place. For example, many political inequities in the United States are a direct result of *states* themselves. The Senate is badly malapportioned because it confers influence to states in a way that over- or under-represents their respective populations. If states did not exist, and the national legislature simply represented people (not political sub-units), political equality would be advanced in the national government. States, however, are fundamental to the nation's creation and operation. It is inconceivable that they would be entirely eliminated. As a result, efforts to make the national government more equitable will very likely need to navigate the continued existence of states. This, like any prevailing path-dependent structure, limits options moving forward. But this truth should not dissuade reformers, as substantial improvements to American democracy are still possible. To paraphrase Voltaire, "Never let the perfect be the enemy of the good."

Unlike many recent books focused on democracy reform, I do not approach this topic from a partisan or ideological perspective. I am not driven by a desire to see one political party improve its position in government. My interest in this book is simply to advance fairness and equality in the American political system. This, and nothing else, is the first principle that guides my diagnosis of problems and proposed solutions. I operate from a belief that our democracy (and therefore our country) is strongest when the national government accurately reflects our collective will.

Let me clarify, however, that my approach is *nonpartisan* rather than *bipartisan*. And what is the difference? In short, a *nonpartisan* approach does not consider partisan attitudes or consequences when assessing problems and potential solutions. Conversely, a *bipartisan* approach considers the interests of both major parties. Consider the following hypothetical example. Party A says the Earth is flat. Party B says the Earth is round. If asked to evaluate these claims, a nonpartisan analysis would quickly conclude that the Earth is indeed round. This determination would be made without regard to the parties' positions. The fact that the conclusion agrees with one party is irrelevant because objectivity and truth are the only important variables. A bipartisan analysis, however, would be hesitant to side with one party over another. Instead, it would likely conclude, "The parties have different perspectives with regards to the shape of the Earth."

So, while I do not approach this book with a partisan or ideological motive, there are instances where my grievances and reform ideas are consistent with those advanced by a political party. More bluntly, in recent years Democrats have clearly been disadvantaged by political inequality across American institutions. Senate malapportionment arguably helps Republicans, who are stronger (as of now) in small, rural states. This advantage extends to presidential elections, where the Electoral College has sent two Republicans—George W. Bush and Donald Trump—to the White House since 2000 despite each losing the national popular vote. House gerrymandering currently favors Republicans nationally, as the party controls the redistricting process in most places that allow it. Since 2010, Republicans have also made it more difficult to vote in many states; party officials and others clearly believe these efforts disproportionately hurt Democratic voters. Finally, the denial of statehood for the District of Columbia likely costs Democrats two senators in each Congress. Given these disproportionate effects, Democrats have recently led efforts to correct associated political inequities. I support these efforts whenever they bring the American political system closer to fairness and equality—not because they help Democrats, but because they move the country closer to its elusive founding vision. In my view, anyone who is willing to put political equality first must be willing to support needed reforms, regardless of which party advances them or stands to benefit in the short run.

Because in the long run, *all* Americans benefit from political equality.

CHAPTER 1

A Fateful Compromise

Nearly every semester, I teach one section of Introduction to American Government to a group consisting mostly of college freshmen. When I get to the class on the Philadelphia Convention, I discuss the Connecticut Compromise.[1] I do not cover all of the Convention's deliberations, but I review the major points. There were competing plans for representation in the new legislature (Congress). Large states mostly supported the Virginia Plan, which called for a two-chamber legislature with representation based on a state's population in both chambers. Small states supported the New Jersey Plan, a one-chamber legislature where representation would be equal (one seat) regardless of a state's size. The Framers struggled to break the impasse but ultimately settled on a historic compromise. The new Congress would have two chambers. One, the House of Representatives, would be based on a state's population. The other, the Senate, would represent states equally regardless of their populations. The House, the "lower chamber," would have more total seats, shorter terms for representatives (two years), and slightly more lenient eligibility requirements. The Senate, the "upper chamber," would have fewer total seats (two per state), longer terms (six years), and slightly stricter eligibility requirements.[2]

At this point, a good number of students from all walks of life generally nod in approval. And I can never blame them. The Connecticut Compromise, on its face, was a sensible deal made by responsible statesmen. Delegates had different interests and found a middle ground. Isn't that what many of us wish our elected leaders would do more often?

But not all compromises are good. If one hypothetical coalition says the sky is blue and another says it is yellow, an even-handed compromise might declare that the sky is green. The middle ground of two positions does not always produce a sensible outcome. Such was the case with the Connecticut Compromise, which established one of the world's most malapportioned legislative chambers. Even worse, because of disproportionate population growth across the states, the degree of malapportionment in the Senate is far worse today than at the time of the Philadelphia Convention.

15

The Senate is hardly the only legislative chamber in the democratic world to suffer from malapportionment. Other countries also have chambers that represent geographic units rather than population, leading to the over-representation of rural areas. While I do not believe malapportionment is *ever* acceptable, two factors make the U.S. Senate a much bigger problem than comparable legislatures abroad. First, the extent of malapportionment is far worse. In the U.S., residents of the smallest state (Wyoming) enjoy 68.5 times as much representation in the Senate as residents of the largest state (California) do. Only two democracies—Argentina and Brazil—have legislative chambers with a higher level of malapportionment.[3] Second, it is typical for upper chambers to feature greater malapportionment than lower chambers in bicameral systems. But most nations with a malapportioned upper chamber grant it disproportionately less power (often significantly less). With the exception of Italy, no other member of NATO or the European Union has an upper chamber whose power evenly matches that of its lower house.[4]

The U.S. Constitution, by contrast, gives the Senate extraordinary powers. In addition to shared powers with the House regarding taxes, the regulation of commerce, immigration, war, and the military, the Senate has the *sole* authority to ratify treaties with foreign nations and confirm federal judges and executive appointees—both of whom are very powerful.[5] Today, senators representing as few as 18 percent of Americans have the ability to form majorities in the Senate. These majorities can advance and block measures that affect all Americans. This is simply indefensible from the perspective of political equality.

In this chapter, I explore the adoption of the Senate and its evolving consequences for American democracy. I explore various avenues for reform, acknowledging that these are only plausible if a broad, vocal, and well-organized coalition of Americans demands greater political equality in their national legislature.

The Philadelphia Convention

On May 29, 1787, just the fifth day of the Philadelphia Convention, Edmund Randolph of Virginia proposed the Virginia Plan, a set of 15 proposals regarding the composition and power of the new federal government. Randolph's proposal is most recognized for its legislative representation plan. Under the Virginia Plan, the new legislature would be bicameral, with state representation in each chamber based on its nonslave population. Representatives in the lower house would be chosen by popular vote, while representatives in the upper chamber would be selected by state legislatures. Advocates of the plan included influential delegates such as James Madison of Virginia, James Wilson of Pennsylvania, and Alexander Hamilton of New York.[6]

The U.S. was unique, however, in that its national government was being created by political units (states) already in place. The delegates operated within a context of path dependence that already granted states equal power in the federal government, regardless of their respective populations. The story can be traced to the First Continental Congress of 1774, which was formed to discuss how the 13 colonies should respond to Great Britain's coercive actions regarding taxation and other matters. Focused on the larger issues at hand, the Congress (without much deliberation) granted each state one vote. John Adams of Massachusetts later commented that determining state representation based on population would have been difficult at the time because the delegates lacked the necessary data.[7] Little did the delegates know that they were setting an important precedent that would be difficult to break. Legislative representation remained equal in the Articles of Confederation, the first national government of the U.S. (created in 1777). With the precedent set, convincing lightly populated states to accept a reduction of their legislative influence at the Philadelphia Convention would therefore be a tough task. Predictably, small states opposed the Virginia Plan, arguing that large state interests would dominate the new national government if they lacked equal representation. Gunning Bedford, Jr., of Delaware cried, "It seems as if Pa. & Va. by the conduct of their deputies wished to provide a system in which they would have an enormous & monstrous influence."[8] Bedford even threatened that if the Virginia Plan were adopted, "the small [states would] find some foreign ally of more honor and good faith, who will take them by the hand and do them justice."[9]

Madison dismissed the concerns of Bedford and others. He believed that even if representation were to be determined by a state's population alone, the considerable checks and balances embedded in the new Constitution would prevent large states from trampling on small states. Furthermore, large states would also not be inclined to "gang up" on small states because interests were not inherently defined by state size. Inhabitants of a state did not have different views on land rights or banking simply because the political unit in which they resided had more (or fewer) people. As a result, there were few issues that perfectly split large and small states at the time. Even the contentious issue of slavery divided along regional lines rather than population size. On this issue, heavily populated Virginia surely had more in common with lightly populated Georgia than it did with heavily populated New York. For Madison and others, diverse interests generally operated *within* each state. There were farmers in both large Pennsylvania and small New Hampshire. There were urban interests in Massachusetts, but also in South Carolina, where Charleston was the fourth largest city in the United States. States did not have interests; states had residents, each of whom had their own personal views and interests. With this in mind, Madison saw no reason why farmers in small states should receive more relative representation than farmers in large states. It made little sense to him that urban business owners should receive less representation in Virginia than they did in Delaware. Why should the same interest be better represented in one place versus another, simply because it is held by a person who resides in a political unit that has fewer people within its borders?

Small states were unpersuaded by Madison and his allies. On June 15, 1787, William Paterson of New Jersey introduced an alternative to the Virginia Plan. The New Jersey Plan, as it came to be known, proposed that the nature of legislative representation in the Articles of Confederation be unchanged. Each state—regardless of its population—would have one representative in a unicameral legislature. Four days later, on June 19, the delegates rejected the plan and voted to proceed with a discussion of the Virginia Plan.

With small states threatening to bolt the convention, Connecticut delegates Roger Sherman and Oliver Ellsworth proposed the compromise that came to define the layout of Congress as we know it.[10] The House would grant representation based on a state's population, while the Senate would represent each state equally (with two seats). House representatives would be elected via popular vote, while senators would be chosen by state legislatures.[11] There was momentum for compromise, as many of the delegates recognized that the issue could effectively cripple the entire Convention. Eldredge Gerry of Massachusetts stated, "We were … in a peculiar situation. We were neither the same Nation nor different Nations. If no compromise should take place what will be the consequence?" George Mason of Virginia agreed, acknowledging, "There must be some accommodation."[12] With the issue still divisive, North Carolina switched its support (from the Virginia Plan) to the compromise, while Massachusetts was divided and forced to abstain. Meanwhile, two of the three New York delegates were absent, leaving the state unable to vote.[13] The so-called Connecticut Compromise was approved, five states to four.[14]

In truth, accommodating small state demands for equal representation in at least one chamber of Congress was likely unavoidable if the Philadelphia Convention were to succeed. It is important to recognize, however, that the creation of a malapportioned Senate was not "a product of constitutional theory, high principle, or grand design." As Robert Dahl notes in *How Democratic is the American Constitution?*, "It was nothing more than a practical outcome of a hard bargain that its opponents finally agreed to in order to achieve a constitution."[15]

Surely, compromises are always necessary anytime people or political entities are entering a union with one another. Some compromises, however, appear more sensible than they are. While the Congress created by the Connecticut Compromise appears to equally balance the representation of people and states, it effectively does more of the latter. First, as I discussed, the Senate was granted considerable powers denied to the House. Senators have always possessed the unique ability to confirm judges and executive nominees, as well as ratify treaties. The power to confirm judges is arguably far more powerful than the Framers intended, as the federal courts now routinely issue decisions that shape public policy. Second, while the House and Senate have equal power over legislation, *both* need to approve bills before they are sent to the president. In effect, this means that if the House—the chamber that more accurately reflects popular opinion throughout the U.S.—passes a measure, the Senate can simply refuse to consider or defeat it.

The House can indeed voice the popular will (though see Chapter 3), but the Senate—with small states enormously overrepresented—can silence it.

Malapportionment Over Time

As I previously argued, states are not actually living, breathing organisms with feelings or even interests. They are collections of people, each with their own views and perspectives. New Hampshire does not have an opinion about tax policy. Rather, the 1.4 million people living in the state each has (or at least has the capacity to have) a position on tax policy. It is therefore misleading to say that the Senate treats each state equally. Rather, it is more appropriate to consider how the Senate treats people within all states. Because each state is given an equal number of senators (two), the Senate effectively represents Americans across the states very differently. Residents in states with fewer people find their views represented by the same number of representatives as residents in states with more people. This is the definition of malapportionment, as those in the smaller states each have more representation per capita than those in larger states.

Consider the following analogy. Two 4th-grade classes are each promised a pizza party at the end of the year if students complete their final projects on time. One class has 30 students. The other has 18. After all students in each class successfully complete their work, the school orders four pizzas for each class. Would that be fair? Of course not. Even though both classes received the same prize, the *classes* are not doing the eating. Rather, the *students* inside the classes are. And in this instance, each student in the class with 30 students will have less pizza to enjoy than each student in the class with 18 students. Students in the smaller class benefit simply because there are fewer of them. The Senate operates on the same basis; the only difference is that the degree of malapportionment is far worse. In fact, if Wyoming and California were the classes in this example, Wyoming would have 10 students and California would have 685 students. If Texas were a third class, it would have 505 students. Nevertheless, four pizzas would be provided to the students in each class for completing their work. Surely, this would be absurd. It would make sense if classes were eating the pizzas, but they are not. Students within the classes are eating. Similarly, *states* do not vote or have interests. *Citizens* within states vote and have interests. Representation in the Senate is a fun pizza party for some and mere crust crumbs for others.

While the Framers knew that they were creating a malapportioned institution with the Senate, the extent of the issue was not nearly as extreme in the founding years as it has become. In the 1790 census, the smallest state, Delaware, had 59,094 residents.[16] The largest, Virginia, had 747,610, making it about 12.65 times as populated as Delaware. In 2020, the smallest state, Wyoming, had about 577,000 residents. The largest, California, had over 39.5 million, making it nearly 70 times as populated as Wyoming. Put another way, the extent of malapportionment between the largest and smallest states in the Senate is now nearly *six times* worse than it was when the Constitution was adopted. Disparities have not simply grown for the smallest and largest states; population differences between states have increased across the board.

Not only has malapportionment grown, but it is also likely to continue

Ratio of Largest to Smallest States (Population)

Shortly after the Constitution was ratified, the largest U.S. state (Virginia) had about 12 times as many residents as the smallest state (Delaware). Today, the disparity between the largest and smallest states is nearly six times greater. In the coming years, the gap is expected to widen even further, making the Senate even more malapportioned than it is today (courtesy American Academy of Arts and Sciences, *Our Common Purpose: Reinventing American Democracy for the 21st Century*).

growing. Because disproportionate population gains are expected to continue in large states such as Florida and Texas, discrepancies in state populations will likely get worse. David Birdsell, dean of the school of public and international affairs at Baruch College, estimates that about 70 percent of Americans will live in the 15 largest states by 2040.[17] In a separate study by the University of Virginia's Weldon Cooper Center for Public Service, researchers concluded that nearly half of the U.S. population will reside in just eight states by this time.[18] While these are only projections, it is widely believed that Americans will continue to congregate in states with large populations. Consequently, the Senate will only get worse from the perspective of political equality.

Why Malapportionment Matters

Political science research has found that Senate malapportionment advantages those residing in small states in various ways. First, because small state senators have equal voting power despite representing fewer people, they are often able to deliver disproportionate benefits for their constituents. In a 1995 study, a team of scholars found that citizens in small states receive more federal funds than those in larger states.[19] At the time, the authors estimated that differences in federal spending between the most over-represented (Wyoming) and most under-represented (California) states amounted to $1,148 per person (in 1990 dollars). Comparable findings were reported in other, more recent studies.[20]

In an extensive 1999 study, political scientists Frances Lee and Bruce Oppenheimer assessed the effects of Senate malapportionment. They divided their analysis between different types of federal programs. Some mandatory programs—including SNAP, Medicare, and Social Security—apply a universal national formula when determining benefits for which a citizen is entitled. For example, regardless of where one lives in the U.S., the income qualifications to receive food assistance under the SNAP program are the same. The retirement age affecting Medicare and Social Security is also identical everywhere. Not surprisingly, Lee and Oppenheimer found that small state residents are not advantaged by these programs. However, many federal programs involve greater annual discretion by either Congress or executive branch agencies. In the former case, Congress may, for example, determine which state and local transportation projects throughout the U.S. receive funding. In the latter case, Congress may simply block grant an amount of money to a federal agency (e.g., the Department of Transportation) and allow it to determine how and where it is spent. In both of these instances, Lee and Oppenheimer found that small state residents receive disproportionate benefits. Regarding federal transportation funding alone, they reported that those living in small states can expect to receive nearly 50 percent more funds per capita (annually) than those living in the largest states.[21]

Beyond federal funds, Americans in small states are privileged by having more access to their senators. The six smallest states basically have three members of Congress representing constituencies the size of a typical House district. Those in larger states have one House member, along with two senators who represent larger—*often much larger*—constituencies. In their study, Lee and Oppenheimer reported that small state residents are more likely to contact their senators with a problem and find satisfaction with the service they receive. Not surprisingly, these residents are also more likely to approve of their senators' performance.

Small state senators also require less funding for their campaigns, as they need to reach fewer voters. Yet because their seats are equally important for determining the overall partisan composition of the chamber, donors from across the country are still eager to fund their campaigns. As a result, small state senators are less burdened by fundraising. This, along with their heightened popularity at home, often provides these senators with additional time to pursue leadership positions in the chamber, something that increases their power even more.

In addition to providing them with more legislative access and material benefits, the Senate also gives greater weight to the partisan preferences of small state voters. While the Senate does not inherently benefit one political coalition over the other, it does tend to favor whichever party has political support in more states at a given time. Of course, having support in more states is entirely unrelated to having the support of more Americans at large. For example, a party could have more support in 30 of 50 states, but still be opposed by 60 percent of Americans if its support is disproportionately concentrated in small states. Between 2015–2021, Republicans managed to maintain a Senate majority despite winning fewer votes in Senate elections nationwide. Between 2014–2018, all 100 Senate seats were up for election once. In these races, Democrats won over 20 million more votes than Republicans. But because Democrats tended to win more populated states during this time, many of their votes did not convert to seats as efficiently. Republicans therefore maintained a Senate majority until 2021, when Democrats seized it by virtue of a 50–50 tie (with Vice President Kamala Harris casting the tie-breaking vote). The policy consequences were enormous. Between 2017–2021, the Republican-led Senate confirmed one-third of the current Supreme Court (as of 2022), confirmed 223 additional federal judges, and approved a $2 trillion overhaul of the U.S. tax code. Furthermore, the Senate blocked popular legislation boosting voting rights (see Chapter 6), expanding background checks for handgun purchases, and addressing climate change. Each bill had strong public support according to various surveys. My intention here is not to judge the wisdom of any particular policy measure, but simply to note that the chamber acted against the broader will of the American people. Given that the Senate is chosen in a manner that weighs some voters more than others, this should not be a surprise.

A Need for Protection?

Is it possible that small states need these aforementioned advantages? One concern that political theorists (and others) have long had about democracy is that majorities have the capacity to dominate—*or tyrannize*—minorities. Those with opinions that deviate from the norm may be left powerless in the face of unrelenting majorities who continue to win elections, pass bills, and appoint judges at odds with their interests. Democracies, therefore, need checks on majority power. The Senate, some argue, is exactly this sort of check, as it protects lightly populated states from heavily populated ones.

There are many reasons why this argument is dubious. First, as I previously discussed, states themselves do not have interests. People within states have interests. And if we look closely, we can see that these interests vary considerably within each state's borders. Too often, we hear about "red states" and "blue states." We see maps depicting states as bright red if a majority of their citizens voted for a Republican candidate and bright blue if a majority voted Democratic. The reality is that *every* state in the U.S. has considerable variation regarding its political attitudes and behavior.

Consider the state of California, often the poster-child for a large, blue state where urban, progressive interests appear to dominate. A number of factors indeed make California generally favorable to Democrats. It has several large cities: Los Angeles, San Diego, San Francisco, San Jose, and Oakland. It has Silicon Valley, Hollywood, and Marin County. Its population is both racially and ethnically diverse. In the 2020 presidential election, the state predictably handed Joe Biden a comfortable victory. Biden won 63 percent of the vote in California, while Donald Trump won just 34 percent. But even though Trump lost California by a massive margin, he still won 6.006 million votes in the state and defeated Biden in 23 counties. To simply label California an urban, blue state is misleading. California produces the country's largest agricultural output. It has small, rural, mountainside villages and ranchers who own guns and want the government "out of their lives." Orange County has a strong conservative tradition; while Trump narrowly lost the county in 2020, Republicans continue to win local races in the area. Kevin McCarthy, the leading Republican in the U.S. House and an ardent Trump supporter, is handily reelected in his California district every two years. And when Trump visited Paradise, California, after devastating wildfires destroyed most of the town's homes in 2018, many were shocked to learn that the community had overwhelmingly supported him in 2016. California is not simply a blue state; it is a state where millions of citizens support Republicans, but millions more support Democrats.

Comparable dynamics are present in every other large state in the U.S. Texas is known as a conservative Republican state (although this is slowly changing) where guns, bibles, fireworks, and rodeos are prevalent. Indeed, each of these things *are* in ample supply in Texas. But if one visits Austin, they will find that the culture has more in common with Brooklyn or Portland, Oregon, than Austin's own outer suburbs. Craft coffee shops with tattooed baristas are abundant. There is micro-brewed beer and lots of indie rock. And when it comes time to vote, Democrats win big. Contrary to popular belief, differences in political preferences are not defined by state. More so, they are defined by the nature of one's community. Democrats are strong in most cities, Republicans are strong in most rural areas, and suburbs tend to be more competitive. Demographics such as race, ethnicity, education, income, and religion are also more predictive of people's political preferences than the state in which they reside.

It is even misguided to typecast *sub-communities* within states. Miami, Florida, is a Democratic city, but the Cuban-American population leans Republican and supported Trump in 2020. In New York City, Democrats handily outnumber Republicans, but Staten Island (one of the city's five boroughs) supported Trump by a 15-point margin in 2020. Philadelphia is a Democratic stronghold, but Northeast Philadelphia is more conservative.

Let me go even one step further. Even when an area is extremely loyal to a political party, there are often major differences between citizens nonetheless. San Francisco is as Democratic as nearly any large city, but Democrats who live in the Presidio hardly align with young voters studying at the University of San Francisco or Black and Latino communities in Bayview–Hunters Point and the Mission District, respectively. Republicans in central Pennsylvania are much more culturally conservative than the high-income, well-educated Republicans living in the affluent Main Line suburbs of Philadelphia.

At the Philadelphia Convention and still today, some have expressed concern that if population determines representation, large states will impose their will on smaller states. My response is simple: which "will" would they impose? Would California impose its urban housing interests, its entertainment industry interests, its big-tech interests, its maritime interests, or its agricultural interests? Would Texas impose its social conservative interests or those of its significant LGBTQ+ community? It is true that some states certainly have overwhelming issues of importance: Iowa and corn, Michigan and cars, Florida and hurricane relief. All of these dominant interests, however, are also abundant in other states. Suppose, for example, that California and Texas wished to "impose" their agricultural interests on smaller states by advancing a tax break for farmers. Would those in small, rural states—like Kansas and Vermont—object? If Florida "imposed" its will to create a national insurance fund for hurricane damage, would citizens in coastal South Carolina mind? The overrepresentation of small states in the Senate does not protect small state interests *because there are no inherently small state interests*. Instead, it arbitrarily lets some citizens shape the federal government more than other citizens, simply by virtue of where they reside on a map.

If there are indeed minority interests that require protection in our democracy, surely there are better examples than citizens who live in less populated political sub-units. One could argue that the poor, the elderly, the young, racial and ethnic groups who have faced a history of discrimination, and the disabled are each minority populations in need of added protection. Each of these groups would theoretically be better candidates for extra representation in the Senate than citizens living in small states. Unfortunately, by offering "protection" on the arbitrary basis of a state's population size, the Senate has often *denied* protection to those who truly need it. Surely, no group was more in need of minority protection in the early years of the U.S. than those who were enslaved. Yet, as political scientist Barry Weingast has observed, the Senate effectively gave "the South a veto over any policy affecting slavery" until 1850.[22] Eight anti-slavery bills were approved in the House between 1800 and 1860, only to be killed in the Senate.[23] Then, after the Civil War, overrepresentation of many southern states in the Senate protected Jim Crow laws denying basic rights to Black Americans. If the Senate is designed to protect minority rights, it has a very spotty track record.

I do agree with James Madison and others that the importance of protecting minority opinions in a democracy should not be shrugged aside. I would simply stress that any safeguards of minority thought should both (1) respect the principle of political equality and (2) check majorities *that pose an actual threat to minorities*. Regarding the latter, we can suspect that majorities surrounding an ideological view or group interest could seek to enforce their common will over minorities. For example, majorities surrounding tax policy, the regulation of business, labor law, abortion policy, or any other political issue would rationally seek to coordinate and adopt policies consistent with their views. Majorities surrounding the interests of particular communities, such as farmers, manufacturers, teachers, retail workers, students, or the elderly would rationally endeavor to do the same. There is no discernible reason or evidence, however, to fear that large states—simply by virtue of their populations— would possess common interests that they would then impose on smaller states.

In the U.S., a number of institutions effectively protect vulnerable minorities while largely upholding the principle of political equality. First, the Bill of Rights—the first ten amendments to the Constitution—explicitly protects citizens from certain intrusions by federal or state governments. Rights surrounding speech, assembly, religion, and treatment in the criminal justice system are surely at risk of violation from majorities. Many Americans often support suppressing unpopular public protests or denying rights to suspected criminals. But because protestors and the accused enjoy constitutionally-ensured rights, they are entitled to protection by the federal courts. And on many occasions, the Supreme Court has protected citizens from popular restrictions that violate their rights. This includes the right to burn an American flag, protest military funerals in public spaces, and view and sell pornographic materials. In each of these cases, majorities wished for different outcomes. A large body of research notes that while judges are somewhat constrained by public opinion and fear of non-implementation of their decisions,[24] they do enjoy considerable discretion and protection when evaluating minority rights. This discretion has been used to expand protections that all Americans enjoy. In fact, as Dahl notes, "...judicial interpretation based on constitutional provisions enormously extends the domain of protected rights—probably beyond anything the Framers could have foreseen."[25]

The structure of the federal government, with three separate spheres of power, also provides protection against a majority gaining and exercising power too quickly or broadly. If a majority view comes to power in the presidency, for example, it will still need to contend with a strong bicameral legislature. Presidents interested in healthcare reform, deregulation, or U.S. policy towards NATO will need to deal with Congress. And typically, they must contend with a Congress where at least one chamber is at odds with them. Unified government in the U.S. has become a rarity, as one party has controlled the presidency, House, and Senate for only 17 of the past 54 years (1969–2022). Even when one party controls both the presidency and Congress, success is not guaranteed. Ideological differences within a party coalition constrain the ability of majorities to enact sweeping changes. And in the event that majorities do successfully approve and implement legislation, it is then subject to judicial review.

Furthermore, the Senate's staggered six-year terms mean that only one-third of its seats come up for election every two years. As a result, it is difficult for majority sentiment to transform the Senate's composition swiftly. This staggering of terms is a prudent way to check majorities from acquiring vast power and implementing significant changes too quickly.

Finally, the will of the majority is also constrained by the considerable inertia that all bureaucracies must endure to enact policy change. Even when legislatures and presidents adopt new laws, there is a complex web of steps required for them to be effectively implemented. These steps often involve multiple federal agencies, all of whom are required to follow established rules when completing their work. This includes establishing processes to receive and review public input, releasing environmental impact statements, and acting in accordance with established labor law. At any step in the process, delays can occur due to lawsuits, personnel changes, or disobedience (or incompetence) within the bureaucracy. Even when majorities act, it takes time for the fruits of their labor to be realized.

Note that each of these aforementioned checks against majority tyranny operate *without* valuing the voices of some Americans more or less than other Americans. Rather than check majorities by counting some people more than others, each does so through requiring extra layers of consensus or slowing the pace of change to ensure that majority support is durable. Furthermore, each of these protections would continue to operate effectively even if Senate seats were allocated according to population.

What About the Filibuster?

The Senate's own rules serve as another check on majority preferences. Because there is no limit on how long a bill can be debated, opposing senators can block a vote on a piece of legislation simply by continuing to talk on the Senate floor (a filibuster). Less dramatically, even a single member's stated opposition to moving forward with a bill (a hold) can prevent it from receiving a vote. While there is a process to end these delays and force a vote (cloture), it requires the support of 60 senators to succeed. As a result, few major pieces of legislation can pass the Senate without the support of three-fifths of the chamber. There are exceptions to this rule, including some that were recently adopted. In 2013, Senate Democrats (then in the majority) changed the rules so that simple majorities could end debate and consider executive and judicial branch nominees. In 2017, a Republican-led Senate extended the same rules to the consideration

of Supreme Court justices. In addition, bills that only address budget-
ary items such as federal tax rates or spending levels can be considered
through the budget reconciliation process, where filibusters and holds are
not permitted. Several major bills, including amendments to the Affordable Care Act (2010), the Tax Cut and Jobs Act (2017), and the American
Rescue Plan Act (2021), were approved through reconciliation. Nevertheless, most legislation cannot be considered in this manner and must clear
the 60-vote cloture hurdle to gain approval.

Some hail the 60-vote requirement as a necessary check on majorities.
And taken alone, filibusters and holds do not present political equality
problems. While they limit the ability of majorities to enact their will, the
cloture threshold is the same for all coalitions wishing to pass legislation.
Rather than advantage one legislator or party, the 60-vote requirement
simply makes it harder for *everyone* to pass legislation. In fact, because
the Senate's malapportionment allows members representing a fairly small
share of Americans to comprise 51-vote majorities, cloture rules sometimes allow senators representing *more* Americans to effectively veto proposals supported by senators representing *fewer* Americans. Suppose, for
example, that national polls show that a bill increasing farm subsidies is
generally unpopular with the public. Nevertheless, 51 mostly small state
senators representing just 26 percent of the U.S. population support it.
Because of the filibuster, senators representing larger states are able to prevent the bill from achieving cloture. In this hypothetical instance, the Senate's cloture requirements actually stopped a measure that did not have
broad support throughout the country. Harvard Law Professor Benjamin Eidelson has reported that most filibusters and holds since the 1990s
have effectively fit this description—events he refers to as "majoritarian
filibusters."[26]

While the Senate's cloture rules do not inherently value some American voters over others, there are several reasons why I still believe the
60-vote requirement should be eliminated. First, while majoritarian filibusters are possible, they are unnecessary because the House already
provides a check on the Senate's legislative action. Consider the previous
hypothetical example regarding farm subsidies. Even if the bill were to
pass the Senate, it would likely fail in the House, which better (though not
perfectly) represents aggregate public opinion in the U.S. Furthermore, in
many cases filibusters and holds are not majoritarian at all; instead, they
often allow small minorities to block very popular bills. The Senate filibuster was a huge barrier to civil rights laws during the 1940s and 1950s.
In recent years, gun control and climate change legislation with overwhelming public support has been blocked by filibusters and holds. And as
I will discuss in later chapters, much-needed reforms to enhance political

equality have been stifled by the 60-vote cloture requirement in recent years. Checks on majority dominance can be prudent, but the bicameral nature of Congress, the president, the courts, and the bureaucracy already provide ample minority protections. In my view, requiring 60 votes in the Senate makes it unreasonably difficult for the wishes of the American people to be actualized by legislation. This has the effect of frustrating voters, leaving them constantly wondering why Congress cannot get anything done. If majorities are generally unable to exert their will, then what exactly is the purpose of democracy?

Reform

In 1995, Senator Daniel Patrick Moynihan of New York commented, "Sometime in the next century the United States is going to have to address the question of apportionment in the Senate." Many other public officials, academics, political professionals, and citizens agree. In reality, however, addressing the Senate's malapportionment problem will be exceptionally difficult. The Constitution, vague in so many ways, is seemingly clear that each state is granted two senators regardless of its size. In a series of 1960s decisions, Supreme Court majorities acknowledged that the Senate was at odds with the rest of the Constitution, but determined that it had no power to correct it because the Senate's apportionment is very clearly defined in the document. In *Reynolds v. Sims* (1964), a landmark Supreme Court decision that ended malapportionment in state legislatures throughout the U.S., the majority opinion noted, "The right of suffrage can be denied by a debasement or dilution of the weight of a citizen's vote just as effectively as by wholly prohibiting the free exercise of the franchise."[27] In other words, weighing some votes less than others is in the same ballpark as denying the right to vote. But while the Senate blatantly distorts the weight of citizen votes by design, the Supreme Court concluded that it was powerless to stop it.

It is generally believed that only a constitutional amendment can address Senate malapportionment. The task is further complicated by Article V of the Constitution, which says, "that no State, without its Consent, shall be deprived of its equal Suffrage in the Senate." This clause has been widely interpreted to mean that all 50 states would need to approve any arrangement that did not treat all states equally in the Senate. In fact, the Senate is the only part of the Constitution believed to be "unamendable" with the support of two-thirds of each congressional chamber and three-fourths (38) of the state legislatures.

So, reform is doomed, right?

Not necessarily, but the odds are admittedly long. Let me begin this next discussion by stressing that no effort to address the Senate's malapportionment can succeed without a broad, visible popular movement that creates a sense of urgency among political actors. Certainly, such a movement does not currently exist. People are not protesting in the streets over unequal representation in the upper chamber. As a result, Senate reform is not something that is likely one or two election cycles away. But if a broad reform effort does eventually develop, anything is possible. Few believed that the abolition of slavery, voting rights for women, the direct election of senators, or Prohibition would ever happen. But each of these reforms came to pass after shifting public support and organized pressure gave elected officials little choice but to relent. In the event that sufficient energy is eventually summoned to advance political equality, Senate reform could happen too.

With this faith in mind, it is worth exploring some potential paths forward. Below, I review four ways that the problem of Senate malapportionment could eventually be addressed.

First, even though Article V demands unanimous consent for changing the Senate's apportionment structure, this unique barrier does not exist when it comes to the Senate's power. Even if seat allocation cannot be altered, the Senate could be weakened through the normal amendment process. Recall that the Senate is unusually powerful for an upper chamber. In fact, of the 23 countries that have been continuously democratic since 1950, only four—Australia, Italy, Mexico and the United States—have powerful upper houses.[28] In most democracies, upper houses are limited to reviewing and delaying legislation, voicing minority opinions, and suggesting amendments. And in most cases, upper houses can ultimately be overruled by lower houses in the event of disputes. In the U.S., a constitutional amendment could limit the Senate's power in numerous ways. The House could assume responsibility for confirming executive and judicial nominees, or perhaps even ratifying treaties with foreign nations. The Senate could relinquish its role in the annual budget process, allowing the more representative lower house to make spending and taxation decisions (along with the president). Any of these reforms would reduce the impact of malapportionment by lessening the scope of decision-making made by the more unrepresentative chamber.

Second, despite the limits of Article V, the Senate's malapportionment could conceivably still be improved without the consent of all fifty states. How?

Here, it is important to understand that the Constitution cannot maintain its legitimacy if it does not evolve with the people and their demands. The courts are not entirely constrained by public opinion (see my earlier discussion regarding rights), but there are limits to the degree to which they can block the will of majorities. When calls are intense enough, elected officials and judges often find a way to make needed reforms fit within the bounds of the existing Constitution. Consider that since the Bill of Rights amendments were ratified in 1791, the Constitution has been amended only 17 times. Many of the most notable changes to the Constitution have come not from new amendments but rather from evolving interpretations of the document. The Interstate Commerce Clause, for example, has always stated that Congress "shall have the power to regulate Commerce with foreign Nations, and among the several States, and with the Indian Tribes." For much of U.S. history, the Supreme Court did not accept this clause as a justification for federal restrictions on industry. In 1936, for example, federal regulations on the mining industry were struck down because mining was not considered "commerce." Beginning in 1937, when a frustrated President Franklin Roosevelt was threatening to "pack" the Court with new justices, the Supreme Court began accepting a more expansive reading of the Commerce Clause. Why? Because the Supreme Court is only as powerful as its legitimacy. By 1937, it was clear that both the political class and the public supported greater regulation of industry. If the Court continued to be out of step with the country, it risked a reduction in its power.

Another example of the evolving Constitution surrounds the "right to privacy." While no such right is explicitly enumerated in the Constitution, the Supreme Court effectively created it in *Griswold v. Connecticut* (1965) using "penumbral reasoning."[29] In essence, the majority argued that while privacy rights are not explicitly protected in the Constitution, there are other rights that imply that privacy must be protected as well. Because the Constitution guarantees due process, free speech, and freedom from self-incrimination, privacy is implicitly protected as well. With this logic solidified, the Court used the newly created "right to privacy" to rule that Connecticut and other states could no longer ban contraception for married couples. Less than a decade later, the right to privacy was used to invalidate state laws banning abortion in *Roe v. Wade* (1973).[30] While the Court overruled *Roe* in 2022, it did not revoke all privacy rights. As these examples demonstrate, constitutional law is malleable. And because the Constitution is so difficult to amend, evolving interpretations by the federal courts have allowed the document to remain current as society has evolved. And if the day comes when a broad majority of the U.S. intensely backs new political equality efforts—including changes to the Senate—we should not be surprised if the federal courts find a way to acquiesce.

What would such compliance look like? Let's consider some possibilities. Imagine that decades from now, a broad majority of the American people support institutional changes to advance political equality. Well-funded interest groups are demanding it. Citizens are marching for it. Before long, candidates find it beneficial to support efforts like reducing malapportionment in the Senate. Support is widespread in Congress and throughout the U.S., but there is still concern that a handful of small states will not submit to ending their equal suffrage in the Senate. At first glance, Article V's Equal Suffrage Clause would seem to end any possibility of reform. But suppose Congress and three-fourths of the states approved an amendment that repealed the Equal Suffrage Clause itself. While there is debate among constitutional law scholars regarding whether this is constitutionally permissible, many believe it likely is. Yale Law School Professor Akhil Amar acknowledges that doing so would be a "sly scheme," but also notes that it would "have satisfied the literal text of Article V and would also have comported with the Constitution's general principle of ongoing popular sovereignty."[31] Richard Albert of Boston College Law School agrees, noting that while many nations—including Germany and Honduras—explicitly ban amendments to their amendment process in their governing documents, the U.S. Constitution does not.[32] If two-thirds of the House and Senate, along with three-fourths of the states, agreed, the rules regarding "amendability" could change. While it is not inevitable that the Supreme Court would accept this reading, remember that this action would be taken amid a national context that overwhelmingly supports Senate reform. Public support would make it difficult for the justices to stand in the way. They would need to consider the court's legitimacy when issuing a ruling.

Once the Equal Suffrage Clause is repealed, Congress and the states would be free to either eliminate the Senate entirely or reform its apportionment structure. Assuming that reformers wished to maintain a bicameral legislature for the purposes of maintaining a check on (at least some) majority actions, reform efforts could keep the Senate's long and staggered six-year terms but simply change the number of seats granted to states. Eric Orts, a professor at the University of Pennsylvania's Wharton School, has proposed that Senate seats be equivalent to a state's percentage of the total U.S. population, with one as the minimum.[33] If this reform were enacted using 2020 census data, 26 states would be granted the minimum one senator, since they each have one percent of the U.S. population or less. Meanwhile, 12 states would continue to have two senators, while eight states would be granted three or four. Finally, the four largest states would see their Senate seats grow more substantially: California would get 12 senators, Texas would get nine, and Florida and New York would each get six. The total Senate would expand to 110 members to compensate for the fact that some small states will still have one seat despite having considerably less than 1/100th of the U.S. population.

While Orts' plan would not eliminate malapportionment in the Senate, it would substantially reduce it while still allowing each state to maintain representation. The result would be an upper chamber that is still distinct from the House due its smaller size, longer terms, and staggered elections. But importantly, the reformed Senate would no longer be distinct for its grossly malapportioned character.

Third, suppose that even in an environment of broad support for democracy reform, a constitutional amendment is unattainable. In this hypothetical scenario, small states are simply unwilling to approve a measure that effectively reduces their citizens' voice in the Senate. Even in this case, Professor Orts believes that his aforementioned Senate reform idea would be possible. In essence, Orts contends that the Constitution has *already* been amended in ways that discredit the Senate's apportionment structure. More specifically, he argues that the various voting rights amendments—the Fifteenth, Nineteenth, Twenty-Fourth, and Twenty-Sixth—have granted their blessing to Senate reform by directing Congress to adopt legislation to protect equal voting rights. While the original intent of Article V of the Constitution is certainly not disputed, Orts argues that "the intentions informing Article V at the founding must be balanced against those behind the voting rights amendments adopted a century or more later. These amendments clearly and repeatedly authorize Congress to protect 'the right of citizens of the United States to vote' against any abridgement 'by the United States.'" Orts notes that the word "abridge" means to "reduce the scope" or "shorten the extent" of something. In his view, because the Senate abridges the equal voting rights of citizens in large states, Congress *already* has authorization—from the various voting rights amendments—to pursue reforms to fix it. Were Congress to approve changes to the Senate's apportionment structure through simple legislation, the Supreme Court could accept the changes using the rationale above. And while such consent may seem unthinkable at the moment, the federal courts have accepted creative interpretations of the Constitution before. And if demands for political equality are one day loud and persistent enough, the courts may have little choice but to accept the will of the people.

Finally, there is one path towards a more representative Senate that most certainly can be advanced without a constitutional amendment. Fundamentally, the Senate is malapportioned because states vary greatly in their population sizes. If every state had the same number of people, the Senate would represent Americans as effectively as the House. Because great differences in state populations exist, however, disparities in representation are great. To the extent that these disparities can be reduced, malapportionment in the Senate could decrease. If demands for Senate reform indeed grow, the easiest path forward may be breaking up large states into several, smaller states. I recognize that this sounds extreme, but there is nothing sacred about state dimensions. In fact, a brief examination of U.S. history demonstrates that states have already been created and split for a variety of reasons. Purchases from foreign nations, wars, scandals, and political considerations have all affected state boundaries in the past. There is no reason—legal or otherwise—why our states must retain the same shapes moving forward.

The Constitution sets the procedure for partitioning existing states or creating new ones from additional territory. Article IV, Section 3 of the Constitution reads, "New States may be admitted by the Congress into this Union; but no new State shall be formed or erected within the Jurisdiction of any other State; nor any State be formed by the Junction of two or more States, or Parts of States, without the Consent of the Legislatures of the States concerned as well as of the Congress." If a state wished to partition itself into multiple states, it could vote to do so. If both chambers of Congress and the president approved the partition, the new states would effectively be created. All of the rights and benefits of statehood—including two senators—would be conferred. The creation of states does not require significant supermajorities in Congress. A simple majority is needed in the House. And while senators can filibuster the creation of new states in the upper chamber, invoking cloture with 60 votes is still more achievable that approving a constitutional amendment. Furthermore, as I discussed, a simple Senate majority could change the chamber's rules for invoking cloture. Recall that in 2013 and 2017, respectively, senators changed the rules so that simple majorities could end debate to consider executive and judicial branch nominees. Even if a future Senate does not entirely end the 60-vote cloture requirement (as I believe it should), it could eliminate it for the consideration of new states. Ian Millhiser, a senior fellow with the Center for American Progress, believes that doing so would be consistent with the filibuster's central function. In 2020, he argued, "The ostensible purpose of the filibuster is to allow senators to continue debating a legislative proposal, and potentially to make changes to that proposal." It was therefore logical, in Millhiser's view, to allow executive and judicial nominees to proceed with a simple majority vote. After all, "Legislation can be debated and amended by senators, but it's not like senators can amend a nominee. There is much less for senators to debate when their only choice is to vote 'yes' or 'no' on a particular individual nominated for a high-level job."[34] The same logic can be applied to statehood bills, which effectively require an up-or-down vote.

Again, there is nothing radical about creating new states. While the map of the U.S. has been unchanged since 1959, a quick review reveals that changes have been fairly common throughout much of American history. Thirty-seven states have been added since the Constitution was ratified. Most of these states were created from U.S. land that was first established by Congress as an organized territory. After some period of time, the territorial government expressed interest in statehood, generally via a ballot referendum of eligible voters. Congress then directed that government to write a state constitution. Once the state's citizens (again, generally by referendum) and Congress accepted the constitution, Congress adopted a measure granting statehood, and the president approved it.[35]

While this general process has governed the establishment of new states, the story of how the U.S. grew from 13 to 50 states is more complex. It is an interesting story, so allow me to digress a bit.

At the time of the American Revolution, the British possessed additional land beyond the 13 colonies. After the war, much of this land was in the contemporary Midwest. Several U.S. states had claims to some of this land. Virginia claimed all of the Illinois Country and Ohio Country. Massachusetts claimed present-day southern Michigan and Wisconsin. Connecticut claimed a small section of land south of the Great Lakes. New York claimed some Iroquois land between Lake Erie and the Ohio River. States without claims to these lands—known as the Northwest Territory—pressured states to renounce all claims before agreeing to ratify the Articles of Confederation. Those without claims were concerned that Virginia, Massachusetts, Connecticut, and New York would continue to expand their territory and gain disproportionate power in a new central government. All four states ultimately obliged and ceded their claims to the federal government during the 1780s.[36] Over the next few decades, the Northwest Territory became the land comprising all or part of six new states: Ohio, Indiana, Illinois, Michigan, Wisconsin, and Minnesota.

Other states emerged from lands once claimed by existing states. Part of western Virginia—known as Kentucky County—eventually petitioned for and was granted statehood by Congress in 1792.[37] Meanwhile, North Carolina ceded western lands to the federal government in 1789, creating the short-lived Southwest Territory. In 1796, citizens from the territory petitioned for statehood; after it was granted later that year, Tennessee became a new state.[38]

The events leading to Alabama and Mississippi becoming states are unique. During the 1790s, Georgia Governor George Mathews and the state's General Assembly scandalously sold large tracts of land—in the so-called Yazoo lands—to political insiders at low prices. The legality of the sales was challenged and ended up in court. But given the complexity of adjudicating the complex land sales (and subsequent sales), Georgia simply ceded all of its claims to the land to the federal government in

1802. Mississippi and Alabama emerged from this territory and became states in 1817 and 1819, respectively.[39] The same year that Alabama gained statehood, the U.S. acquired Florida from Spain. It would become a state in 1845.

In 1803, President Thomas Jefferson agreed to the Louisiana Purchase from Napoleon-led France. The land acquired from that purchase—at the cost of just $15 million—included land that would become all or part of 15 U.S. states. The entire states of Arkansas, Iowa, Kansas, Louisiana, Missouri, Nebraska, and Oklahoma would emerge from the vast territory, along with parts of Colorado, Minnesota, Montana, New Mexico, North Dakota, South Dakota, Texas, and Wyoming. The massive tract of land was divided into territories for various idiosyncratic reasons. For example, the Kansas and Nebraska Territories were established in an (ultimately disastrous) attempt to balance the increasingly tense North-South split regarding slavery in 1854. Senator Stephen Douglas of Illinois, the author of the Kansas-Nebraska Act, believed that inhabitants of each new territory should be able to decide whether slavery would be permitted. He assumed, however, that northernmost Nebraska would oppose slavery, while southernmost Kansas would allow it. He was correct about Nebraska, but Kansas saw intense violence between pro and anti-slavery forces, escalating the conflict that led to the Civil War.

The Dakota Territory was originally expected to become one state, but ultimately split. One of the reasons, according to historian Steven Bucklin, was that corrupt state legislators moved the territory's capital in 1883. When it was moved from Yankton to Bismarck, those in the southern part of the territory (where most settlers lived) became resentful. This, combined with the fact that the regions were increasingly tied to different commercial hubs, helped fuel the split before South and North Dakota became separate states in 1889. It also helped that Republicans had just gained control of both chambers of Congress and the White House in the 1888 elections. Newly elected Republican President Benjamin Harrison was more than happy to sign bills creating two new states expected to be loyal to his party.[40]

Many U.S. states owe their admission at least partially to President James Polk. In 1846, after threatening war over the territory, Polk's government negotiated the Oregon Treaty with Great Britain. In the process, land was secured that would become the states of Oregon, Washington, and Idaho, as well as parts of Wyoming and Montana.

Just months earlier, Polk had led the U.S. into war with Mexico. After gaining independence from Spain in 1821, Mexico controlled the vast territory known as Texas. The territory was very sparsely populated by Mexican settlers, leaving them far outnumbered by indigenous peoples. Hoping to increase the number of settlers and add protection from native tribes potentially hostile to its government, Mexico enacted the General Colonization Law in 1824. This allowed—and even encouraged—Americans to settle Texan land. Before too long, the American settlers became disgruntled with an increasingly centralized Mexican government and sought independence. After a crushing defeat at the Alamo in 1836, Texan rebels were victorious at the Battle of San Jacinto and effectively gained independence (though Mexico did not recognize it). Beginning in 1837, Texan officials sought U.S. statehood. The U.S. did not immediately grant it, however, for a variety of reasons. Primarily, abolitionists and those concerned with further igniting North-South disagreements over slavery worried about adding a large slave state. In 1845, however, the U.S. Congress obliged Texan wishes and granted statehood. Naturally, this led to heightened conflict with Mexico, who promptly broke off diplomatic relations. Mexico not only still laid claim to Texas but also believed the Texan border to be further north (at the Nueces River) than the U.S. claimed (at the Rio Grande River). President Polk ordered General Zachary Taylor to the Rio Grande in January 1846, seemingly to instigate military conflict with Mexican troops. After the U.S. was predictably attacked by Mexican soldiers, Polk requested a declaration of war, which Congress overwhelmingly gave him. The U.S. invaded Mexico, conquering Mexico City in 1847 and securing full surrender from the country in 1848. By winning the war, the U.S. not only solidified Texas as a state, but also muscled Mexico into ceding the land that became all of California, Nevada, and Utah, as well as parts of Arizona, Colorado, New Mexico, and Wyoming.[41, 42]

The establishment of both West Virginia and Nevada as states resulted from the politics of the Civil War era. When Virginia voted to secede from the Union in 1861, most delegates from the state's northern and western counties opposed the action. The region, which had long felt isolated from the state government, was generally less supportive of slavery. After a series of conventions (the Wheeling Conventions), several dozen counties in this region decided to formally split from Virginia, remain in the Union, and petition for statehood. In 1863, Congress and President Lincoln granted statehood to West Virginia. The following year, in the days leading up the 1864 presidential election, congressional Republicans worried that Lincoln could be defeated by Democrat George McClellan. They quickly approved statehood for Nevada, a territory that had just 6,857 people![43] This both added a few additional electoral votes to Lincoln's column and expanded the number of Republican senators.[44]

Two states live outside the continental U.S. In 1867, the U.S. acquired Alaska from Russia for $7.2 million. While the purchase was originally derided as "Sewards' Folly" (a reference to William Seward, the secretary of state who negotiated the purchase), the eventual discovery of gold and oil made Alaska an incredible bargain.[45] Hawaii was acquired by much more controversial means. An independent nation led by Queen Liliʻuo-kalani, Hawaii's government was overthrown by European and American business leaders on the island with the assistance of the U.S. minister, John L. Stevens, in 1893.[46] In 1898, Congress approved the annexation of Hawaii despite the opposition of most native Hawaiians. The islands became the Hawaii Territory, a title they still had at the time of the Japanese bombing of Pearl Harbor in December 1941. Nearly two decades later, in 1959, Congress finally granted statehood to both Alaska and Hawaii.

If nothing else, this brief overview makes it clear that the establishment of the 50 U.S. states was largely idiosyncratic. States have been added for all sorts of reasons, many of them (e.g., the politics of slavery) completely irrelevant and inapplicable today. Partisan, ideological, and regional politics were often a consideration. Furthermore, the developments that led to some states growing (in population) much more than others were generally unanticipated at the time of statehood. California, for example, became a state in 1850 before the construction of the Transcontinental Railroad or modern dams. Florida's population has undoubtedly grown because of the invention of air-conditioning, while Texas owes some of its substantial growth to an unanticipated twentieth-century oil boom. Had the population growth of these states been anticipated, there may have been initial calls to divide these geographies into multiple states. But this, of course, could not be known.

If states can be established and shaped as a result of slavery disputes, capital relocations, and wars incited upon neighboring governments, surely the cause of political equality is worthy of adjusting some state boundaries. Not only would state partitions improve political equality, but they would also improve representation for citizens. It is simply indefensible to expect senators from California and Texas to represent 30–40 million residents, particularly when over ten percent of senators are representing less than one million residents. The Framers could have never anticipated these sorts of disparities in state populations. Thankfully, they created a process through which the problem can be addressed.

Any future attempt to partition states should be done for the purpose of improving political equality, not advancing the partisan interests of one particular coalition. Of course, I am not naïve. Politics *always* matter, and the rules are never neutral; surely some would be advantaged or disadvantaged by any change in the number of states. However, the effort should not be led with this intention in mind. One intriguing idea was presented in 2018 by Burt Neuborne, a professor at the NYU School of Law and the founding legal director of the Brennan Center for Justice.

Under Neuborne's plan, Congress would pass a law (the Democracy Restoration Act) stipulating that whenever the census identifies states with populations that exceed the least populous state by more than a certain ratio, each of those states would have the option of dividing in half. Eligible states could still refuse to split, but if they did choose to partition, the decision would have advance blessing from the federal government. Any potential split would require the support of majorities in *both* of the two new states being created.[47]

Neuborne's proposal is a novel way to decrease malapportionment in the Senate through a transparent, consistent framework. Rather than Congress arbitrarily deciding to allow some states to split, but not others (perhaps for partisan reasons), this approach would offer blanket support to any large states wishing to do so. In my view, the reform should also require any split to create two states with similar partisan divisions as the original state. For example, Florida is a competitive state with similar numbers of Democratic and Republican voters. If Florida chose to split, it would therefore need to create two new politically competitive states (as measured by recent election results). New York is a state where about 60 percent of voters generally support Democrats in national elections. If the state were to split, it would need to create two states with this rough partisan breakdown. This approach would prevent partisan gerrymandering of new states. Of course, states are already permitted to split however they wish, so long as both the new states and Congress approve. While states would retain this right, the pre-approval conferred by Congress through the Democracy Restoration Act should, in my view, only apply if the above conditions are met.

Neuborne offers several suggestions regarding the population ratio that would trigger the new law. It could be set to 20:1, meaning that any state with at least 20 times more people than the smallest state would be eligible to split into two states. Under these terms, seven states—California, Florida, Illinois, New York, Ohio, Pennsylvania, and Texas—would currently qualify for a fast-tracked partition. In fact, because their populations are more than 40 times greater than the smallest state, two states—California and Texas—could theoretically split twice (creating four states in each case).

I would argue that the threshold should be set even lower than 20:1. If the ratio were set to 10:1, 14 states would be able to divide themselves into two new states. Meanwhile, the seven largest states—noted above—would gain the right to split multiple times. Five—Florida, Illinois, New York, Ohio, and Pennsylvania—would be permitted to split twice (creating four states each), while both California and Texas would be able to split three times, creating eight states from their current territories. The Senate's structural inequality would not be eliminated through these hypothetical partitions, but it would be reduced in a meaningful, partisan-blind way.

Conclusion

Any honest assessment of the Philadelphia Convention should conclude that the Connecticut Compromise was necessary to advance the U.S. Constitution. The Framers can be faulted for many things, but the decision to accept this deal was defensible given the circumstances. Because states were equally empowered under the Articles of Confederation, small states had the political power to demand equal representation in the upper chamber. And so they did. Recognizing why the Framers acted in 1787, however, is a far cry from rationalizing the Senate's malapportionment today. George Washington's crossing of the Delaware River was impressive in 1776, but today I would encourage him to take the bridge or perhaps airdrop his troops into central New Jersey. Much has changed since 1787. And these changes make the Connecticut Compromise more problematic today for at least two important reasons. First, the degree of malapportionment is much greater than it was at the time the Senate was created. The population difference between the largest and smallest states has grown from 12:1 in 1790 to nearly 70:1 today, with no sign of slowing down. Population is expected to continue clustering in large U.S. states, with up to 70 percent of Americans expected to reside in just 15 states by 2040. In other words, the Senate will only become *less democratic* with time.

Second, notions of equality and democracy have changed markedly since the Framers met in Philadelphia. The idea that all adult citizens should determine the composition of their government (let alone equally determine it) was not yet appreciated in 1787. Slavery was prevalent, women were considered second-class citizens, and even large numbers of white males were unable to vote. Today, our culture and government generally acknowledge that equality is an important ingredient of democracy. But while this value is now widely expressed, not all relics from a prior time have been eradicated. The Senate, clothed in immense power, is an unfortunate example.

Improving political equality in the Senate will ultimately take a great deal of public awareness and passion for change. Legal creativity will be required, progress may be incremental, and solutions are destined to be imperfect. But any progress helps modernize American democracy and ensure that the national government better reflects the collective will of the people.

CHAPTER 2

Everybody's President

On November 8, 2016, Republican Donald Trump shocked the world by defeating Democrat Hillary Clinton in the contest to serve as the nation's 45th president. The race had been widely interpreted by media officials, academics, political consultants, and others as a choice between two unpopular candidates, but one in which Clinton would surely prevail. Trump's campaign—full of personal insults, outlandish tweets, blatant distortions, and appeals to sexism and racism—was unlike anything the country had ever seen. In the early days of his campaign, he said Senator John McCain—a former POW in Vietnam—was only "a hero because he got captured," adding "I like heroes who weren't captured."[1] He made crude remarks about Fox News reporter Megyn Kelly, noting (after an interaction with her) that "she had blood coming out of her eyes. Blood coming out of her ... wherever."[2] When a class action lawsuit alleged that Trump's eponymous university was "a basically fraudulent endeavor," Trump argued that the federal judge in the case—Gonzalo Curiel—was incapable of being impartial because he was Latino.[3] Trump attacked the appearance of many of his Republican opponents during the presidential nomination contest, mocked a disabled reporter while on stage at a rally, and referenced the size of his genitals during a televised debate. His well-attended rallies consisted of testosterone-laden, stream-of-consciousness rants against the media, politicians, liberal elites, and others. And on October 11, 2016, just weeks before the general election, video surfaced of Trump bragging to *Access Hollywood* reporter Billy Bush about committing sexual assault. While Trump had rabid supporters, his campaign never appealed to a majority of Americans. By the time November 2016 rolled around, about 60 percent of Americans (including many Republicans) had an unfavorable view of him.

While most Americans disliked Trump, Hillary Clinton's campaign was troubled too. From March 2015 onward, the media scrutinized her clumsy use of a private email server while serving as secretary of state. Her husband, former President Bill Clinton, had become a liability as well. His charitable foundation, despite spending billions on humanitarian programs around the globe, faced criticism for a lack of transparency and accepting money from controversial donors. Progressives had always viewed Hillary Clinton with suspicion, and her 2016 Democratic nomination contest with Senator Bernie Sanders only exacerbated claims that she was too moderate, too corporate-friendly, and too cautious to bring meaningful change. Her acceptance of millions in speaking fees from Wall Street corporations—including $675,000 for three speeches at Goldman Sachs alone—only helped feed this narrative. To make matters worse, media coverage of her campaign—as was the case in 2008—was littered with sexism. Despite her troubles, however, Clinton appeared to have a comfortable lead against Trump less than two weeks before Election Day. Then, just ten days before the election, the FBI announced that it was reopening the investigation into her use of the private email server. While Clinton was ultimately cleared (for a second time), she entered the election a wounded candidate limping to the finish line. She was still expected to win, but likely by a smaller margin than once imagined.

Ultimately, Clinton did not win. Trump won narrow victories in Florida (1.2 percentage points), Michigan (0.23), Pennsylvania (0.72), and Wisconsin (0.77), securing 75 electoral votes in the process. The final Electoral College margin of victory was 306–232 in favor of Trump.[4] After Clinton's stunning loss, the Monday morning quarterbacking was incessant. Clinton was slammed for failing to campaign adequately in the vital Rust Belt states that Trump captured. Her handling of the email controversy was considered a disaster, while her corporate speeches were seen as appallingly short-sighted and tone-deaf. Her choice of Tim Kaine—an inoffensive, center-left senator from Virginia—as her running mate was assailed for failing to mobilize progressives. Her campaign was called lazy, too data-driven, too arrogant, and too careful. Even President Obama, who had campaigned heavily for Clinton, remarked,

> Good ideas don't matter if people don't hear them…. I won Iowa (in 2008) not because the demographics dictated that I would win Iowa. It was because I spent 87 days going to every small town and fair and fish fry and VFW hall, and there were some counties where I might have lost, but maybe I lost by 20 points instead of 50 points…. There are some counties maybe I won that people didn't expect because people had a chance to see you and listen to you and get a sense of who you stood for and who you were fighting for.[5]

Clinton, his comments implied, had not worked as hard as he had.

Many of the criticisms directed towards Clinton were unquestionably valid. It was widely understood that Clinton's campaign did not connect with many Americans, including some who typically vote for Democrats. She did indeed campaign lightly in the Rust Belt. Her meager efforts to appease Bernie Sanders' supporters reeked of arrogance. In light of the email scandal, the Clinton Foundation, and her Wall Street speeches, Clinton was easily painted as a corrupt insider detached from the problems of "Main Street."

Somewhat relegated to the background, however, was the fact that American voters did indeed *prefer* Clinton. By no means was their preference overwhelming, but it was decisive. Once all votes were counted, Clinton had 2,868,686 more than Trump, good for a 48.2 percent—46.1 percent plurality. For at least the fifth time in American history, a candidate whom voting citizens preferred was denied the presidency because of the Electoral College.

Trump, who had once called the Electoral College "a disaster for democracy," was now its biggest defender, tweeting that it is "actually genius in that it brings all states, including the smaller ones, into play." His contradictory statements reflect something all too common in American politics. Citizens and leaders alike often view the efficacy of institutions through a prism of how it affects them politically. The Electoral College was bad, according to Trump, when it reelected Barack Obama in 2012. But when it launched Trump into the White House in 2016, it was indispensable to our democracy. Democrats are not immune from such hypocrisy either. Their calls to eliminate the Electoral College grew after the institution denied them the White House in both 2000 and 2016.

Because it fails to treat all voters equally, the Electoral College is a deeply problematic institution. Let me stress that it is not fundamentally misguided *because* it helped elect George W. Bush in 2000 or Donald Trump in 2016. Rather, it is problematic because it is an antiquated, illogical, confusing and, most importantly, unfair method to select presidents.

In this chapter, I explore how the Electoral College came to be, how it works today, and why I believe it runs contrary to democracy's promise of "one person, one vote." Finally, I explore reform efforts currently underway, addressing both their attributes and potential for success.

The Framers and their Intentions

As I have previously argued, I do not believe that compromises forged by 1780s elites should always determine the structure of 2020s political institutions. While I believe the Constitution represented impressive democratic progress in 1787, parts of the document were (and in some cases, are) at odds with modern conceptions of human equality. The Constitution upheld the privileged position of aristocrats, allowed women to be sidelined from civic life, and relegated most Blacks to the cruel and

humiliating condition of slavery. Through various constitutional amendments, Supreme Court interpretations, and the actions of federal and
state governing bodies, the document has been updated and refreshed in
important ways. The Electoral College, however, continues to pick presidents. This is particularly ironic given that the Framers were not even
enthusiastic about it when it was created.

Defenders of the Electoral College often cite the wisdom of the Framers, implying that the 56 men who drafted the Constitution saw the institution as the unquestioned best way to select a president. This line of
thinking is wholly incorrect. More accurately, as John Roche observed in
1961, the Electoral College was merely a "jerry-rigged improvisation which
has subsequently been endowed with high theoretical content."[6] In other
words, it was a patchwork compromise that later generations have sought
to reframe as ingenious.

The Framers were divided on the question of presidential selection in
ways that reflected broader disagreements at the Convention. In general,
there were three camps. Some, including James Wilson of Pennsylvania,
believed that a national popular vote made the most sense. Noting that
governors were selected by citizens in both Massachusetts and New York,
Wilson argued that direct election had proven to be a "convenient & successful" method of executive selection.[7] While none of the Framers had a
modern conception of voting rights, Wilson and others believed that eligible voters—in most states, white men with property—should be permitted to express their preference for president. All of the votes across the 13
states would be counted, and the person with the most supporters would
be president. Today, we call this a *popular vote*, and we use this method
to elect our senators, our House members, our governors, our state legislators, our mayors, our freeholders, our schoolboards, and even our student councils. At the Philadelphia Convention, however, Wilson received
pushback. Too many delegates doubted the ability of citizens to make a
prudent decision given the challenges of limited information and communication at the time. Some delegates from the smaller states worried that a
national popular vote would fail to give them a sufficient voice in choosing
the president. In many ways, this critique was an extension of the opposition voiced towards the Virginia Plan. As Professor Shlomo Slonim noted
in 1986, "The smaller states were no more prepared to concede to the large
states domination of the process of selecting a chief executive than they
were prepared to allow them to dominate the legislature."[8]

The importance of slavery to this discussion cannot be ignored.
Speaking for North Carolina, then a slave state with a relatively small population, delegate Hugh Williamson rejected a popular vote because "slaves
will have no suffrage."[9] To be clear, Williamson was not lamenting that

slaves would be unable to vote. He was angry because slaves—who would certainly be unable to vote—would not bolster a state's say in choosing the president nonetheless. James Madison, otherwise inclined at the time to support a popular vote, shared these concerns. He stated, "The latter [Southern States] could have no influence in the election on the score of Negroes."[10] Without the necessary support, visions of a national popular vote were abandoned.

A second camp advocated for state legislatures to select the president. Citizens would vote for their state representatives and senators, who would then vote for president. Concerned that this method would make presidents beholden to local interests, the Framers abandoned it without much debate.

James Wilson served as a Pennsylvania delegate at the Philadelphia Convention in 1787. He believed that U.S. presidents should be elected through a popular vote, but not enough of his fellow delegates agreed. After the Constitution was ratified, he would serve as an associate justice on the U.S. Supreme Court for nine years (Smithsonian American Art Museum, CC PDM 1.0: *https://creative-commons.org/publicdomain/mark/1.0/).*

A third camp—the largest—argued for a parliamentary method of executive selection. The president, it was argued, should be chosen by Congress. Such a method would enhance the power of those living in small states, as their disproportionate influence in the Senate would be reflected in the presidential selection process. This idea was ultimately rejected, however, because some worried that it would overly empower the legislature and violate the separation of powers. Gouverneur Morris, a delegate from Pennsylvania, commented that there were "concerns for the independence of the president if he were elected by the Congress." Furthermore, as Morris added, corruption might be more likely "if the president were chosen by a small group of men who met together regularly."[11]

With the Convention deadlocked on the question of presidential selection, the Committee on Unfinished Parts took up the issue. In other words, presidential selection had been relegated to the backburner, and it was time to make a decision. Deadlocked, the Framers did what functional legislative bodies do. They argued, negotiated, and came to a compromise. The result was acceptable to most delegates, but it was hardly a point of pride to them. As historian Jack Rakove commented in 2000, "The Electoral College was cobbled together at the last minute and adopted not because the Framers believed it would work, but because it was less objectionable than two more obvious alternatives: election of the president by the people or by Congress.... It had no advantages of its own."[12]

As constructed, the Electoral College would grant each state a number of presidential electors equivalent to its House delegation (which would vary by population) plus its two senators. The compromise appealed to smaller states, who would be overrepresented relative to their population. The extent of malapportionment would, however, be less than that found in the Senate. Larger states would still have more electors, but not as many more as population proportions would dictate. For example, Virginia initially had about 12 times as many people as Delaware, but would have only about 3.3 times as many electors.

Each state would have the responsibility of choosing electors "in such manner as its Legislature may direct." In other words, states had broad latitude to decide who in their state would be charged with casting its votes for president. In the 1789 election, four states—Delaware, Maryland, Pennsylvania, and Virginia—allowed eligible citizens to directly vote for the state's electors. Connecticut, Georgia, South Carolina, and New Jersey allowed state legislators to choose the slate.[13] By 1800, state legislative selection actually became more popular; in that election, 10 states (out of 16) employed it. As a result, fewer Americans voted for president in 1800 than in 1796. At the start of the nineteenth century, a majority of American adults—even white, land-owning men—were not voting for president.

The Framers actually doubted that the Electoral College would ultimately select presidents. Instead, many assumed that electors would often support "favorite sons," or politicians from their home states. In this event, because no candidate would receive a majority of the total electoral votes available, the election would be thrown to the House of Representatives. There, each state delegation—regardless of its size—would have one vote for president. According to the original Constitution, House delegations could choose from any of the top five electoral vote winners nationwide. Taken as a whole, the Electoral College was designed to give states the ability to filter presidential candidates, narrowing the competition to five. Then, the House—with an equal voice for each state—would make the final selection.

Very quickly, the Framers' vision for the Electoral College crumbled. Two primary reasons are to blame. First, political parties soon developed. While the Framers had hoped to avoid permanent party coalitions from emerging, it soon became clear that in a majoritarian system, parties were essential to advancing commonly-held policy objectives. Through coordination, like-minded politicians could unite to support one another's elections, increase their numbers in legislatures, and work together to pass bills favorable to all members. Today, many often cite the Framers' opposition to parties in an attempt to distance or protect them from the partisan strife we see in today's politics. This is misguided. The same Framers who initially despised political parties eventually formed and expanded America's first major parties. John Adams and Alexander Hamilton were prominent Federalists; Thomas Jefferson and James Madison were Democratic-Republicans. Even George Washington, while never declaring himself a partisan, was very clearly an adherent to Federalist principles.

As a two-party system developed in the 1790s, the Federalists and Democratic-Republicans began nominating candidates for president every four years. Across the states, electors were chosen with an understanding that they would support one of the two major presidential candidates. In 1796, for example, those voting for electors understood that they were choosing adherents of either John Adams or Thomas Jefferson. And with only two major candidates seeking office, one was very likely to win a majority of electors. This was at odds with the Framers' original vision of the Electoral College, which they believed would fail to choose a final winner and instead kick the election to the House of Representatives. In a world of two-party government, the process would rarely make it that far.

The second development at odds with the Framers' vision was the democratization of voting that came in the early 1800s. After 1800, more states gradually allowed eligible citizens to vote for their state's electors. Ten states permitted direct election by 1816; by 1836, all but South Carolina did.[14] In addition, more states expanded the pool of eligible voters by dropping property requirements. Between 1812 and 1821, four new states entered the Union with universal suffrage for white males, while four older states dropped their existing property requirements.[15] Opponents of expanded voting rights were loud and, in limited instances, successful at blocking reform. In Massachusetts, an aging John Adams helped reject universal manhood suffrage at the state's 1821 constitutional convention. At Virginia's convention in 1829, John Randolph bluntly declared, "I am an aristocrat. I love liberty. I hate equality.... I would not live under King Numbers. I would not be his steward—nor make him my taskmaster."[16] Democracy—even for white men—was still not a universally accepted concept. Nevertheless, while foes like Adams and Randolph successfully delayed some state efforts, the momentum to drop property requirements ultimately prevailed. By 1840, over 90 percent of adult, white males in the U.S. were able to vote for presidential electors.[17] While women (in all states after 1807)[18] and Blacks (in most states)[19] were excluded from voting, the electorate increased substantially.

The interaction of these two developments is significant. By 1840, white male citizens went to the polls and chose electors aligned with one of two presidential candidates. They did so with the clear understanding that one candidate would secure the backing of a majority of the nation's electors and become president. The idea of elites choosing electors who would narrow the field before House delegations chose the president was fully disregarded. The system intended by the Framers—*with only lukewarm enthusiasm*—was dead. And to a large extent, it was the Framers themselves who perpetuated its extinction! It turns out the Framers were not as stubbornly married to the Framers' ideas as some citizens and commentators in the twenty-first century appear to be.

The Electoral College Today

Recall than an institution fails the test of political equality when it values the input of some citizens more than others. The modified Electoral College that emerged in the early-mid 1800s does this in numerous ways. While this reformed version is indeed more participatory than its predecessor (because citizens can vote for electors), it is still far from a model democratic institution. In this section, I focus on six central problems with today's Electoral College from the perspective of political equality. These include (1) malapportionment, (2) misfires, (3) punishment for high turnout, (4) census lags, (5) faithless electors, and (6) contingency elections.

Malapportionment

The Electoral College suffers from a malapportionment problem for a few reasons, but most centrally because it factors Senate seats into its state allocation formula. Because every state has exactly two senators regardless of population—the chief malapportionment sin of the U.S. Constitution—discrepancies are often massive. Consider again the smallest and largest states in the U.S.—Wyoming (3 electors) and California (54 electors). In 2020, Wyoming had one elector for every 195,369 residents. In California, there was one elector for every 711,723 residents.[20] This means that each resident of Wyoming had over 3.6 times as much influence over

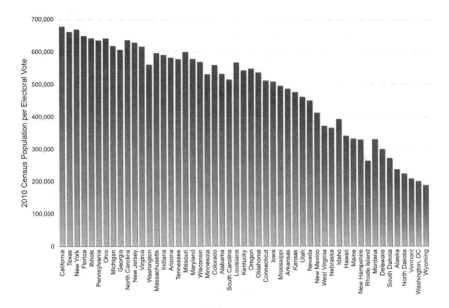

As the population of a state rises, the number of residents per elector increases substantially. Today, each resident of the smallest state (Wyoming) has nearly four times the influence as each resident of the largest state (California) in the Electoral College (Perl Coder, CC BY-SA 4.0: *https://creativecommons.org/ licenses/by-sa/4.0/deed.en*).

choosing electors as each resident of California. Other state disparities are significant as well. The above figure shows the number of residents in each state per electoral vote. As I discussed in Chapter 1, population disparities between the states are much greater than they were in 1787, meaning that residents of large states are much more devalued today than they were when the Constitution was adopted.

Too often, reactions to these disparities reflect partisanship, tribalism, and geographic defensiveness. (I don't like California, so this is a good system!) I am susceptible to gut reactions as well, but let's try to set those aside for a moment and just consider the profound unfairness at work here. Under the Electoral College, voting-age residents have more or less say over who becomes president simply based on where they live. Vermonters have considerably more say than Texans; Montanans have more influence than Floridians. Despite the fact that the president of the United States has equal power over all Americans, he or she is chosen through a process that weighs some voices more than others. Presidents sign tax laws, make decisions about troop deployments, and issue executive orders that fundamentally affect the lives of Americans throughout the country. President George W. Bush's decision to invade Iraq committed the tax dollars, service, and (in nearly 5,000 cases) lives of Americans without regard to their home state. Service members from North Dakota were no more at risk than those from North Carolina or New York. President Obama's executive order creating the Deferred Action for Childhood Arrivals (DACA) program in 2012 applied equally to undocumented children throughout the country. And when President Trump banned transgender persons from serving in the military in 2017, members of this community were equally affected in California and Wyoming. If Americans are equally subject to a president's decisions, shouldn't they all have an equal opportunity to determine who that president will be?

The sorts of distortions created by the Electoral College sound absurd when applied to other hypothetical circumstances. Imagine if a town decided that the votes of older voters would count more than younger voters when selecting a mayor. Or that the votes from certain neighborhoods would be valued 3.6 times more than others. Stepping outside of politics, imagine if football games counted points scored in the second quarter more than those scored in the fourth. Or what if golf matches weighed strokes on the sixth hole differently from the other 17 holes? As crazy as it sounds, this is basically how the Electoral College works.

Misfires

The most noticeable problem with the Electoral College from a political equality perspective, of course, is that the national popular vote winner does not always win the election. While some historical cases are open to debate, by my count this has occurred on five (possibly six) occasions—1824, 1876, 1888, 1960 (debatable), 2000, and 2016. The U.S. has had 59 presidential elections, meaning that in about ten percent of all cases, the winner has not been the preferred choice of the voting public.

Electoral vote distortions, or "misfires," occur for two primary reasons. First, because some votes (those in small states) effectively count for more, candidates can conceivably win enough support from small states that it helps them secure an Electoral College majority despite losing the national popular vote. Second, 48 of the 50 states now allocate electoral votes on a winner-take-all basis, meaning that the candidate who wins the most popular votes in a state wins all of that state's electors. The margin of victory in a state is immaterial; the goal is simply to win the most votes in individual states.[21] As a result, candidates can secure Electoral College majorities without winning a plurality of popular votes nationally. Consider the following example. Suppose for simplicity's sake that the entire U.S. consisted of three states—Delaware, New Jersey, and Pennsylvania—in 2020. Delaware had the minimum three electoral votes, while

New Jersey and Pennsylvania had 14 and 20, respectively. Now imagine if Joe Biden had won his home state of Delaware and New Jersey by 100,000 votes each. In Pennsylvania, however, assume that Donald Trump secured a small victory margin of 10,000 votes. In this example, Trump is elected president because he wins in the Electoral College by a margin of 20–17. He wins despite the fact that Biden earned more popular votes—190,000 more, to be exact.

This is a simplified example, but it reflects what can occur on a larger scale in presidential elections. Candidates receive the same benefit if they win a state by a single popular vote or by hundreds of thousands (or millions) of votes. Therefore, candidates who win larger states (with more electoral votes) by small margins have the potential to reach 270 electors without winning national popular vote pluralities or majorities.

As I noted, Electoral College misfires have occurred at least five times in U.S. history. Below is a brief discussion of each instance, including a discussion of why some cases are a bit more complicated.

In 1824, Andrew Jackson handily defeated John Quincy Adams in the national popular vote, 41.4 percent to 30.9 percent. Both percentages are unusually low because 1824 actually featured four candidates vying for the presidency. The election was held during a bizarre (and brief) period in U.S. history where one political party—the Democratic-Republicans—had come to dominate. The 1824 campaign saw the party splinter, with four candidates—Jackson, Adams, Treasury Secretary William Crawford, and House Speaker Henry Clay—all seeking the White House. Because no candidate earned an Electoral College majority, the election was thrown to the House for the second time (1800 was the first). Adams was elected in the House after 13 of 24 state delegations chose him. Some cried that Adams had entered a "corrupt bargain" with Clay whereby the latter was promised the position of secretary of state in exchange for throwing his support to Adams. Nevertheless, Adams became the country's sixth president despite losing the initial popular vote badly to Jackson. Some historians do not consider 1824 a true Electoral College misfire because six states—Delaware, Georgia, Louisiana, New York, South Carolina, and Vermont—still did not choose their electors through a statewide popular vote. In other words, we cannot fully ascertain the nation's preferences if several states did not allow them to be recorded. This is a fair point, but based on the popular vote that *was* recorded, Jackson was overwhelmingly favored over Adams.

The 1876 presidential election was held in the waning days of the Reconstruction period. After the Civil War ended in 1865, federal troops occupied the former Confederate states to varying degrees in an attempt to quell racial violence and enforce civil (including voting) rights for Blacks.

Momentum for such action had begun to slow during the 1870s, particularly after a financial panic hit in 1873. As years passed after the Civil War, Northerners were increasingly content to allow the South (i.e., the white South) to govern itself again at the expense of civil rights. In this context, Democrat Samuel Tilden defeated Republican Rutherford B. Hayes in the popular vote, 50.9 percent–47.9 percent, in the 1876 election. Tilden led in the Electoral College by 19 votes, but 20 remaining electoral votes were disputed. In three former Confederate states—Florida (with four electoral votes), Louisiana (8), and South Carolina (7)—reported returns favored Tilden (the favored candidate of the white South), but there were widespread reports of electoral fraud and threats of violence against Republican voters. Because the Republican-led federal government still controlled state electoral commissions in the South, they subsequently disallowed enough Democratic votes in each of the three states to make Hayes the winner. One additional electoral vote in Oregon was disputed after the elector was declared illegal for being an "elected or appointed official." With the results disputed, Congress formed a 15-member electoral commission to determine the fate of the disputed electoral votes. Five members each were selected from the House, Senate, and Supreme Court. By an 8–7 margin, the commission ultimately granted all 20 disputed electoral votes to Hayes, giving him enough to win in the Electoral College by a 1-vote margin, 185–184. Hayes therefore became the second president elected despite losing the national popular vote.

In 1888, incumbent Democratic President Grover Cleveland won the popular vote against his Republican challenger, Benjamin Harrison. In the Electoral College, however, Harrison prevailed, 233–168. Harrison's narrow victory in New York, then the state with the highest electoral vote count, helped him secure victory despite winning just 47.8 percent of the national popular vote.

The 1960 election is rarely cited as an Electoral College misfire, but there is an argument that it should be. Democrat John Kennedy was victorious in the Electoral College by a count of 303–219. Kennedy is often credited with earning 34,220,984 popular votes compared to just 34,108,157 for his Republican opponent, Richard Nixon. The truth is a bit more complicated. In the state of Alabama, the actual number of votes received by Kennedy is difficult to determine because of unusual circumstances there. Typically, when citizens vote for president under the Electoral College system, they are actually voting for a slate of electors committed to the candidate of their choice. For example, when a majority of Michigan voters chose Joe Biden in 2020, they were actually electing Biden's slate of 16 Michigan electors. This slate then formally voted for Biden in Lansing (the state capital) in December. It is through this process that the winner-take-all nature of the institution works. In 1960, however, Alabama chose to use a different process. In that state, the 11 Democratic elector candidates ran not as a slate, but as individuals. Six ran as unpledged, and five pledged to support Kennedy if they won. Alabama voters could vote for all 11, or they could choose to only support the unpledged or Kennedy electors. Most voters selected something close to the full slate, meaning that they voted for both the Kennedy and uncommitted electors. Ultimately, all 11 electors were chosen by the state's voters, as each received more votes than any of Nixon's Republican electors. In the Electoral College, the Kennedy electors were faithful to the candidate, while the uncommitted electors voted for independent segregationist Harry Byrd, a senator from Virginia. Typically, Kennedy is assigned 318,303 votes (the votes won by the most popular Kennedy elector). Allotting Kennedy this count gives him the narrow national popular vote victory noted above. This accounting, however, is generous to Kennedy because it gives him the full popular vote of any citizen that cast a vote for his most popular elector, even if they also voted for (or even preferred) uncommitted electors with no intention of supporting him. It will never be fully known how many Democratic voters in Alabama in 1960 preferred Kennedy to uncommitted, but the number is certainly less than 100 percent, given Kennedy's stated support for civil rights and the fact that Alabama's electorate was almost entirely white. If the true number of Kennedy supporters was at least 112,828 fewer than the 318,303 for which he is credited, the difference would be large enough to give Nixon the national popular vote victory. In my view, this was likely the case given Alabama's politics at the time, but the circumstances were strange enough that 1960 can only be considered a possible Electoral College misfire.

Forty years later, Democratic Vice President Al Gore lost a close election to Texas Governor George W. Bush by a 271–267 vote in the Electoral College. The election is mostly remembered for the chaos surrounding the vote in Florida. Had Gore won Florida and its 25 electoral votes, he would have eclipsed 270 electoral votes and become president. The Gore campaign argued that in several Democratic-leaning counties, ballots were discarded even when the intent of the voter was clear. More specifically, ballots were thrown away if the paper chad had been punctured, but not fully removed from the ballot. Gore demanded a recount that would count all ballots for which "the intent of the voter" could be determined; his request was granted by the Florida Supreme Court. However, the U.S. Supreme Court overruled this judgment in a 5–4 ruling.[22] The High Court determined that (1) there was not enough time for a recount and (2) allowing a recount in some (but not all) Florida counties would violate the Equal Protection Clause of the Fourteenth Amendment.

The "hanging chad" ballots were not the only election irregularity in Florida in 2000. A flawed ballot in Palm Beach County likely led some of Gore's supporters to vote for Reform Party (far-right) nominee Pat Buchanan. Meanwhile, thousands of (mostly Black) Florida residents were improperly disenfranchised before the election by being mistakenly classified as felons. In the end, none of it mattered. Bush was certified as the winner in Florida and therefore the Electoral College. Al Gore, the first (not last) victim of the Electoral College in the twenty-first century, retired from politics and devoted his career to the global climate crisis, winning a Nobel Prize and an Oscar for his 2006 film, *An Inconvenient Truth*.

The 2016 election, which I discussed at the start of the chapter, was at the least the fifth case of an Electoral College misfire. And in terms of total votes, it was easily the largest. No candidate has ever won as many more votes than his or her chief competitor and still lost a presidential election than Hillary Clinton. For all of Clinton's missteps in 2016, she was decidedly preferred by a plurality of U.S. voters in that election. No discussion about "why she lost"—which seemingly dominated every talk show, newspaper column, Twitter handle, and dinner table conversation for weeks after the 2016 election—should have led with any other reason than the mere existence of the Electoral College. Donald Trump's narrow victories in Florida, Michigan, Pennsylvania, and Wisconsin—all by 1.2 percentage points or less—landed him 75 electoral votes. More generally, Trump won his states by less than Clinton won hers, so his accumulation of electoral votes was far more efficient. Clinton won more votes, but not in the right places. This explanation only makes sense, of course, in the context of a system that values the voice of some Americans more than others. Regardless of what one thinks about Hillary Clinton or Donald Trump, such an institution is simply incompatible with modern conceptions of basic fairness and democracy.

Punishment for High Turnout

Chapter 6 will discuss the state of voter participation in the U.S. with considerable detail. For now, however, let's just say that turnout in the U.S. is generally underwhelming by global standards. While 2020 turnout (66.7 percent) was unusually high, most industrialized democracies routinely see higher rates of voter participation in national elections. Explanations are many, but generally include a lack of electoral competition, winner-take-all elections, voter apathy, the inconvenience of voting, and too many elections. While I will punt our larger discussion of turnout, I will note here that while turnout is generally poor to mediocre, it does vary across the U.S. Some states routinely record turnout rates over 70 percent in presidential elections, while others are typically stuck below 50 percent. In addition to its other aforementioned democratic deficits, the Electoral College effectively punishes voters in states with relatively high levels of participation.

Consider the following case from the 2020 election. Hawaii and Maine are similarly sized states in terms of population. Each has a bit over one million residents and, as a result, four electoral votes. Maine, however, routinely has one of the highest turnout rates in the nation. In 2020, it was 76.3 percent of all eligible voters. Hawaii, by contrast, had one of the lowest 2020 turnout rates in the country, at just 57.5 percent. Maine recorded 819,461 votes, while Hawaii recorded only 574,469 votes. Because a state's total number of electors is set by the size of its congressional delegation, it does not change depending on the number of citizens who choose to participate. So, in 2020, 819,461 voters had to share four electoral votes in Maine, while only 574,469 got to share four electoral votes in Hawaii. Each participating citizen in Maine had considerably less influence than each participating citizen in Hawaii. Maine voters were effectively devalued for the mere reason that there were more of them, per capita. Put another way, Mainers were punished because a large number of them chose to do their civic duty.

Census Lags

The Electoral College undervalues the voices of citizens in both large states and states with high turnout rates. In addition, the institution hurts the voting power of citizens in states with high population growth rates. Let me explain. Recall that a state's number of electors is equivalent to its number of House seats, plus two. The number of House seats is determined based on the results of the census, which is conducted every ten years. However, if a state grows quickly after a census is taken, its House delegation (and therefore its electoral vote count) is still not adjusted until after the following census. These lags create notable disparities. By the 2020 election, Texas—based on its population—should have had 38 House seats and 40 presidential electors. Because its electoral vote count remained set by the 2010 census until after the 2020 census was completed (which was after the 2020 election), it had just 38 presidential electors. Colorado, Florida, Montana, North Carolina, and Oregon—all of whom grew quickly between 2010 and 2020—also had fewer electoral votes in 2020 than their population shares justified. Meanwhile, California, Illinois, Michigan, New York, Ohio, Pennsylvania and West Virginia—all of whom grew at slower rates after 2010—had more electors in 2020 than an updated census would have dictated. Because the census is taken only every ten years, electoral vote allocations are nearly always a bit out of date. If a national popular vote were used to elect the president, a state's population growth would be irrelevant because all citizen votes would count equally, regardless of where voters resided.

Faithless Electors

While the Constitution is clear that each state has the right to choose electors "in such manner as its Legislature may direct," it is vague on the question of whether states can compel electors to vote a certain way. Since the early 1800s, however, states have structured their rules so that electors are very likely to support the candidate who wins the state's popular vote. Parties or candidates choose their own slates of electors. So, when Joe Biden won the most popular votes in Rhode Island in 2020, his four electors were chosen to cast the state's four presidential votes in December. These four individuals had been selected by the Rhode Island Democratic Party, meaning that they were a fairly safe bet to honor their pledges and vote for Biden. (They all did.) Sometimes, however, electors go rogue, becoming *faithless electors*. In 2016, a record seven electors violated their pledges (three more attempted to do so), costing Trump two votes and Clinton five. Faithless electors did not affect the outcome of the 2016 election, nor any that preceded it. But Robert M. Alexander, a professor at Northern Ohio University, cautions that many electors do believe that they have the right to stray from their state's vote (and their implicit pledge). After conducting a survey of 2016 electors, he reported that 21 percent gave at least some consideration to defecting.[23]

Thirty states and the District of Columbia have adopted laws requiring electors to be faithful to their pledged tickets. In some of these states, faithless electors are immediately replaced, meaning they are effectively unable to stray from their pledges. In most states, however, faithless electors merely face a fine of $1,000 or less. After the 2016 election, both Colorado and Washington levied $1,000 fines against their respective faithless electors. The electors sued, arguing that according to the Constitution, electors could not be compelled to support a particular candidate. The Supreme Court ultimately heard the case in *Chiafalo v. Washington* (2020), ruling unanimously that states are permitted to punish faithless electors. Writing for the majority, Justice Elena Kagan said, "Nothing in the Constitution expressly prohibits states from taking away president electors' voting discretion … the power to appoint an elector (in any manner) includes power to condition his appointment, absent some other constitutional constraint."[24] The ability to punish electors, however, does not mean that additional states must adopt such restrictions or that those with laws will make them stricter. In the absence of those developments, faithless electors in many states will continue to have enormous power to deviate from the will of their state's voters.

Contingency Elections

Recall that the Framers believed that the Electoral College would generally fail to choose a winner. Instead, electors were expected to mostly select "favorite son" candidates from their home states or regions. Then, following the protocol laid out by the Constitution, the House—with each state delegation having one vote—would choose from the five leading electoral vote winners. The rapid rise of a two-party system meant that the Framers' vision never really came true. Instead, most elections have seen a candidate secure an Electoral College majority. Only twice in U.S. history—1800 and 1824—has the institution failed to produce a winner. The 1800 election occurred before the Twelfth Amendment (1804), which placed the president and vice president on separate ballots. Under the original Constitution, electors each had two votes for president and the candidate who finished second in the electoral vote count became vice president. As a result, when Democratic-Republican electors each voted for Thomas Jefferson and Aaron Burr in 1800, it produced a tie.[25] It took 36 ballots before a majority of House delegations chose a candidate (Jefferson).

The aforementioned 1824 election was unusual because four candidates earned electoral votes, with none earning a majority. The House eventually chose John Quincy Adams, who had lost the popular vote by more than ten points.

Because each of these cases occurred early in U.S. history, Americans have little awareness of how contingency elections work in the event that the Electoral College fails to produce a winner. And while contingency elections have not been necessary in nearly 200 years, the possibility remains. In fact, in 2004, had Iowa, Nevada, and New Mexico—which were all very competitive—gone to Democrat John Kerry instead of President George W. Bush, an Electoral College tie would have resulted. More recently, if Joe Biden had lost the swing states of Arizona, Nevada, and Pennsylvania in 2020 (all of which he won by less than 2.5 points), he and Donald Trump would have tied with 269 electoral votes.

A contingency election, if needed, would make the Electoral College look like a model democratic institution. Each state delegation in the House would receive one vote, regardless of its size. This means that the 52 California representatives would need to coordinate and decide how to cast their *single vote*. Meanwhile, representatives from the six smallest states—Delaware, Vermont, Wyoming, North Dakota, South Dakota, and Alaska—would simply have a vote all to themselves. Nearly forty million Americans living in California would be represented by the same number of votes as less than 600,000 Americans in Wyoming. Other disparities between the states would be massive as well. Twenty million Floridians would have the same voice as 643,000 Vermonters. Twenty-nine million Texans would be represented by the same number of votes as less than 900,000 South Dakotans. The democratic deficit would be equivalent to that seen in the Senate, as all states would have equal value regardless of population.

Another reason why a contingency election would be unfair involves the District of Columbia. By virtue of the Twenty-Third Amendment, D.C. has had three presidential electors since 1964, the same as the smallest U.S. states. However, D.C. is not a state. As a result, it would have no voice in a contingency election. The roughly 700,000 residents of the District—who pay more annual federal taxes than the residents of 21 states!—would have no say in choosing the president.[26] In Chapter 4, I will discuss the broader issue of representation in the District of Columbia, as well as in the U.S. territories.

Beyond being wildly undemocratic, contingency elections have the potential to be exceptionally chaotic. The Constitution is clear that a candidate must receive the support of a majority (26) of House delegations in order to be elected. Given the state of partisanship in the U.S., this could be very difficult to obtain. Imagine that in the 2020 election, Joe Biden had lost the swing states of Arizona, Nevada, and Pennsylvania, creating a 269–269 Electoral College tie. The election would have been thrown to the House, where Democrats maintained a majority of members, but Republicans controlled a majority (27) of state delegations. In this event, the House very likely would have granted the presidency to Trump. But suppose both Democrats and Republicans had each controlled exactly 25 delegations. In this example, which candidate would have received the support of 26 delegations? Which House Democrats would have voted for Trump? Or which House Republicans would have voted for Biden? Delegations would also be unable to consider compromise candidates since the Constitution only allows them to choose someone who finished in the top three in electors.[27] It is difficult to see how the situation could have been resolved in time for the January 20, 2021, inauguration. Ultimately, a contingency election was not needed in 2020. And it may not be needed in our lifetimes. But the possibility is very real. And if it does happen, it will likely be a democratic and logistical nightmare.

Addressing the Naysayers

Any one of the above six concerns regarding an institution's democratic viability would be reason enough for concern. The Electoral College possesses all six. Nevertheless, while a majority of Americans consistently support adopting a national popular vote, there are many supporters of the existing system. Some have simply determined that the Electoral College helps their party in contemporary times and therefore have little interest in seeing beyond partisan politics. Others, however, have less overtly political concerns about replacing it. I do not believe it is helpful to dismiss these honest apprehensions without fair consideration. In fact, by responding to them, I believe the case for eliminating the Electoral College only becomes stronger. Below, I raise several of the most common arguments against eliminating the Electoral College and address them.

"If we have a national popular vote, New York and California will determine the election."

When I published an op-ed in the *Richmond Times-Dispatch* in 2020 calling for the abolishment of the Electoral College, this was the most common retort I found in my inbox. Clearly, many citizens worry that a national popular vote would elevate heavily populated states (these two, in particular) to the extent that the rest of the country would not matter. There are a number of reasons why this argument is flawed.

First, while California is indeed the most populated state in the U.S., New York is just the fourth. Both Florida and Texas have more residents and electoral votes than New York. Given current growth projections, each of these two states is expected to grow at a faster pace than New York in the near future. Any "advantage" that a national popular vote would bestow on large states would be felt in Florida and Texas more than in New York.

Second, this argument implies that individuals who live in larger states should have *less* influence than those who do not. I see no valid reason why an American—simply by virtue of residing in a place that has a high population—deserves to be devalued when choosing a president who will have power over them. Is a 50-year-old farmer in upstate New York less American than a 50-year-old farmer in Kansas? Does an elderly woman in California deserve to have less than half of the voting power as an elderly woman in Rhode Island? The suggestion that large states such as California and New York would themselves "gain" power from a national popular vote is misguided. A national popular vote would not consider states as political entities *at all*. Instead, it would recognize only citizens.

California, New York, and other large states would not benefit from end-ing the Electoral College; instead, citizens living there would finally be granted the same voting power as those residing in smaller states.

Third, it is often implied—mostly by conservative media and political figures—that California and New York are universally populated by radi-cal left-wingers who despise everything about the states who live between them. Not so fast. As I discussed in Chapter 1, states (including these two) are hardly monolithic. California is the leading agricultural state in the U.S., producing more than $13 billion more in annual food value than the second leading state (Iowa).[28] Less than half of New Yorkers live in New York City, and Republicans are favored throughout the rural parts of the state; Trump won 41 of the state's counties in 2020 (Biden won just 21). Make no mistake, both California and New York are majority Dem-ocratic states, but they also include considerable numbers of Republican voters. Donald Trump received 6,006,429 votes in California (34 percent) and 3,251,997 votes in New York (38 percent) in 2020. However, Trump received no electoral votes from either state, meaning that over 9 mil-lion of *his* voters were effectively disenfranchised in these states. With a national popular vote, these votes would have gone into his national tally.

"If we have a national popular vote, candidates will only care about (and campaign in) cities."

I understand why critics have this concern. With a system that values overall votes, candidates would seemingly have little incentive to spend time in rural areas where comparatively few votes exist. Under the Elec-toral College, the argument goes, rural areas are bolstered, forcing candi-dates to care about them and their issues.

There are several problems with this argument. First, under the Elec-toral College, candidates do not campaign more in small, rural states. While citizens in lightly populated states do effectively see their votes count for more, there is still no reason for candidates to campaign any-where that is not electorally competitive. Individual citizens in Wyoming indeed count more per electoral vote than any other citizens in the coun-try, yet the state has not seen a presidential candidate visit in recorded memory. The reason is that it has been a solidly Republican state for decades. Candidates campaign solely in places where they do not know whether they will win a plurality of the votes. The only small states that have received any candidate attention in recent years are New Hampshire and Nevada, and this is because both parties have seen a path to victory in them. Candidates spend most of their time in larger, swing states—Flor-ida, Michigan, North Carolina, Pennsylvania—where the most electoral votes are in question. While the Electoral College enhances the value of citizens in small states, the winner-take-all nature of the institution means that candidates will still not focus on them unless their state is competitive.

Relatedly, candidates already campaign disproportionately in urban areas. Most campaign events are typically held in cities located within competitive states—places like Philadelphia, Pennsylvania; Las Vegas, Nevada; Raleigh, North Carolina; and Detroit, Michigan. With a national popular vote, candidates would likely continue to hold the bulk of events in population centers since these are the easiest places for large numbers to congregate. (This is why sporting events and concerts are generally held there too.) But in this case, events would likely be held in a broader range of cities throughout the country.

But even though campaign events would continue to be disproportionately held in cities under a national popular vote, this does not mean candidates would ignore other areas or their concerns. Why? It is a simple numbers game. The population of the 100 largest cities in the U.S.—going all the way down to Tacoma, Washington, with 220,000 residents—is still less than 20 percent of the country's population. A national campaign focused only on urban issues would never be a winning strategy. Furthermore, even if this was not the case, candidates (under any system) are not incentivized to merely target places with the most voters. Rather, they are incentivized to target *persuadable* voters. In the U.S., persuadable voters are generally found disproportionately in suburban areas, which means that candidate policies—under a national popular vote—would be more likely to cater to them (as they arguably already do). But rather than candidates focusing on narrow targets in a handful of swing states only, they would be forced to consider issues of interest to persuadable voters across the U.S.

"If we have a national popular vote, states (and their issues) will not matter."

Without question, the Constitution emphasizes the protection of state sovereignty. States existed before the national government and only begrudgingly ceded power to Washington (well, first New York and Philadelphia) in the 1780s when it became clear that more national coordination was necessary. As a result, the original Constitution and the Bill of Rights protect state sovereignty in many ways. State legislatures were initially charged with electing U.S. senators (until the Seventeenth Amendment). States have their own equal representation in the Senate. And under the Tenth Amendment, "The powers not delegated to the United States by the

Constitution, nor prohibited by it to the States, are reserved to the States respectively, or to the people."

That states mattered to the Framers is not a disputed fact. However, this should not be the end of the discussion. First, political culture and democratic norms have changed substantially since the 1780s. The idea that states have particular interests that capture the attention of presidential candidates in a national campaign is overstated. As Robert Alexander has noted, "differences among states have become less marked over time. Communication, transportation, and the mass media have minimized differences throughout the United States."[29] Of course there are differences throughout the country, but they are rarely defined by state borders. As I discussed in Chapter 1, states cannot be pigeonholed into particular characteristics. States are not wholly agricultural, industrial, urban, rural, highly educated, or elderly. There are far more interests within states than across them. Agricultural interests are powerful in heavily populated states such as California, New York, and Texas. Urban interests are plentiful in small states such as New Mexico and Rhode Island. If the Electoral College demands that candidates pay attention to "state interests," it is increasingly unclear which interests would even grab their attention. And while some states certainly have overwhelming issues of importance (e.g., Pennsylvania and fracking, California and wildfire prevention, Iowa and corn), all of these dominant interests are also found in other states. A national popular vote would simply allow candidates to value these issues (and others) in proportion to the degree to which they affect Americans as a whole.

Furthermore, as political scientist George Edwards has observed, "partisanship and ideology drive divisions in American politics far more so than one's state residency."[30] If you look at an electoral map that divides the U.S. into counties, what becomes clear is that political disagreements in the U.S. are not fundamentally between states. Rather, they are largely based on demographic differences—race, ethnicity, education, etc.—that are often revealed through density. Urban areas, whether in Alabama, Arizona, California, Maine, or New York, tend to be diverse and overwhelmingly Democratic. Rural areas, whether in inland Oregon, central Pennsylvania, or western Maryland, tend to be Republican strongholds. The politics of upstate New York are far closer to rural Indiana than Brooklyn. Suburbs almost anywhere are more mixed, with more progressive communities often living closer to the associated urban center.

The regional divide on slavery that defined so much of early U.S. politics is a relic of the past. Visit a coffee shop, craft brewery, or college campus in nearly any city in the U.S. for long enough, and you will likely overhear progressive chatter. Attend a high-school football game in upstate New York, rural Georgia, West Texas, or even inland California, and you will likely find that the fans' median politics lean in a more conservative direction. When you consider the variation that exists within states, it makes more and more sense to simply count all votes—wherever they are submitted—the same.

It is important to note that while a national popular vote would fully shift the focus of presidential campaigns from states to people, it would do nothing to reduce state autonomy on *policy*. Even though their relative power has been reduced since the ratification of the Constitution,[31] states retain considerable leeway in adopting their own laws. States have varying laws regarding driving, marijuana, alcohol, prostitution, physician-assisted suicide, state taxes, renters' rights, divorce, in-state college tuition, unemployment benefits, Medicaid, the death penalty, and much, much more. A national popular vote would not restrict this autonomy from the federal government at all; it would simply mean that for the purposes of selecting an executive for the federal government, all citizens would have equal power regardless of where they live.

Reform

Efforts to reform or eliminate the Electoral College are as old as the country itself. In fact, according to FairVote, more proposed amendments regarding the Electoral College have been proposed than for any other subject of constitutional reform.[32] All efforts to fully replace the institution, of course, have failed. As I have discussed, amending the Constitution is exceptionally difficult. There are formidable obstacles to gaining the support of two-thirds of each chamber of Congress, along with 38 state legislatures. In this case, there are always some citizens and officials who are simply uncomfortable with ending the traditional system, even though it already operates in a way at odds with the Framers' design. Second, some agree with the Electoral College's biases, believing that a federal republic should value states as political entities even at the expense of malapportionment.

Third, politics matter. Political actors are not likely to support a reform that they do not believe will serve their interests. Those representing small states face pressure to defend a system that overvalues their people. Officials in swing states are understandably hesitant to surrender the disproportionate attention that candidates heap upon them every four years. Most importantly, if members of a political party come to see the Electoral College as benefiting them, they are more likely to protect it. In a polarized political environment, this dynamic is especially true. Since the 2000 and (especially) 2016 elections, when Republican presidents were elected despite losing the national popular vote, Republicans (citizens and elites alike) have clearly become more supportive of the Electoral College. Following the 2000 race, 75 percent of Democrats said that they preferred a national popular vote to the Electoral College, though just 41 percent of Republicans agreed. By 2011, with the 2000 election further in the rear-view mirror, 71 percent of Democrats and 53 percent of Republicans supported adopting a national popular vote.[33] Then, after Trump's surprise victory in 2016, the numbers changed markedly. In a survey conducted in December 2016, 81 percent of Democrats supported a popular vote, while just 19 percent of Republicans did so.[34] Then President-elect Trump, the beneficiary of the Electoral College in 2016, contradicted past statements and called the institution "genius."

For a brief period after President Obama's reelection in 2012, Republicans appeared to be the party with concerns about the Electoral College. After Obama's victory, media coverage stressed the apparent lock on the Electoral College that Democrats had. Commentators highlighted that as long as Democrats continued to win the Rust Belt states of Michigan, Pennsylvania, and Wisconsin, as well as the newly Democratic-leaning states of Nevada, New Mexico, and Colorado, they would be difficult to beat in the near future. Rather than suggest a national popular vote, however, Republicans in many places suggested that states allocate their electors in a manner similar to Maine and Nebraska, with candidates securing one elector for each House district that they win. Republicans were attracted to this idea because they would be able to secure electors in states where several of the House districts were favorable to them, but the overall state was not. The idea was particularly appealing in the 2010s because many Republican-controlled state legislatures had effectively gerrymandered their state's House districts following the 2010 census. (Chapter 3 will address gerrymandering with more detail.) By doing so, they often drew districts in a way that efficiently allocated Republican votes to maximize seats won. In fact, Republicans won a majority of House seats in 2012 despite losing a majority of votes in House races nationwide. Democrats vehemently opposed this suggested reform, but it ultimately failed due to a lack of sustained support within the Republican Party.

Brief discussions after 2012 notwithstanding, most efforts to reform the Electoral College have focused on replacing the institution with a national popular vote. Reform came closest in the late 1960s, a time of broad reform across U.S. political institutions and culture. In 1969, there was brief bipartisan support in Congress for a constitutional amendment to elect presidents based on the popular vote. The House passed it 339–70, with more than 80 percent of each party's voting members lending their support. Unfortunately, small state senators from both parties filibustered the amendment, and it never received a vote.[35] Had there been a stronger demand from the public to reform the system, the Senate may have been forced to consider it. After all, substantial blocs in Congress also tried (successfully for a while) to defeat proposals for the direct election of senators and women's suffrage before each was enshrined in the Constitution.

In recent years, an intriguing reform idea has emerged that would effectively advance a national popular vote without a constitutional amendment. In 2001, a coalition of law professors started outlining an Electoral College workaround that became the National Popular Vote Interstate Compact (NPVIC). In 2007, the Maryland Legislature became the first to approve it, and it was signed into law by then-Governor Martin O'Malley. In the years since, 15 additional states and the District of Columbia have entered the agreement. Under the compact, states pledge to give their electors to the winner of the *national* popular vote, regardless of which candidate the state's voters supported. The compact would only take effect when (and if) a sufficient number of states join so that the national popular vote winner is guaranteed to be elected president. This would occur when the number of electors possessed by NPVIC member states equals or exceeds 270. Under the NPVIC, the Electoral College would technically remain in place, but it would always act in accordance with the national popular vote. Because each state already has the power to choose electors "in such manner as its Legislature may direct," no constitutional amendment would be necessary. As of 2021, NPVIC member states have a combined 195 electoral votes, nearly 72 percent of the total needed for the compact to take effect.

As of 2021, each state that has joined the compact is a Democratic-leaning state, further confirming that Electoral College reform has become extremely partisan since Trump's 2016 victory. Before 2016, the effort was still mostly led by Democrats, but not entirely. In fact, Republican-led assemblies in both Arkansas and Oklahoma most recently passed the NPVIC in 2009 and 2014, respectively.[36] In order for the compact to achieve its objective, one of two things will likely need to happen: (1) Democrats will need to win majorities in several additional state legislatures, including some that are not solidly Democratic states, or (2) support will need to become at least marginally bipartisan so that Republicans can help pass it in some states. The challenge is deepened by the fact that support is not automatic in Democratic-led states either. In 2019, Democratic Governor Steve Siolak of Nevada vetoed the NPVIC. In doing so, he stated, "Once effective, the National Popular Vote Interstate Compact could diminish the role of smaller states like Nevada in national electoral contests…. In cases like this, where Nevada's interests could diverge from the interests of large states, I will always stand up for Nevada."[37] Nevertheless, the NPVIC's odds are certainly much better than the passage of a constitutional amendment.

Even if approved, the NPVIC would face additional obstacles. Article I, Section 10 of the Constitution notes that states may enter "compacts" or "agreements" with one another, provided that compacts are then approved by Congress. The Supreme Court has limited congressional power on this question somewhat, ruling in *U.S. Steel v. Multistate Tax Commission* (1978) that compacts are only subject to congressional sign-off if (1) they increase state power at the expense of federal power or (2) affect "our federal structure."[38] Whether the NPVIC would fall into these categories is unclear. On one hand, the Constitution already lets states choose electors as they see fit, so it does not appear as though state power is *increasing*. On the other hand, the NPVIC does seek to change the federal nature of presidential elections by empowering the people and devaluing the importance of states as political units. It is certainly possible that Congress would therefore need to grant its approval. If required, obtaining passage in the House and Senate would add a formidable obstacle to the NPVIC taking effect. However, it would still pale in comparison to garnering two-thirds of each congressional chamber and the support of 38 state legislatures—as an amendment would require.

A larger obstacle for the NPVIC is that the Supreme Court will likely need to rule on its constitutionality. Recent precedent offers some hope for the NPVIC. When the Court ruled on the constitutionality of faithless electors in *Chiafalo v. Washington* (2020), Justice Elena Kagan's majority opinion said, "Nothing in the Constitution expressly prohibits states from taking away presidential electors' voting discretion … the power to appoint an elector (in any manner) includes power to condition his appointment, absent some other constitutional constraint." This statement, included in an opinion that eight of nine justices joined, appears to reinforce the idea that states have broad latitude when it comes to assigning electors.

However, it is also possible that the Court will consider additional factors when evaluating the NPVIC. First, the Court previously ruled in *U.S. Term Limits, Inc. v. Thornton* (1995) that states could not limit the terms that U.S. House representatives serve.[39] While the Constitution does not expressly prohibit such limits, the Court noted that term limits would permit states to circumvent the constitutional provisions that allow Congress to determine the qualifications of its members. The majority opinion noted that the Framers did not spend "significant time and energy in debating and crafting Clauses that could be easily evaded" and "manipulated out of existence." One could envision the Court reaching a similar determination about the NPVIC.

Second, some believe the NPVIC may violate the Guarantee Clause of the Constitution, which states that the "United States shall guarantee to every State in this Union a Republican Form of Government." Critics believe the NPVIC would deprive voters in non-compacting states of a republican form of government because the states that join it would effectively determine the outcome of an election in a manner for which the non-compacting states had not consented.

Third, the *Bush v. Gore* (2000) decision applied the Fourteenth Amendment's Equal Protection Clause in ruling that Florida could not recount the votes of some counties, but not others. While the majority opinion in this case was expressly limited to the particulars of the 2000 election, some believe its logic could apply to the NPVIC. If a national popular vote were effectively determining the presidential election, it is possible the Court could find "equal protection" problems with the fact that states have varying election laws. Policies regarding voting rights for ex-felons and the mentally disabled, as well as ID requirements, registration rules, and absentee voting differ significantly from state to state. While this is permitted under the Electoral College system where states are empowered, the Court could find it problematic within the structure of a national popular vote.

Finally, some critics argue that the compact might violate Sections 2 and 5 of the Voting Rights Act (VRA) of 1965 by diluting the votes of racial and ethnic minorities. On the surface, this critique seems implausible because the Electoral College clearly devalues the votes of Blacks and Latinos. In fact, the over-weighting of rural areas means that the Electoral College effectively values Black and Latino votes more than ten percent less than white votes.[40] However, as I will discuss in Chapter 6, the Voting Rights Act is triggered whenever a change is seen as disadvantageous to a community of Black or Latino voters. As a result, even if the shift to a popular vote advantages these communities overall, if it reduces their current voting power *anywhere*, it could be struck down. Hypothetically, the Court could find that Blacks in Delaware, for example, would be disadvantaged by the NPVIC. Because Delaware is a small state, its citizens (including its Black citizens) would see the power of their individual vote reduced by the NPVIC. Even though all votes across the U.S. would now be treated equally, the change (and relative reduction) in voting power for racial and ethnic minorities in some places might be problematic under the VRA.

In my view, none of these issues should distract from the central issue at hand. The Electoral College is wrong because it does not treat all citizens equally. The NPVIC, while complicated, would have a very straightforward outcome. Every American choosing to vote for president would see their vote count equally. It is commonplace for opponents to use convoluted legal explanations in an effort to shed doubt on the efficacy of an idea. My advice is to resist falling into this trap. The Electoral College, in practice, is illogical and unfair. A national popular vote, which the NPVIC would effectively produce, is built around the concept of fairness and equality.

Relatedly, Americans should not be dissuaded by the fact that the NPVIC's success may require creative manipulations of the Constitution. The honest reality is that achieving change in the U.S. political system often does. Because the Constitution is so dated and amending it is so cumbersome, many important social and political changes in the U.S. have depended (and still depend) on cleverly interpreting the meaning of its words. And it is precisely because constitutional law is evolving and fungible that the Constitution continues to have power at all. If the courts clung to the Framers' original intent, or even the intent of later amendments and acts of Congress, they would be forced to deny political changes demanded by large majorities of the American public. Both the Constitution and the courts would consequently risk the loss of public confidence and legitimacy. Courts require legitimacy because without it, those in elected positions have little reason to follow their decisions. Today, as I discussed in Chapter 1, there are many staples of U.S. law that rest on evolved interpretations of our founding document. The fact that the NPVIC would likely need some creative justifications of its own to pass constitutional muster is not a sign of its weakness. Rather, it is simply a necessary response to a political system that is highly resistant to statutory change.

While there are no guarantees regarding its behavior in future cases, the Supreme Court has issued bold rulings on behalf of political equality in the past. Recall that in *Reynolds v. Sims* (1964), the Court issued a landmark ruling declaring that state legislative chambers must be roughly equal in population. The ruling cited the Fourteenth Amendment's Equal Protection Clause in declaring that state legislatures must follow the principle of "one person, one vote." In his majority opinion, Chief Justice Earl Warren wrote, "Legislators represent people, not trees or acres. Legislators are elected by voters, not farms or cities or economic interests."[41] The ruling required many states to dramatically transform the structure of their legislatures. Prior to the ruling, malapportionment was appallingly bad in some cases. In California, the six million residents of Los Angeles County had just one member in the state senate, the same as the 400 people living in Alpine County. In the Idaho Senate, the smallest district had 951 people, while the biggest had 93,400. In Nevada, the smallest senate seat represented 568 people, while one urban district had approximately 127,000 residents. Following the ruling, many states were aghast at what they considered an activist court decision. U.S. Senator Everett Dirksen of Illinois led a fight to pass a constitutional amendment to overrule the decision, but it ultimately failed. With one historic ruling, the Supreme Court greatly enhanced political equality in a way that few thought possible just a few years before.

If the NPVIC ever reaches the Supreme Court's chambers, the justices will be much more likely to craft and accept bold interpretations of the Constitution if there is apparent public pressure to do so. In the past, the High Court's interpretation of economic regulation, racial integration, the rights of same-sex couples, and more has evolved once the public's evolution has become clear. If Electoral College reform becomes part of a broader movement to revitalize American democracy, it should have a fighting chance in court.

As unlikely as big structural changes can seem given the constraints of our political system, they *are* possible and they *do* happen. Remember— the stars only need to align once.

Conclusion

Path dependency is very powerful because it leads us to grant legitimacy to things to which we have become accustomed. It makes sense that the first six keys on a keyboard are QWERTY. Of course Election Day is a Tuesday. And when we elect the president, we use the Electoral College because... we always have! Once something becomes normalized, its features and flaws fail to shock us as they should. Things begin to make sense that should not. When old traditions are eventually broken, people often begin to realize how little sense the former system made. They can even become shocked and embarrassed that they had not realized it before. Surely, for example, many Americans now find it hard to believe that they once opposed same-sex marriage or even racial integration. Because old traditions become so embedded, it is important to take a step back and try to assess them objectively. In this chapter, I have tried to do so regarding the Electoral College.

It is easy for some Americans to openly disagree with the Framers. They may cite their opposition to racial or gender equality, their elite and sheltered position in society, or simply the large amount of time that has passed since the crafting of the Constitution. But for some Americans, breaking with the Framers is hard. This is understandable, as we are taught to see George Washington, James Madison, Thomas Jefferson, and a few others as practically divine figures. Their pictures hang in our classrooms. Their faces are on our money. And some of them even have their faces carved on a mountain! When it comes to the Electoral College, however, one can seek change and still not divorce themselves from the Framers. As I have tried to document, the Framers were hardly in love with the institution. In reality, they could not garner sufficient support for a national popular vote or congressional selection and settled on a compromise. Their compromise reflected the politics of their time—highly-regional and stained by slavery. There is no reason to believe that the Framers would make the same deal if they operated in today's political climate. We should not bind ourselves to a compromise designed to accommodate interests that no longer exist.

Furthermore, the Electoral College designed by the Framers is already gone. Once the two-party system emerged and states allowed voters to select their electors, the system was transformed away from a tool for state elites to narrow presidential selection down to five (as the Framers intended). Instead, it became an indirect (though inequitable) way for eligible citizens to select the president.

Today, rather than brilliantly accommodate the federal nature of our republic, the Electoral College neither reflects the Framers' intentions nor modern conceptions of political equality. Instead, it values the votes of some citizens more than others in completely arbitrary ways. Citizens count for less if they live in states with high populations or particularly engaged citizens. They are entirely ignored by candidates unless the state in which they reside happens to have a roughly equal number of Democratic and Republican voters. They stand at the whims of having their votes ignored by presidential electors who are entirely unknown to the public. They are at risk of a contingency election so unfair and potentially chaotic that it could risk the legitimacy of the person elected. And most egregiously, they sometimes (twice in the last six elections) see a candidate they collectively preferred reduced to a concession speech after an election. The Framers may not have been ready for a truly democratic presidential selection process; they operated in a time when such conceptions were almost entirely foreign.

What is our excuse?

CHAPTER 3

In Search of Fair Districts

When compared to the Senate and the Electoral College, the U.S. House of Representatives appears to be a model democratic institution. Seats are determined by state population, meaning that residents are (almost) equally represented in the chamber. Residents in California, Texas, and other large states—hugely underrepresented when choosing senators and the president—finally have the proper amount of say when it comes to the House.

While the above sentiment is true, the story has always been more complicated. House districts have a long history of malapportionment; until the 1960s, states often stacked more residents in some districts versus others in order to heighten or depress the representation of particular groups. While the most egregious malapportionment issues have since been addressed by the Supreme Court and Congress, some remain. Furthermore, political equality in the House is currently threatened by the proliferation of partisan gerrymandering.

Gerrymandering, while complicated, is basically the manipulation of electoral district boundaries for the purpose of aiding a political party or other group. Of the many democratic inequities covered in this book, gerrymandering is quite possibly the least popular with the American public. A recent survey indicated that less than 10 percent of Americans support it.[1] The idea of one political party drawing legislative districts in a manner that blatantly seeks to expand their advantage is difficult to defend with a straight face. Unlike the Senate or the Electoral College, there are few high-minded defenses of the practice. Partisan gerrymandering does not advance (or even claim to advance) federalism, guard against tyranny, or protect small states. Despite its widespread opposition, however, gerrymandering has worsened in recent years due to improved technology, heightened partisanship, Supreme Court rulings, and inaction by Congress. Today, state legislative majorities—who typically draw districts for both the U.S. House and their own chambers—are both motivated and well-equipped to construct district maps that confer massive advantages

71

to their respective parties. This is problematic. If some voters have a disproportionate ability to shape legislative power (and therefore policy), political equality is not present.

In this chapter, I discuss the mechanics of the U.S. House and its districts. I pay close attention to history, exploring important acts of Congress and Supreme Court cases that have shaped the system in place today. I chronicle changes that have improved political equality in the chamber, as well as continuing challenges that threaten it. I conclude the chapter with a series of recommended reforms. Thankfully, making the House more responsive to the people does not require a constitutional amendment, a Supreme Court ruling, or even further action by individual states. The Constitution gives Congress enormous power to enact meaningful change in this area through simple legislation.

State Apportionment

The House of Representatives was designed to be the federal institution most closely aligned with the passions of the people. Article I, Section 2 of the Constitution states, "The House of Representatives shall be composed of Members chosen every second Year by the People of the several States, and the Electors in each State shall have the Qualifications requisite for Electors of the most numerous Branch of the State Legislature." In other words, if a citizen is eligible to vote in elections for their state house—which is always the state chamber with more seats—they must be permitted to vote for the U.S. House. Because all states have always permitted eligible citizens to vote for their lower house, eligibility for the U.S. House has followed the same principle.

Under the terms of the Connecticut Compromise, the House is apportioned according to state population. Article I, Section 2 notes, "Representatives ... shall be apportioned among the several States which may be included within this Union, according to their respective Numbers." The Constitution also stipulates that all states must have at least one House seat. While there is no limit placed on the overall size of the House, the Constitution does require that there be no more than one seat for every 30,000 residents in a state.

In order to assign districts, the U.S. government must know how many people live in each state. So, every ten years, it completes a new census, a massive undertaking that utilizes mail, phone calls, online submissions, and even door knocks to record the population of each of the nation's communities. While the U.S. Census is a highly professional operation, the results are certainly imperfect. First, marginalized communities (e.g., the homeless) are underrepresented. Second, research shows that nearly a quarter of Americans fear that their census responses will be used against them. And because particular groups—racial and ethnic minorities and immigrants—are more likely to be both marginalized and fearful, they tend to be systematically undercounted. One study estimates that the 2010 census missed 2.1 percent of Blacks, 1.5 percent of Hispanics and 4.9 percent of Native Americans on reservations. Meanwhile, nearly one percent of whites may have been counted twice![2] The implications of inaccurate counts are severe, as the census is used to determine not only U.S. House seats, but also legislative apportionment at the state and local level. In addition, over 300 federal and state funding programs use the census to determine how much to allocate to particular communities.[3] Biases in the census are undoubtedly a form of malapportionment.

After the first census was completed in 1790, Congress quickly increased the size of the House from 65 to 105 seats. While Congress did not increase the chamber in proportion to the nation's population growth in the years that followed, it did continue to gradually authorize seat expansions. By 1911, the House had grown to 435 seats. Following the 1920 census, it was expected that the chamber size would be increased again. Politics, however, would prevent this expansion. In the decade between 1910 and 1920, millions of immigrants—mostly from southern and eastern Europe—moved to U.S. cities to work in factories and, eventually, assist the U.S. effort in World War I. When it came time to reapportion the House after the 1920 census, Republicans feared that this growth would result in states with large immigrant populations gaining considerable influence in the House. According to Michael Waldman, president of the Brennan Center for Justice at NYU, Republicans were pressured by "prohibitionists who feared the influence of alcohol-tolerant cities" to prevent this from happening.[4] As a result, the Republican majority simply refused to reapportion the House following the census. States that had grown significantly since 1910 were denied proper House representation until 1932. Before the next census took place, however, Congress passed the Permanent Apportionment Act of 1929. The law (1) established an automatic method for apportioning House seats following a census and (2) fixed the House at 435 seats. The latter decision was reportedly made because there were "not enough chairs" in the House to allow further expansions.[5] The House has therefore remained fixed at 435 seats since 1911.[6]

After each census, states are awarded a number of seats based on the share of the country's population that resides within their borders. States can therefore gain, lose, or keep their House seats following a census. In fact, states can *lose* seats even when they *grow* in population. For example, during the 1990s, every U.S. state grew in population. The following decade (2000–2010), only Michigan declined in population. Because many states grew more slowly than others, however, their share of the country's population declined. More than 1.5 million more people lived in New York in 2010 than in 1990, but the state still had four fewer House seats by 2010 because other states grew much faster. Growth was particularly strong in the South and Southwest during this period; Florida and Texas gained four and six seats, respectively.

From a political equality perspective, House apportionment is more equitable than either the Senate or the Electoral College. It does, however, have some notable imperfections. First, because the census is only conducted every 10 years, population shifts are not immediately reflected in House apportionments. For example, the 2020 census awarded Florida 28 House seats. But suppose that by 2024, the state has grown to the point where it should have 30 seats. In this event, there is no mechanism to immediately make this update. Any shifts in population during the 2020s can only be reflected after the 2030 census takes effect in 2032.

Second, because every state must have at least one district regardless of its population, several states—Vermont and Wyoming—feature at-large districts that are smaller than the average district nationwide.[7] Wyoming's at-large district represents 577,000 people, though the average House district includes nearly 760,000. Third, because seats cannot be partially awarded, states can narrowly gain or lose seats during the apportionment process. In small states, the difference can be significant from the perspective of representation. Montana, for example, had nearly 989,000 residents according to the 2010 census, but was granted only one House seat. The reason was that while Montana was much larger than states like Wyoming and Vermont, it was not large enough to demand a second House district. Rhode Island, however, with 1.057 million residents—only 68,000 more than Montana—narrowly met the cutoff to receive a second seat.

An End to (Most) House Malapportionment

Many are surprised to learn that the Constitution does not actually discuss House districts at all. Instead, Article I, Section 4 simply declares, "The Times, Places and Manner of holding Elections for Senators and Representatives, shall be prescribed in each State by the Legislature thereof; but Congress may at any time make or alter such Regulations...." This broad clause has been interpreted to mean that once states are given a certain number of House districts, their legislatures may determine how they will be created. Congress, however, retains the power to supersede the discretion of states with regard to the "Times, Places, and Manner" of elections.

Congress initially gave states broad latitude to determine how they constructed their House seats. There was no requirement that each district represent the same, or even a similar, number of residents or citizens. If a state had two districts, one could represent 500,000 residents, while the other represented just 100,000 residents. Districts could be *contiguous*, meaning that one could travel from any point in the district to another point without crossing the district's boundaries, or they could be comprised of disconnected communities throughout the state. States could divide their territory into distinct districts, each with a single representative. Alternatively, states could simply set all districts as "at-large" districts. With this design, all House districts would represent the entire state, as senators do. The difference is that instead of having two, a state would have as many representatives as their population dictated. States could also have plural-member districts that did not comprise the entire state but still elected multiple members. In fact, some of the original 13 states used both at-large and plural-member districts in the first congressional elections.[8]

Early Congresses established a tradition of approving a new House apportionment law after each census. Until the 1840s, these laws simply stipulated how many House seats each state would have. In 1842, Congress set the first major limits on the districting process, as states were required to create "single-member districts." Plural-member districts were banned, while at-large districts would only be permitted in states with just one House district. The law also required that all districts be geographically contiguous. The law was poorly enforced, however, as four states—Georgia, Mississippi, Missouri, and New Hampshire—held at-large House elections soon after it was approved.[9] The lack of enforcement was undoubtedly aided by significant doubts that some—including President John Tyler—had about whether Congress indeed had the legal authority to require "single-member districts."[10] In an apparent contradiction of the 1842 law, an 1844 report from the House Committee on Elections determined that members in the four violating states had been "duly elected" and could therefore be seated. The single-member requirement was dropped in 1850, but restored again in 1862.

Congress continued to exercise its power to regulate House elections. In 1872, it mandated that House districts have, "as nearly as possible, equal population." In 1901, Congress required that districts be both compact and contiguous, seemingly to prevent states from creative designs that were technically contiguous, but not compact.[11] A contiguous district simply means that all parts are connected, while a compact one implies that a district's constituents live about as near to one another as possible. Echoing previous efforts, however, neither the 1872 nor 1901 laws were always enforced. In 1929, when Congress capped the size of the House at 435 seats, it neither repealed nor reauthorized the aforementioned requirements regarding equal population and compactness. In 1932, the Supreme Court ruled in *Wood v. Broom* that, unless otherwise stated, the provisions of each apportionment law only affect the apportionment cycle for which they are written. As a result, all requirements regarding how states allocate their House seats were deemed to have lapsed. Several states, including New York, Illinois, Washington, Hawaii, and New Mexico, created at-large House districts in the years that followed.[12]

By the 1960s, many states had significantly malapportioned House seats. Seventeen states had at least one House district that included more than twice the residents living in the smallest district.[13] In six states, at least one district was three times more populated than the smallest one. And two states—Michigan and Texas—had districts that included more than four times the residents living in the smallest district. State legislatures generally created malapportioned House districts to embolden either their party or particular demographic groups, an act of gerrymandering. Nearly all cases of extreme malapportionment involved over-representing rural communities at the expense of urban communities. This generally had the effect of marginalizing more racially diverse communities who disproportionately populated cities. In their 2016 book, *Gerrymandering in America*, Anthony McGann and his co-authors note that "the overrepresentation of rural, white voters was one of the foundations of the one-party, Democratic South."[14]

State legislatures also designed malapportioned districts to protect sitting incumbents. Recall that states have the power to draw districts for both their own state legislative chambers and the U.S. House. Naturally, a state legislature empowered to draw its *own* districts has an incentive to maintain districts that allow members to continue winning their seats. It may be less obvious why a state legislature would wish to protect U.S. House incumbents, but there are logical reasons why this also occurs. First, for partisan reasons, state representatives want to see incumbents of their own party continue to hold U.S. House seats. Relatedly, state and national representatives often have personal and professional relationships that may motivate the former to assist the latter in maintaining their seats. Finally, state legislators—who have less at stake when drawing U.S. House districts—are often happy to defer the redistricting workload to U.S. House members themselves. Former U.S. House Representative Phil Burton of California once candidly remarked, "The most important thing you do, before anything else, is you get yourself in a position to draw lines for [your own] district. Then, you draw them for all your friends."[15]

The 1960s saw significant advancements on behalf of democracy. By the end of the decade, Congress had finally protected voting rights for Blacks, extended the presidential vote to the District of Columbia, and banned the poll tax. During the early 1960s, the Supreme Court also issued some of its most consequential decisions on behalf of political equality. The decisions would eliminate the worst cases of malapportionment in both the U.S. House and across state legislatures. The Court's efforts began in *Baker v. Carr* (1962). The case involved a lawsuit by Charles Baker, a citizen, against the state of Tennessee. Baker argued that the Tennessee Legislature had violated the state's constitution by failing to redistrict its seats for decades, resulting in some districts that contained far more residents than others. Baker resided in a Shelby County district that had about 10 times as many residents as some of the state's rural districts. He argued that this malapportionment violated the Fourteenth Amendment's Equal Protection Clause. Tennessee countered that the case involved a "political question" that could not be adjudicated through the courts. Nearly a year after the case was argued, the Supreme Court ruled 6–2 that redistricting and apportionment *were* judiciable matters (i.e., issues that courts could address).[16] While the decision did not immediately declare a standard for redistricting, it set the stage for two cases that did so.

In 1963, the Supreme Court heard the case of James Wesberry, a voter living in the Fifth U.S. House District of Georgia. Wesberry argued that because his House district had a population more than twice as large as others in the state, his influence was effectively diluted. In a 6–3 ruling, the Court agreed. Writing for the majority, Justice Hugo Black quoted Article I, Section 2 of the Constitution, which states, "The House of Representatives shall be composed of Members chosen every second Year by the People of the several States." Black and his colleagues determined that this language implies "that as nearly as is practicable one man's vote in a congressional election is to be worth as much as another's." As the chamber "of the people," the House was not intended to be manipulated by state legislatures to create bias toward particular parties or groups.[17] As a result, states throughout the U.S. would finally be forced to draw districts that represented all citizens equally. Unlike the aforementioned apportionment acts that Congress had occasionally approved in years past, this ruling would be well enforced.

While the focus of this chapter (and to a large extent, this book) is on representation in the national government, the Court's next decision regarding apportionment in state legislatures (*Reynolds v. Sims*) is too important to ignore. In 1963, voters in Birmingham, Alabama, sued their state, arguing that the state's legislative districts denied them equal representation. Alabama gave each county one senator, regardless of the county's population. Alabama was hardly the only state with a heavily malapportioned state legislature. One town of 38 residents in Vermont elected the same number of state representatives as Burlington, Vermont, a city of 33,000 people. In Georgia, assembly districts contained between 1,876 and 185,422 constituents.[18] The Idaho Senate had one district with more than 93 times as many residents as another, while the Nevada Senate featured a disparity of more than 200 to 1. In an 8–1 ruling, the Supreme Court declared in *Reynolds* that the Fourteenth Amendment required that states draw legislative districts roughly equal in population. In one of the most pro-democracy statements to ever appear in a Supreme Court opinion, Chief Justice Earl Warren wrote that "the right of suffrage can be denied by a debasement or dilution of the weight of a citizen's vote just as effectively as by wholly prohibiting the free exercise of the franchise." Counting some votes less than others, Warren argued, is essentially the same as denying the right to vote. Warren and the majority insisted that representation in legislative bodies is inherently about *people*, writing, "legislators represent people, not trees or acres. Legislators are elected by voters, not farms or cities or economic interests."[19] Allowing some citizens to have more representation than others does not protect minority interests; it just treats some people as more important than other people.

In sum, *Baker* declared that the Court had a right to review malapportionment cases. *Wesberry* interpreted Article I broadly to conclude that equal representation in the House is required. *Reynolds* was the closing act that did not disappoint. Going beyond Article I, the Court boldly declared that the Fourteenth Amendment's Equal Protection Clause protects citizens from malapportionment in all levels of government. Rather than rely solely on a technical interpretation of Article I, *Reynolds* unequivocally deems political equality a first principle. The decision is unambiguous—when governments at any level create or perpetuate malapportioned legislatures, they violate citizens' rights in the process. While the Court deemed that nothing could be done about the U.S. Senate given its clear mandate in the Constitution, all other legislative bodies would henceforth need to abide by the principle of "one person, one vote."

After his retirement, Chief Justice Earl Warren called the three apportionment cases of the early 1960s the most important cases decided during his tenure.[20]

With "one person, one vote" now enshrined in the drawing of House districts, Congress passed a measure in 1967 requiring that all seats—except those in states with only one district—be single-member districts. Hawaii and New Mexico, the only two multi-district states who still had at-large House districts, were required to replace them with distinct, single-member seats of roughly equal population. Since the law's passage, no state has seriously attempted to challenge this requirement.

Political Gerrymandering

While the Warren Court largely ended House malapportionment in the 1960s, its decisions did not formally address other forms of political gerrymandering. Even when districts contain the same number of residents, there are still ways for those designing them to empower some voters over others. Consider the following hypothetical example. State A is a state that leans Democratic. While election results vary each year, about 55 percent of the state typically supports Democrats, while 45 percent support Republicans. Democrats control the state legislature and therefore have the power to draw the state's six congressional districts. Democratic support is mostly concentrated in and around the state's major city, while the vast rural area surrounding it is heavily Republican. In Scenario 1, Democrats draw six

Earl Warren served as Chief Justice of the U.S. Supreme Court from 1953 to 1969. During that time, he authored a number of landmark opinions that redefined the meaning of the Constitution. While his opinions also ended segregated public schools, banned anti-miscegenation laws, and enhanced protections for the accused, Warren referred to the three malapportionment cases of the 1960s as the most important of his tenure (TradingCards NPS, CC BY 2.0: *https://creativecommons. org/licenses/by/2.0/*).

equally-populated districts consisting of roughly 55 percent Democrats and 45 percent Republicans. This requires some of the districts to look rather odd, as Democrats achieve this outcome by creatively combining their own urban strongholds with various rural communities. In this scenario, Democrats are likely to win all six of the state's House districts. Here, Democrats employed "cracking," or a process whereby a majority party spreads the other party's supporters across multiple districts in order to deny them the opportunity to win seats.

In Scenario 2, Democrats instead choose to "pack" one district with Republicans, giving the opposition party a 90–10 percent majority in this district. In doing so, they concede that this single district will likely vote Republican, but further ensure that the other five districts will be solidly Democratic. In fact, in this scenario, each of the other five districts could be about 65 percent Democratic, making it unlikely that any would vote against the party even in a Republican-wave year. This packing scenario would likely be preferred by the state's Democratic U.S. House incumbents, as their seats would be more secure from Republican competition.

Through either cracking or packing, the Democratic majority in these examples effectively gerrymandered their state's House districts to maximize their party's advantage. While clever, this exercise is highly undemocratic. To appreciate why, it is important to reflect on how votes are converted to power in Congress. In the U.S., voters elect House members, who consolidate their power through membership in political parties. In the House, the party with the most seats controls the chamber, including its leadership positions, its committees, and the legislative agenda. If districts are drawn in a way that creates bias towards one party, then political equality cannot exist. Let me be clear how I define *bias*. I apply an approach developed by political scientists Andrew Gelman and Gary King in 1994. In their model, a state's districts are not biased simply because one party has a better chance to win more seats than the other. In states with more Democrats or more Republicans, the more popular party *should* generally win more seats. Rather, districts contain bias if support for one party produces a different number of seats than the equivalent amount of support for the other party could. Let's return to the hypothetical state discussed above. Suppose again that Democrats win 55 percent of the statewide popular vote in a House election one year, winning five of six races (83.3 percent). Because they employed packing (Scenario 2), Democrats lost one overwhelmingly Republican district, but won each of the other five districts with about 65 percent of the vote. Two years later, Republicans have an unusually strong year led by broad dissatisfaction with a Democratic president. In this election, 55 percent of the state supports a Republican House candidate. However, because the state's districts are biased in favor of Democrats, the votes do not efficiently convert into seats. Republicans win one district with 95 percent of the vote, but earn just 47 percent of the vote in the other five districts, losing them all. Republicans improved their performance in all districts, but the extra votes did not earn them a plurality in any new districts. This scenario is a classic example of bias. Democrats won five of six seats when they won 55 percent of the statewide vote. But Republicans won just one of six seats when they earned the same statewide support. The system did not treat the parties fairly, meaning it also failed to treat voters fairly.

The Constitution does not explicitly stipulate that voter preferences must be equitably aggregated into party power in the House. In fact, the Constitution does not mention parties at all. But parties are (and have always been) central to aggregating political preferences and converting them to policy in the United States. Candidates run on party labels and are nominated by parties. Over 99 percent of all members ever elected to the House have caucused with a major party. Upon election to the House, majority party members consolidate their power to determine the chamber's leaders. They ensure that all committees are led by one of their representatives, and that each committee has more of their members overall. Majorities shape legislation, determine when it receives a vote, and act cohesively in an effort to shape public policy. Of course, bipartisan compromises and crossover voting occur, but House policy is overwhelmingly determined by the will of the majority. Consequently, if Democratic and Republican voters do not have an equal opportunity to shape House elections, then the House fails to accurately represent not only parties, but the people. As McGann and his co-authors note, "If we have partisan elections, it is not logically possible to treat every voter equally without also treating each party equally."[21]

While the *Wesberry* decision did not directly address partisan gerrymandering, many assumed that the ruling implied that the practice was not constitutionally permissible. If creating a malapportioned legislature was unconstitutional because it diluted the political power of some voters more than others, then how could partisan gerrymandering—which effectively does the same thing—be allowed? Perhaps because they assumed it would not be permitted by the federal courts, states created House districts with little partisan bias in the two decades following *Wesberry*. In *Davis v. Bandemer* (1986), the Supreme Court considered whether the Indiana Legislature had violated the Equal Protection Clause with its post–1980 state legislative maps. While the Court ruled that Indiana's districts did not constitute a violation, it did affirmatively state that partisan gerrymandering claims were "judicable," meaning that the Court had the power and ability to strike district maps that were sufficiently biased in favor of one party. While the majority opinion did not elucidate a clear standard for evaluating such claims, state legislatures appeared to continue respecting the possibility that courts could strike biased maps; partisan bias during the House redistricting that followed the 1990 census was again fairly limited.[22]

After the 2000 census, there was a slight bias towards Republicans during the following round of redistricting. One way of quantifying bias is to estimate what share of seats each party would have won if it earned exactly 50 percent of the House vote nationally. McGann and his co-authors estimate that Democrats would have won slightly over 48 percent of the 435 House races if they had won 50 percent of the national vote in 2002; Republicans would have won nearly 52 percent of all seats with the same national vote share.[23]

During the twenty-first century, several factors have converged to make partisan gerrymandering a larger problem than it was during the 1970s–1990s. First, the Supreme Court has reversed itself on the question of whether partisan gerrymandering is judiciable. In *Vieth v. Jubelirer* (2004), a plurality of justices (four) ruled that partisan gerrymandering claims were non-justiciable because there is no "judicially discoverable and manageable standard" for determining when a sufficient degree of partisan bias has occurred to the point of violating one's constitutional rights. Justice Anthony Kennedy agreed with the plurality that no standard currently existed, but he did not foreclose the possibility of a workable standard emerging.[24] McGann and his colleagues argue that *Vieth* gave states a green light to engage in more blatant partisan gerrymandering. More bluntly, in their view, the ruling "return[ed] to state legislatures much of the power to manipulate districts and engineer political outcomes that they had before *Baker v. Carr*."[25]

The legal ability for states to maximize partisan gain through the redistricting process was quickly married with both motive and opportunity. Capitalizing on the unpopular Iraq War and the beginning of the Great Recession at the end of President George W. Bush's term, Democrat Barack Obama was handily elected president in 2008. Democrats also recorded impressive victories in congressional, gubernatorial, and state legislative contests that year. But by 2010, President Obama and the Democrats faced electoral headwinds due to a slow recovery from the Great Recession, the rise of the Tea Party, backlash from the Affordable Care Act, and apathy from some of their own supporters. Sensing an opportunity for big gains, Republicans invested $30 million in REDMAP, a project designed to help the party (1) take control of state legislative chambers and (2) aggressively gerrymander state legislative and U.S. House maps following the 2010 census. The plan worked exceedingly well. Republicans swept the 2010 midterm elections, gaining 63 House seats, six Senate seats, 680 state legislative seats, and six governorships. With control of both the state legislature and governor's mansion in 21 states (compared to just ten for Democrats), the party fully controlled redistricting in many states. With the help of consultants, lawyers, and very sophisticated software, Republican majorities designed maps that nearly ensured the party would win a disproportionate number of House seats. The effort was aided by vast technological improvements over prior redistricting rounds. John Ryder, the Republican Redistricting Committee chair during the 2010 cycle, noted, "When I started doing this in the mid–70s … we were using handheld calculators, paper maps, pencils, and really big erasers. It was pretty primitive."[26] By 2010, the process was quite sophisticated. The "Big Data" revolution meant that parties and their operatives knew much more about voters and their preferences than a decade or two before, allowing for more precise maps. Rather than rely solely on aggregate partisan data at the town level, operatives were able to consider the political leanings and voting likelihood of specific blocks and households.

In 2012, the new Republican-drawn maps produced expectedly biased results. While Democrats won 1.4 million more House votes than Republicans across all 435 races, Republicans maintained a comfortable majority (234–201) in the chamber. Some states were particularly egregious. In North Carolina, 51 percent of voters chose a Democrat in their respective House race, yet only four of the state's 13 districts elected a Democrat. The same was true in Pennsylvania, where a majority chose a Democratic House candidate, but Democrats won just five of the state's 18 races. In Ohio, Republicans won 52 percent of the House vote but netted 12 of 16 seats. In each case (and others), Republicans had packed Democratic voters into a small number of districts, allowing them to win these easily so Republicans could secure narrower (but still generally comfortable) victories in the others.

Partisan gerrymandering is not unique to Republicans. Democrats effectively gerrymandered Maryland's eight House districts, allowing the party to win seven of the state's eight seats in 2012 despite losing about 40 percent of the statewide vote. But Democrats were unable to replicate this effort in many states because they fully controlled very few state governments (ten). Furthermore, the largest Democratic state—California—did not permit partisan gerrymandering. While the state still sent 38 Democrats and only 15 Republicans to Congress, the margin likely could have been greater with an aggressive Democratic gerrymander.

The general consensus for most of the 2010s was that the Republican House majority was safe because so many states were effectively gerrymandered. Several factors intervened, however, to allow Democrats to retake the chamber in 2018. First, disapproval of President Trump was extremely high; as a result, motivation among Democrats to vote in 2018 was much greater than is typical for a midterm election. In fact, turnout was higher in 2018 than in any midterm race since 1914. Second, Trump's rise had cost Republicans some traditional support in suburbs across the U.S. When these areas became more favorable to Democrats, some of the Republican seats that had been drawn after 2010 became vulnerable. Third, as I will discuss later in the chapter, several states were forced by courts to redistrict before the 2020 census was conducted. The resulting maps ultimately netted the Democrats additional seats.

In 2019, having seen the effects of aggressive, sophisticated partisan gerrymandering, the Supreme Court again ruled on the constitutionality of the practice in *Rucho v. Common Cause*. Justice Kennedy, who had previously suggested that a standard could be developed for evaluating the constitutionality of partisan gerrymandering, had retired the previous year. Ultimately, a 5–4 majority ruled that while partisan maps may be "incompatible with democratic principles," the federal courts cannot review such allegations because they involve "non-justiciable political questions." Writing for the majority, Chief Justice John Roberts confirmed what the Court had suggested in *Vieth*—the courts cannot adjudicate political gerrymandering disputes because there are no "judicially discoverable and manageable standards for resolving them."[27]

While the Supreme Court took bold steps to end House malapportionment and advance political equality in *Baker*, *Wesberry*, and *Reynolds* in the 1960s, it refused to defend democracy from the insidious threat of partisan gerrymandering in 2019.

This is not, however, the end of the story. The Supreme Court has placed limits on one form of redistricting—*racial gerrymandering*. And in recent years, a growing number of states have taken meaningful action on their own to reduce partisan bias in their redistricting practices.

Racial Gerrymandering

In addition to diluting a party's vote, legislative districts can also be drawn to reduce the influence of other groups, including racial and ethnic minorities. In this area, Congress and the Supreme Court have set important limits. While no federal restriction bans cracking or packing for partisan gain, neither of these practices is acceptable if they dilute the electoral power of a racial or ethnic minority group.

Before the 1960s, many of the most extreme cases of malapportionment overvalued white communities and undervalued Black communities. This, combined with the absence of voting protections in the South, effectively disallowed Blacks in the region from holding any meaningful political power. A century after the Civil War, Congress passed and President Lyndon Johnson signed the Voting Rights Act (VRA) in 1965. The law, which I will discuss more in Chapter 6, barred states from adopting any law or practice that restricted voting rights on the basis of race. Literacy tests were explicitly banned, and states with a history of discrimination were required to receive preclearance (or pre-approval) from the U.S. Justice Department before changing any voting laws. The law is considered to be one of the most effective civil rights acts ever enacted in the U.S.

Within two years of its passage, voter registration in jurisdictions targeted by the law soared from 29.3 percent to 52.1 percent among Blacks. Between 1965 and 1985, the number of Blacks elected to office in the 11 former Confederate states rose from three to 176.[28]

The Voting Rights Act plays an important role in the redistricting process. Section 2 of the law explicitly bans "vote dilution," or state actions which reduce the effect of a person's vote. When Congress amended Section 2 in 1982, it stipulated that minority groups had the right "to elect" candidates of their choice. It was not enough for states to permit racial and ethnic minorities to vote; they also had to ensure that their votes amounted to political power. The clause was an attempt to prevent cracking on the basis of race. Recall that cracking is the process of splitting up a group into multiple districts so that they are unable to elect their preferred candidate in any district. The Supreme Court interpreted the scope of the 1982 VRA amendments in *Thornburg v. Gingles* (1986). The majority ruled that in some cases, states could be required to create "majority-minority" districts under the Voting Rights Act. A "majority-minority" district is one where a majority of voting-age citizens belong to a distinct racial or ethnic minority group. Under *Thornburg*, states can be required to form these districts when (1) the racial or language minority group "is sufficiently numerous and compact to form a majority in a single-member district," (2) the minority group tends to vote similarly, and (3) the majority votes sufficiently "as a bloc" to allow it to defeat the minority's preferred candidate.[29] After the 1990 census—the first to follow *Thornburg*—the number of "majority-minority" districts in the U.S. rose from 32 to 51. The average non–white population share of these districts was 55 percent.[30]

The Supreme Court has placed limits, however, on the extent to which states may go to create majority-minority districts. In *Shaw v. Reno* (1993), the Court ruled that districts cannot be "unexplainable on grounds other than race." In other words, districts need to make geographic sense. States are subject to litigation if they group together non-compact communities for the sole purpose of creating a majority-minority district.[31] The majority in *Shaw* noted that while not inevitably true, "bizarrely shaped" majority-minority districts are strongly indicative that race alone was considered.[32] In 2014, for example, a federal district court struck down Virginia's U.S. House map because its 3rd District grouped heavily Black communities in Richmond, Hampton, Newport News, and other jurisdictions together in order to create (or in this case, sustain) a majority Black district. Multiple communities in Southeast Virginia were isolated from the rest of the district, making the district non-compact. The Supreme Court declined to hear an appeal of the case in 2016, and the state was required to redraw its

House map before that fall's elections. The resulting map allowed Democrats to win three additional seats in the state by 2018.[33]

In the Virginia case and others, the federal courts have often found that the creation of *arbitrary* majority-minority districts—whereby disconnected communities are combined to create one—can actually dilute a minority group's influence. By packing large numbers of a minority group into a single district, a state can effectively reduce that group's potential influence in other districts. Under the banner of fostering minority representation, a state legislature could pack minority voters into a single district and make it easier for the non-favored party to win the state's other seats. This is particularly possible when the racial group overwhelmingly votes for the same political party, as is the case with Black voters in the U.S. As I discussed, packing is a common method of partisan gerrymandering. In fact, Republicans secured most of their post–2010 redistricting gains this way. But if the federal courts detect this motive *on the basis of race* (not just politics), they can strike down the scheme if there is a valid legal challenge. Under the Voting Rights Act, plaintiffs need only show that districts had the *effect* of diluting a minority group's vote. Even if doing so was unintentional, states can still have their district maps struck down by courts on this basis.

The criteria regarding race and redistricting can be confusing and contradictory, but in general, states *should* create majority-minority districts when it is possible to create a geographically compact one. When doing so would require creative boundaries and the amalgamation of disconnected communities, however, majority-minority districts are considered suspect and subject to legal challenge. As legal scholar Patricia Okonta has noted, "There is a delicate balance between race conscious redistricting that enables Black voters to elect their preferred candidate and those schemes that are designed to dilute Black political power throughout the state."[34]

Some have suggested that the requirement to draw majority-minority districts when feasible inherently hurts Democrats. Because majority-minority communities are almost always heavily Democratic, grouping too many of these voters into single districts effectively "wastes" Democratic votes that could have helped win other districts. Research suggests that this concern is not entirely unfounded, but it is a bit overblown. While many majority-minority districts are indeed non-competitive, this is difficult to avoid given that Democrats are often overwhelmingly favored (by all races and ethnicities) in urban communities. In a fair system, one in which community preferences are accurately reflected by district lines, there *should* be heavily Democratic districts in urban communities. This only presents a party bias problem if one party's voters are packed into a district, while the other's are strategically divided so that seat gains can be maximized. Consider the example of Pennsylvania. Creating a majority-minority district in Philadelphia does group a large number of Democrats together. But so long as rural, heavily Republican parts of the state are also appropriately combined to create a heavily Republican district, the partisan bias in the state cancels itself out.

While it is true that it is harder for Democrats to actively gerrymander districts in states with majority-minority district requirements (because they cannot efficiently split minority communities in an effort to win multiple districts), research finds that fair district maps are absolutely possible. Political scientists Micah Altman and Michael McDonald found that it was possible to create unbiased districts in Ohio after the 2010 census despite the need to form majority-minority districts.[35] Iowie Chen and Jonathan Rodden reached a similar conclusion in a 2013 study focused on Florida.[36] Meanwhile, in their aforementioned book, McGann and his colleagues note that while New York, New Jersey, California, and Illinois all had majority-minority districts after the 2010 census, none had a biased House map.[37]

State Regulations

So long as states draw evenly-apportioned, single-member House districts that do not dilute the power of racial or ethnic minority groups, they are free—as far as the federal government is concerned—to design maps as they like. Many states, however, have opted to include additional restrictions when completing the process. These restrictions sometimes remove state legislatures from the mapmaking process entirely. In other cases, they set limits on the sorts of communities that can be divided or the shapes that districts can take. While states often have different restrictions for redistricting their own statehouses and U.S. House districts, I will continue to focus on the latter.

In most states (30), state legislatures directly determine U.S. House district lines. In three additional states—Iowa, Maine, and Utah— an advisory commission recommends district lines that state legislatures ultimately must approve. These 33 states effectively allow partisan gerrymandering since elected majorities ultimately approve the maps, though some do require legislative supermajorities for approval. In most of these states, governors have the power to veto approved plans, but in several—Florida, Maryland, Mississippi, and North Carolina—they do not.[38]

Meanwhile, 11 states—Arizona, California, Colorado, Hawaii, Idaho,

Michigan, Montana, New Jersey, New York, Virginia, and Washington—do not allow state legislatures to control the redistricting process. Instead, each uses either an independent or bipartisan commission to draw House district lines. Finally, six states have only one congressional district, so redistricting power for the House is not applicable.[39]

Beyond power to draw the maps, states differ with regards to other limitations on redistricting. Nineteen states require districts to respect political boundaries, meaning that they should not divide counties, cities, towns, or ward lines. Thirteen states require that those constructing maps at least consider keeping "communities of interest"—or groups of people with common cultural, racial, ethnic, or economic interests—together when carving district lines.

Some states also regulate the shapes that districts may take. Recall that as early as 1842, Congress required that all House districts be geographically contiguous. Interestingly, Congress never reapplied these rules after they last expired in 1929. Twenty-three states have opted to require contiguity, though most states without the mandate generally draw contiguous districts nonetheless. In reality, contiguity is a fairly low bar to cross. So long as two places are connected by any amount of land or water, the standard is met. Suppose a hypothetical House district in Ohio included parts of Cleveland and Cincinnati, along with a narrow strip of land connecting them. Technically, this district would be contiguous. A much stricter standard is "compactness," which requires that constituents residing within a district live as close to one another as possible. If Ohio required compact districts (it does not), the hypothetical district above would clearly violate the standard. Only 18 states currently require compact House districts.[40]

Finally, two states—Arizona and Washington—formally encourage those drawing House districts (independent commissions in both cases) to create "competitive" districts where Democrats and Republicans are relatively even. Both states only require this consideration when doing so is "practicable," meaning if the state leans heavily towards one party, the commission would not be expected to create evenly-matched districts.[41] Many political commentators have called for more states to adopt a competitiveness requirement, arguing that such districts increase both voter turnout and legislative accountability. While I understand this argument, it is unclear to me why districts *should* be competitive if the area in which they represent is not. For example, does it make sense to join San Francisco with conservative communities in the Sierra Nevada mountains simply for the sake of party competition? I find it more sensible for San Francisco to be able to elect a progressive member of Congress, while more conservative communities can elect someone with corresponding views.

These districts will not necessarily lack competition, but it will likely come at the party primary stage, rather than in the general election.

Reform

The House, by its very design, is better positioned than the Senate to reflect the will of the people. States have a certain number of seats based on their population as determined by the decennial census. And since the 1960s, the chamber has been comprised of single-member districts with roughly equal populations. Nevertheless, the House is far from perfect from the perspective of political equality. First, even in a post–*Wesberry* world, there are instances when some House districts represent considerably more or less people than others. This occurs for several reasons. First, while the U.S. Census is a highly professional operation, it does fail to accurately count everyone. Because disadvantaged communities are disproportionately undercounted, some House districts are actually representing more people than official data would indicate (or that is appropriate). Problems were exacerbated in the 2020 census, when the Covid-19 outbreak disrupted the normal process for counting people. Furthermore, a nonpartisan taskforce of the American Statistical Association concluded that the Trump administration further jeopardized the 2020 count through a series of political actions. These included (ultimately unsuccessful) attempts to ask respondents if they were U.S. citizens,[42] the appointment of several political figures to high-level positions within the traditionally nonpartisan Census Bureau, and attempts to end the count prematurely.

Second, even if the census were perfectly accurate, it only occurs once every ten years. As a result, there is lag regarding when population shifts among the states are reflected in House seat counts.

Some malapportionment issues arise from the state allocation process. Because all states must have at least one district, some (e.g., Vermont, Wyoming) have a seat with a smaller population than those found in other states. In addition, there is always a mathematical cutoff when determining the number of seats each state receives. If a state—particularly a small state—narrowly reaches or misses the population threshold to gain an additional district, the impact can be significant. Montana had just one House district after the 2010 census despite a population of over one million people for most of the decade that followed. Rhode Island, with fewer than 100,000 more residents than Montana, had a second seat. On a per capita basis, Rhode Islanders therefore enjoyed nearly twice the representation in the House during this time as Montanans did.

Radical changes to the House, which would necessitate a constitutional amendment, could address these problems (and more). Currently, states are an important part of determining representation in the House, as seats are first allocated to them. But why is this necessary? The House is designed to represent "the people," so there is actually no reason for states to serve as intermediaries. Imagine a system where voters throughout the U.S. could vote for the party that they wished to see control the House every two years. After the election, each party would then receive a percentage of the 435 seats proportionate to its vote share. All voters would have the same influence over the chamber regardless of where they resided. No voter would feel as though their vote was meaningless because they lived in a non-competitive district. Issues created by census inaccuracies or lags would not matter because seat allocation to states would be obsolete.

Proportional representation certainly has appeal from the perspective of political equality, but it does raise new issues. Among them, it complicates the nature of constituent representation. Once a party earns seats, which parts of the country (or districts) would elected members represent, if any? One solution is a mixed-member proportional (MMP) system, which combines single-member districts with a national system of proportional representation. This approach, used by Germany and other nations, essentially gives each citizen two votes—one to decide the representative for their single-seat constituency and one for a political party. Seats in the legislature are then filled equally by constituent representatives and general party representatives (based on the percentage of nationwide votes that each party receives). Under MMP, malapportionment problems caused by census inaccuracies, census lags, and state allocation would still exist. However, their effects would be blunted because half of House representation would be determined by a party's national vote share—something entirely unaffected by these issues.

As I have noted, history has proven that aggressive electoral reforms that seem unachievable can become a reality with time. It is this faith that undergirds many of the proposals in this book. However, much like the reforms suggested in Chapter 1 regarding the Senate, the adoption of an MMP system in the United States is admittedly ambitious. It is difficult to imagine that 38 states—the number needed to amend the Constitution—will willingly cede influence over congressional representation anytime soon.

Thankfully, House apportionment can be improved through simple acts of Congress. In the near term, Congress must take steps to de-politicize the next census. Requiring an independent group of researchers to review the agency's data before it is finalized—something that the

American Statistical Association (ASA) has recommended—would mark an important step.[43] And if there are indications that the unusual circumstances surrounding the 2020 census led to a particularly unreliable count, Congress should consider authorizing an entirely new census sometime before 2030. A so-called "middlecade" census is something Congress would be well within its power to authorize. While such a move would be unprecedented, the consequences for incorrect assessments of population—for both apportionment and programmatic purposes—are simply too great to delay correcting.

Congress also has the power to more equitably assign House districts to states. Recall that Congress capped the size of the House at 435 seats in 1929. Since this cap was adopted, the U.S. population has increased from about 122 million to 331 million—a 171 percent increase. As a result, House districts continue to include more and more people. As of 2022, the average House representative now serves nearly 760,000 constituents. Only India, with 1.4 billion people, has legislative districts that represent more citizens than the U.S.[44] There are strong arguments that the House should be enlarged, perhaps considerably, for representation purposes alone. Many have argued that expanding constituencies make House members less responsive to citizen needs.[45] It has even been suggested that large, more heterogeneous districts exacerbate inequality because poorer citizens rarely comprise a large share of a district.[46] These concerns reflect a fear expressed by James Madison during the founding era. Madison worried that members representing large districts "would not possess enough of the confidence of the people, and would be too sparsely taken from the people, to bring with them all the local information which would be frequently wanted." Madison actually proposed a Congressional Apportionment Amendment in 1789 that would cap House districts at 50,000 persons. Along with 11 other amendments, it was approved by Congress in 1789. Ten of these 12 amendments (known as the Bill of Rights) were quickly ratified by the states, but the Apportionment Amendment fell one state short of ratification. Today, with more states in the Union, an additional 27 states would be needed for ratification. No time limit was placed on state consideration, so technically it could still be ratified if states were to take action.

Let me be clear—I do not believe that Madison's Congressional Apportionment Amendment would constitute good public policy today; with 50,000 residents per district, there would be over 6,500 districts in the U.S. House! However, I do believe Congress should consider a more modest reform to better ensure that districts are more similarly sized. The so-called "Wyoming Rule" would continue to grant each state at least one representative (as is required by the Constitution), but shrink the size of the average district nationwide so that it equaled the population of the smallest state. For example, according to the 2020 census, Wyoming is smallest state with about 577,000 residents. The overall population of the U.S. is about 331 million people. As a result, the House would be expanded to 574 seats, with the average seat containing 577,000 persons rather than the current 760,000. Seats would continue to be allocated to states based on population, but the smallest states would no longer have districts with fewer constituents than other states. This reform would increase the House by 32 percent, hardly a radical expansion given that the chamber's size has remained stagnant for over 100 years. Adopting the Wyoming Rule would not solve all malapportionment problems with the House, but it would move the chamber closer to political equality. Furthermore, it would have three positive side effects. First, by shrinking the size of districts nationwide, representation should become easier for members, particularly if their staffs and budgets remain the same size. Second, campaigns should become a bit less expensive for individual House seats, perhaps freeing members from some (not all) of the burdens of fundraising. Finally, if the Electoral College remains in place for the immediate future, a larger House helps ameliorate its own malapportionment problems. Let me explain. If the House grows, but the Senate does not, then the share of a state's electoral vote count determined by population increases. For example, if the House grew to 574 members, Wyomingites would still have more influence in the Electoral College than Californians, but the disparity would drop from 3.6 times to 2.9 times. Again, progress, not perfection.

Congress has the power to increase the size of the House through simple legislation; no amendment is necessary. Doing so would not be historically unusual. Recall that until 1911, the House routinely grew every ten years as population continued to expand.

Expanding the House would address malapportionment, but partisan gerrymandering requires further action by Congress. Despite acknowledging in *Rucho v. Common Cause* that the practice may be "incompatible with democratic principles," the Supreme Court determined that partisan gerrymandering is not judicable because there is no "judicially discoverable and manageable standard." This was a deeply unfortunate judgment. If the High Court felt a responsibility to apply the Constitution in a way that advanced political equality—as the Warren Court once did—it surely could have found a standard. The Supreme Court has adopted and applied complicated standards for evaluating the president's emergency powers, obscenity, the constitutionality of majority-minority districts, and much more. Because voters cannot be treated equally unless parties are treated equally, the most obvious standard would evaluate claims of unconstitutional gerrymandering on the basis of whether they failed to provide one party's voters with the same opportunity to convert votes to seats as the other party. If Democrats can win 55 percent of a state's House vote, but fail to win roughly the same number of seats as Republicans would win *with the exact same vote share*, then that could be deemed a violation of the Equal Protection Clause.[47] As the Court has done when evaluating malapportionment claims, a margin of error would certainly be applied. And while one could argue that a threshold for acceptable bias would be arbitrary, judges must draw legal lines as a matter of course. In his 2006 dissent in *LULAC v. Perry*—a case that effectively extended the holding in *Vieth*—Justice Stevens suggested that the Court adopt a ten percent deviation from symmetry standard. Under this plan, if a state drew district lines allowing Republicans to win 50 percent of its House seats with just 35 percent of the state's overall vote (while Democrats would need 65 percent of the state's vote share to win the *same number of seats*), this map would be constitutionally suspect. Again, this sort of standard would be no less arbitrary than those applied by the Supreme Court in all sorts of cases. Unfortunately, the Roberts Court (or five justices, to be precise) chose to pass the buck.

As the majority opinion in *Rucho* made clear, however, Congress and the states possess the power to address this issue. And more states are taking action. As recently as 2000, no states drew House districts in a nonpartisan or bipartisan way. Today, 11 do so. In all but one case—Virginia in 2020—the reform was enacted solely through a statewide ballot referendum. Not surprisingly, state legislators are generally reluctant to concede an important power that they possess. In Virginia, Democrats had campaigned on nonpartisan redistricting in 2019 when they were in the minority in both chambers of the state legislature. Upon taking the majority later that year, Democrats hedged on the issue, knowing that adopting an independent commission would effectively strip the party of its newly-acquired power during the next round of redistricting. A slim 54–46 majority—now consisting of mostly Republicans and nine Democrats—approved a nonpartisan redistricting amendment in March 2020. Voters had the final say in a November 2020 referendum, where they overwhelmingly supported it.

There are two reasons, however, why relying on states to solve this problem is less than ideal. First, there are few remaining states where statewide ballot referenda could create an independent redistricting commission (under existing state laws). Most of those with this ability have already acted to do so. And given the process in Virginia, it is clear that persuading legislatures to strip their own power will be a formidable (though not impossible) challenge—particularly on an issue that has a difficult time maintaining salience with the public.

The second reason concerns asymmetric adoption. As I have stressed, American democracy is practiced through political parties. In the U.S., as a result of a winner-take-all design, it does so through *two* major parties. Preferences are expressed through citizen votes for party candidates, who then consolidate power and advance like-minded policy objectives. As a result, political equality simply cannot exist unless the two major parties have equal opportunities to gain and exercise power. Popularity must convert to power in the same manner for each party. State gerrymandering reforms are laudable, but any true solution must be national because it is the entire U.S. House that collectively advances bills for the chamber. If some states have districts with partisan bias, but others do not, the House remains biased. This is particularly problematic if one party (or its voters) is more likely to allow partisan gerrymandering than the other. Currently, most of the states that have approved nonpartisan or bipartisan redistricting reforms are Democratic-leaning states. These include California and New York, the largest and fourth-largest states in the U.S. If voters are creating fair districts in states where Democrats are favored, but biased districts in states where Republicans are favored, the result is a tremendous House advantage for the latter.

With this in mind, the only true path for ending partisan gerrymandering lies with Congress, who has the power to do it across all states through legislation. Recall that Article I of the Constitution declares, "The Times, Places and Manner of holding Elections for Senators and Representatives, shall be prescribed in each State by the Legislature thereof; but Congress may at any time make or alter such Regulations…." The Supreme Court majority in *Rucho* confirmed—though no doubt ever existed—that the latter clause permits Congress to rectify partisan gerrymandering.

In both 2019 and 2021, the House took the first step in doing so. The For the People Act (H.R. 1), a broad measure also targeting voter suppression (see Chapter 6), campaign finance inequities (see Chapter 7), and much more, was approved by the chamber. If ultimately signed into law, the bill would mandate that every state use independent commissions when drawing House districts. The House vote was extremely partisan, with all but one Democrat supporting the bill in 2021 and all Republicans opposing it. The public was less divided, as 67 percent of Americans expressed support for the measure.

Because there are many components of the For the People Act, it is difficult to determine which factors led to support or opposition to the bill. But if a stand-alone independent redistricting bill had been considered in 2021, Republicans likely would have opposed that as well. Their reasons—both public and private—are predictable. Publicly, Republicans would likely appeal to federalism, arguing that redistricting should be left up to the states. More quietly, they would object to reducing a considerable electoral advantage that they currently enjoy. In fairness, if the circumstances were reversed, Democrats would likely be in no rush to reform redistricting rules either. While they are generally more reliable supporters of electoral reform, the aforementioned case of Virginia proves that Democrats are also not eager to forfeit advantages conferred by partisan gerrymandering.

In the current environment where Democrats *are* disadvantaged by partisan gerrymandering, reforming the system has two paths. First, Democrats could approve reforms at a time when they control the House, Senate, and presidency. Doing so would likely require the party to end the 60-vote cloture requirement in the Senate, as it is exceedingly unlikely that it will enjoy a 60-vote majority in the chamber anytime soon. As I have stated, I believe allowing simple (51-vote) majorities to govern in the Senate would improve the quality of American democracy. Not only would majorities gain the ability to enact popular economic and social policies, but efforts to improve political equality—such as those included in the For the People Act—would have a much-improved chance of passage.

Second, opponents of partisan gerrymandering could bring so much attention to the issue that politicians in *both* parties eventually find it difficult to resist reform. We already know that Americans overwhelmingly oppose partisan gerrymandering when they learn more about it. If armies of passionate, mobilized citizens demand that candidates and elected officials address the issue, it could be very difficult to ignore.

In my view, either course of action is justified as a means to ending the scourge of partisan gerrymandering. The simple fact that proponents of redistricting reform overwhelmingly come from one political party (today, at least) does not mean that reform would create an advantage for one party. To the contrary, truly nonpartisan or bipartisan redistricting commissions would increase partisan *fairness* in the House. And when parties are treated fairly, their supporters (citizens) are as well.

CHAPTER 4

Second-Class Americans

In August 2005, I moved to Washington, D.C., to begin my graduate studies at Georgetown University. In the eight years that followed, I received my master's and PhD in Government, worked for a non-profit organization (The Sunlight Foundation), got married, and made lots of terrific friends. When I first moved to the city, I was excited to take advantage of (free!) Smithsonian museums, visit monuments on the National Mall, and eat lunch in Lafayette Park outside the White House. Young and wide-eyed, I envisioned meeting politicians and media figures and becoming endlessly ensconced in all aspects of American politics and policy. But ultimately, while I checked off plenty of bucket list items while living in the District, those are not the things I remember most about my time there.

My wife and I lived in the Northwest part of the city, just a few blocks from the National Cathedral. When away from Georgetown's campus, I could often be found at Saxby's on 35th Street or at Politics & Prose in the Chevy Chase neighborhood. For lunch, I would often visit convenient (and inexpensive) local joints like Rocklands, Surfside, and Cava. My friends and I spent hundreds of hours (and thousands of dollars) at The Tombs, a classic college bar in Georgetown. Thomas Sweet, only a few blocks from there, had great soft serve ice cream. I loved my little barbershop, Camillo, in Tenleytown. I got plenty of parking tickets, but with time learned how to (mostly) avoid them. I frequently patronized the Avalon Theatre, Pearson's Liquors, and the public swimming pool in Tenleytown. Every other year, I had my car inspected. I called the fire department when our carbon monoxide detector would not stop beeping. (I should have just changed the battery.) I filed a police report when my laptop was stolen. I reported for jury duty at least four times. I lived through an earthquake, Snowmageddon, a derecho, Hurricane Irene, and enough oppressive summer days for one lifetime.

My life in Washington was hardly glamorous. I worked, spent time with friends, stayed in touch with family, and established roots in my community. Even though I studied American politics, my life was not defined by living in the nation's capital. The same is true for a vast majority of residents in the District today. National politics are the local industry, similar to entertainment in Los Angeles, finance in lower Manhattan, and country music in Nashville. But to view the District as simply the seat of the national government is misguided. Washington, D.C., like any city or town in the U.S., is a community. It is a place filled with distinct neighborhoods, fifth-generation families, local sports teams, native cuisine (half-smokes!), farmers' markets, diverse cultures, and persistent debates about development, inequality, safety, housing prices, and schools.

The glaring difference between Washington and other cities and towns in the U.S. is a lack of representation. While citizens living in Washington are able to vote for president by virtue of the Twenty-Third Amendment, approved in 1963, they have no representation in the U.S. House or Senate. Citizens are therefore unable to have a voice in legislative debates regarding taxes, war, healthcare, or any of the other national policies set by Congress. Even worse, Congress often uses its control over the District to advance policies clearly at odds with the wishes of the city's constituents. This blatant and shameful lack of democracy for nearly 700,000 Americans is simply indefensible. And this injustice, now over two centuries old, is not even sanctioned by the Constitution! There is no indication that Alexander Hamilton, Thomas Jefferson, and James Madison intended to disenfranchise citizens when they agreed to establish Washington, D.C., as the nation's capital in 1790.

The solution to this problem is both straightforward and achievable—the District of Columbia must be granted statehood. The city's residents overwhelmingly support statehood; Congress has no moral right to deny representation to American citizens who demand it.

Residents of the District of Columbia are not the only Americans without the full rights of citizenship. There are five inhabited U.S. territories—American Samoa, Guam, the Northern Marianas Islands, Puerto Rico, and the U.S. Virgin Islands—that have no say in selecting any federal officeholders. Collectively, the territories have a population of nearly 3.6 million people. With the exception of the 46,000 residents of American Samoa, those born in the territories are U.S. citizens. But because they lack national representation, the territories are often neglected by the federal government. Full political equality would seem to demand that the territories be granted statehood as well. It is important to consider, however, that the territories (at least four of them) were effectively colonized by the U.S. Respect for democracy demands that the people of these communities—and no one else—determine their own political futures. Territorial residents should not be forced to submit to statehood if they do not desire it. There are many residents in the territories who worry that full integration with the U.S. would compromise cherished traditions and cultures. But when those living in the territories *do* support it, statehood should absolutely be granted. In 2020, Puerto Rico opted for statehood in a non-binding island-wide referendum, with 52.5 percent of voters supporting the option. Congress must respect the principles of democracy and self-determination and provide Puerto Rico with a binding opportunity to choose statehood or another political arrangement. Failure to do so would not only perpetuate political inequality; it would also be a shameful human rights violation.

If reservations about statehood persist in the other four (much smaller) territories, democracy could be advanced through other means. Even when territorial residents have hesitated about full integration, they have generally expressed a clear desire to have a louder voice in national affairs. Voting representation could be extended to the territories for U.S. House and presidential elections (if a national popular vote is eventually adopted). Because the Senate represents states, this type of representation could reasonably be reserved for territories opting to pursue statehood. But by inviting Americans in the territories—who pay federal taxes and fight in foreign wars—to have a louder voice in their national government, the U.S. would move closer to representing the collective will of its people and advancing political equality.

Representation in
the District of Columbia

Article I, Section 8 of the Constitution gives Congress the power to establish a federal capital and hold exclusive jurisdiction over it. As part of the Compromise of 1790, James Madison, Alexander Hamilton, and Thomas Jefferson agreed that the federal government would pay each state's remaining Revolutionary War debts in exchange for establishing the new national capital in the southern United States. In essence, northern states conceded the location of the capital in exchange for the assumption of debts, of which they had a disproportionate amount. That year, Congress passed the Residence Act, authorizing the creation of a national capital—the District of Columbia—on the Potomac River. The District would be formed from land donated by the states of Maryland and Virginia.[1] While much of the District was undeveloped, two towns—Georgetown, Maryland and Alexandria, Virginia—were already thriving communities. In 1800, Congress met in Washington, D.C., for the first time; later that year, President John Adams moved into the newly-constructed White House.

There is ample evidence that the Framers never intended to deny voting rights to the District. In fact, writing in *Federalist* No. 43, James Madison wrote that people living in the District of Columbia "will have their voice in the election of the government which is to exercise authority over them."[2] This promise, however, was not kept. In 1801, Congress passed the District of Columbia Organic Act, which formalized its control of the District. Notably, the bill stripped citizens of their previously held Maryland or Virginia residencies. As a result, they were no longer able to vote in congressional elections. As the District of Columbia was not a state, it lacked its own seats in the House or Senate (or votes in the Electoral College). The 14,000 residents of the District were effectively denied any representation in the federal government that they hosted.

While there were efforts to advance voting representation for the District as early as 1888, nothing changed until 1960. By then, the city's population was nearly 764,000 residents. While District residents were known to lean Democratic, the party's advantage was not considered significant. As a result, by the late 1950s, both major parties supported allowing District citizens to vote in presidential elections. Remarkably, a constitutional amendment passed in both the House and Senate by a voice vote! By March 1961, the required 38 states had approved the Twenty-Third Amendment, granting the District a number of presidential electors equivalent to the smallest U.S. state. Soon after the amendment was adopted, several factors—mostly centered on race—converged to make the District an overwhelmingly Democratic city. First, the percentage of the city's residents identifying as Black grew substantially in the 1950s and 1960s. Second, after the Voting Rights Act passed in 1965, voting awareness increased among Blacks throughout the U.S., leading to higher turnout. The larger Black electorate in the District was also more Democratic than it had previously been, as support for the party grew in response to its actions on behalf of the Civil Rights Movement (including the Voting Rights Act itself). Since 1964, the District has given its three electoral votes to Democratic presidential candidates in each election.

In 1976, prospects for full voting rights in the District looked promising. Both the Democratic and Republican Party platforms endorsed congressional representation. Two years later, Congress passed a constitutional amendment to provide the District with full voting representation in both the House and Senate. Support was bipartisan; while more Democrats supported it than Republicans, it was backed by prominent Republican Senators such as Bob Dole of Kansas, Barry Goldwater of Arizona, and Strom Thurmond of South Carolina. Despite its passage, Democratic Senator Ted Kennedy of Massachusetts expressed doubt that the amendment would ultimately gain support from the necessary three-fourths of states because of the District's "four toos." The city was, he feared, "too Black, too liberal, too urban, and too Democratic" for many state legislatures to rally behind.[3] And while a sufficient number of states had supported the Twenty-Third Amendment, this was before the city became more racially diverse and reliably Democratic. As it turns out, Kennedy was correct. After only 16 states—including none with Republican state legislative majorities—ratified the amendment within the seven-year window, it expired.

Some noted that supporters were never able to build momentum behind the effort across the country. After the amendment expired, an editorial in *The Washington Post* angrily noted, "This country apparently assumes that the District of Columbia is composed of nothing more than a bunch of bureaucratic paper-shufflers for the federal government. We ourselves have done blessed little to let the national public know about the citizens who were born here and who will die here, who raise and educate their children here, who build their churches here, who deliver their services here, and above all who struggle as hard as other American citizens to meet their responsibilities and fulfill their dreams here."[4] Creating change—particularly constitutional change—in the U.S. is exceptionally difficult. Without a strong public demand, which the District of Columbia Voting Rights Amendment clearly lacked in the late 1970s and 1980s, it is nearly impossible.[5]

In 1970, less than a decade after the District earned the right to vote in presidential elections, Congress used its power to grant it a non-voting delegate in the House. This delegate could serve on committees and speak on the House floor, but could not vote on any legislation. Three years later, Congress granted the city "home rule." The District would have its own mayor and city council, but Congress still held the power to overrule its decisions. Furthermore, the city was barred from taking certain actions that most local governments in the U.S. are free to adopt. The District was forbidden, for example, from taxing those who work in the city but live elsewhere. It was barred from changing the city's height limit on buildings, something that has made affordable housing in the city a greater challenge. Finally, over 50 percent of the city's property—managed by the federal government—was exempt from local taxation. This inability to tax so much territory has meant hundreds of millions of dollars in lost revenue each year.

On many occasions, Congress has inserted itself into the local government's affairs. In 2014, the District's residents overwhelmingly (69 percent) supported marijuana legalization in a ballot referendum. The initiative allowed those 21 and older to possess up to two ounces of marijuana. But Congress has prohibited the policy from fully taking effect. In recent years, Congress has also sporadically barred the District from using local tax dollars to fund abortion services and clean needle exchange programs.[6] And on multiple occasions since 2004, Congress has funded a program that provides funds ($20 million a year) to District students to attend private schools; the program is generally unpopular in the city, as most residents would prefer that the funds be used to improve public schools.[7] Whether the District's policy preferences regarding marijuana, abortion, or school vouchers constitute "good public policy" is immaterial. In a democratic society, citizens should be able to exercise their collective will. On each of these issues, the District's tax-paying residents were unable to have the same input that citizens around the country enjoy.

District citizens have been denied basic democratic rights despite consistently meeting the same demands of citizenship that those in the fifty states do. District residents pay full federal income and payroll taxes. In fact, the combined tax receipts paid by District residents is routinely higher than that paid by the residents of many U.S. states. In Fiscal Year 2019, according to the Internal Revenue Service (IRS), District residents sent more money (over $27 billion) to the federal government than the residents of 21 states.[8] District residents not only pay their fair share of taxes, but they also willingly take up arms for their country. In fact, more than 4,000 District residents were killed in the Second World War and Korean War (combined), while at least 250 residents have been killed in conflicts abroad since. And of course, the total number who have fought and been wounded in these conflicts is much higher. District residents have served despite having no voice when Congress authorizes wars, considers funding for troops, or sets policies regarding veterans.

In the late 2000s, the issue of D.C. voting rights received renewed attention. In 2009, the Senate approved a bill that would provide the District with voting representation in the House. In addition, the bill would have added an additional House seat in heavily Republican Utah, which had just missed obtaining a fourth House seat after the 2000 census.[9] With the Utah provision included, the Senate approved the measure with the support of nearly all Democrats and six Republicans. The Senate bill, however, also included language that stripped several gun control measures that the District had implemented. This language was ultimately enough to prevent its passage in the House. After the 2010 census, Utah gained a fourth House seat by virtue of its population growth, effectively killing this solution for advancing House representation in the District.

Since 2010, supporters of voting rights have consolidated their efforts behind full statehood for the District of Columbia. In 2020, the House approved statehood for the first time in a 232–180 vote. The new state, if approved, would be named Washington, Douglass Commonwealth, after abolitionist Frederick Douglass. Sadly, the vote was almost entirely partisan. All but one House Democrat backed the measure, while every voting Republican opposed it. Democratic House Speaker Nancy Pelosi commented, "The fact is people in the District of Columbia pay taxes, fight our wars, risk their lives for our democracy and yet, in this state they have no say, they have no vote in the House or Senate about whether we go to war and how those taxes are exacted."[10] Republicans cried that Democrats were simply seeking to expand their power by adding reliably Democratic seats to the House and Senate. Republican Senate Majority Leader Mitch McConnell vowed not to consider the measure in the Senate, comparing D.C. statehood to "full-bore socialism." Republican Senator Tom Cotton of Arkansas argued that while the District has more residents than Wyoming, the latter deserves voting rights more because it is a "working class state," rather than the home of those who work in national politics.[11] Cotton's statement was problematic for several reasons. First, the vast majority of District residents do not work for the federal government or in politics at all. Second, the District has a very large working-class population. Tens of thousands of tax-paying residents clean houses and hotels, serve food, sweep streets, exterminate pests, repair pipes and houses, fix potholes, and work in public safety. Third, even if this were not the case, why would any U.S. citizen deserve to lose their voting rights because of the type of work that they do?

Passage of D.C. statehood had been gaining momentum for years, but the effort received renewed focus in 2020 as the nation experienced a wave of protests targeting police brutality against Black Americans. The issue of D.C. voting rights is a matter of both political and racial equality. Of the nearly 700,000 residents in the District, more than half are non–white. About 46 percent of the population identifies as Black, a figure that is nearly four times the national percentage. After the House approved statehood, Stasha Rhodes, the campaign director for 51 for 51, stated "The protests across America aren't just a call for policing reform ... [they are] also a call to challenge the very institutions that allow White supremacy and racism. The fact that ... 700,000 mostly Black and Brown people do not have a vote in Congress is racism."[12]

Even if majorities in the House and Senate (along with the president) were to agree to approve D.C. statehood in the near future, the federal courts could present an obstacle. Some, including prominent organizations such as CATO and the Heritage Foundation, believe that the Constitution—the Twenty-Third Amendment in particular—does not currently permit statehood for the District. In a paper published by Heritage, attorney R. Hewitt Pate noted that the Twenty-Third Amendment's reference to "the District constituting the seat of Government" establishes the current

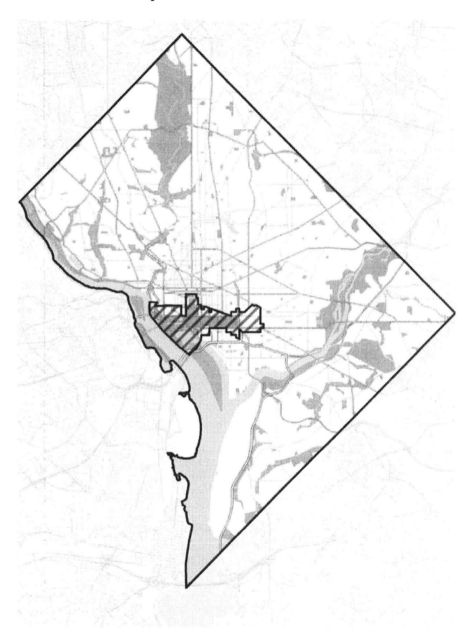

If approved as a new state, Washington, Douglass Commonwealth, would include all of the District's current territory, with the exception of the striped area. This territory, which is comprised of mostly government buildings and the National Mall, would remain a federal district (District of Columbia Office of Planning).

District of Columbia as a "permanent constitutional entity."[13] While this is true, nothing in the Constitution prevents Congress from expanding or contracting the District's size. Even a much smaller federal district—one consisting of only government buildings and public spaces—could both "constitute the seat of Government" and be a "permanent constitutional entity." The District's boundaries have been shrunk before; in 1846, the town of Alexandria was removed from the District and returned to Virginia. If the District were indeed shrunk again, its former territory—consisting of the areas where people reside—could become a new state.

Critics also note that the Twenty-Third Amendment grants three presidential electors to the District. Therefore, if Congress shrinks the District in order to establish a state, the remaining District—consisting mostly of monuments and government buildings—would still be entitled to three electoral votes in presidential elections. These would be in addition, of course, to those held by the new state (Douglass Commonwealth) that was once part of the District. There is a solution to this problem as well. The Twenty-Third Amendment provides that the District's electors shall be appointed "in such manner as Congress may direct." As writer Ian Millhiser has noted, Congress could simply approve a law (not an amendment) declaring that these three electors will go to whichever candidate wins the national election. These votes would simply pad the total of the winner and have no impact on the presidential election's outcome.

Representation in the U.S. Territories

When Hurricane Maria slammed into Puerto Rico in 2017 and left 2,975 residents dead, many Americans did not realize that their own country was suffering. To be clear, most Americans undoubtedly saw the news coverage and recognized that Maria was a devastating storm. Rather, 47 percent of Americans did not know that Puerto Ricans *were* American citizens.[14] This survey spoke to a broader truth in the U.S.—the five inhabited territories and their residents are often an afterthought in the states.

It is not the purpose of this book to document the long and complex history of the U.S. and its overseas territories, but a crash course is warranted. As I discussed in Chapter 1, the U.S. has possessed territories for most of its history. In fact, 31 of the 37 states added after the Constitution was ratified were territories (or part of territories) at one time. These territories consisted of western (or Midwestern, in today's parlance) land controlled by the U.S. after the American Revolution, as well as land later acquired through foreign purchases and wars. In these cases, the process of advancing from a territory to a state generally followed a series of steps. First, Congress established an area as an organized U.S. territory. In doing so, the territory became a full part of the U.S., meaning all federal laws and constitutional rights applied. After the territory expressed a preference for statehood, Congress empowered the territorial government to craft a state constitution. Once both Congress and a majority of the territory's eligible voters approved the resulting constitution, both houses of Congress formally approved a resolution affirming statehood. The last U.S. territories to become states were Alaska and Hawaii in 1959.

Today, the U.S. holds five inhabited territories: American Samoa, Guam, the Northern Marianas Islands, Puerto Rico, and the U.S. Virgin Islands. The combined population of the territories is nearly 3.6 million people, with the vast majority (roughly 90 percent) residing in Puerto Rico. Unlike previous examples, however, it is far from clear that statehood is inevitable for these five territories. Each remains "unincorporated," meaning that residents are not fully subject to federal laws or afforded full constitutional protections. Rather, Congress has complete control over the territories, meaning that it has discretion over which features of American law apply.

The story (at least the short version) of how the U.S. obtained its current territories, as well as how they came to be "unincorporated," begins in the late 1800s. By that time, Cuba had been fighting for its independence from Spain for several decades. With reports of (real and exaggerated) atrocities committed by Spain blanketing U.S. newspapers, the population supported U.S. intervention on the side of the Cubans. Other considerations also built momentum towards war. Teddy Roosevelt, then serving as assistant secretary of the Navy under President William McKinley, believed war could help establish the U.S. as a global power. He and others also believed that Spanish aggression only 90 miles from the U.S. violated the spirit of the Monroe Doctrine. That 1823 policy declared that the U.S. would not accept efforts by European governments to retake or expand possessions in the Americas. While Spain already possessed Cuba, its failure to maintain legitimacy with the people suggested that it no longer effectively controlled the island. Finally, some business interests, frustrated by the Spanish government, saw an opportunity for better investment opportunities in an independent, U.S.-aligned Cuba.

After the U.S. sent the USS *Maine* battleship to Havana in January 1898 to protect its interests during the ongoing Cuban revolt, the ship mysteriously exploded the following month, killing 266 men. While the cause of the explosion was (and remains) unclear, major newspapers—engaging in "yellow journalism"—called the explosion an attack. Support for war increased even more, with "Remember the Maine! To hell with Spain!" becoming a national rallying cry. Ultimately, the U.S. entered the war and defeated Spain after just four months of fighting. Cuba was granted its independence within just a few years, though the U.S. did secure a perpetual lease of 45 square miles at Guantanamo Bay. The site remains a U.S. naval base, gaining prominence during the War on Terror as detainees were held indefinitely at the base's detention camp without a trial and, in some cases, tortured.

While the U.S. entry into the Spanish-American War had centered on Cuba, the Treaty of Paris that settled the conflict resulted in the U.S. obtaining additional territory. Spain ceded Puerto Rico, as well as the Pacific possessions of Guam and the Philippine Islands (the U.S. paid Spain $20 million for the Philippines). These Spanish acquisitions were not the only U.S. acquisitions of 1898, or the years that followed. As the U.S. was fighting Spain in 1898, Congress also annexed the Republic of Hawaii. Just a few years earlier, Hawaii's monarchical government led by Queen Lili'uokalani had been overthrown by European and American business leaders with help from U.S. diplomats.

The following year, in 1899, the U.S. would add five Samoan islands (named American Samoa in 1911) to its list of territories. The U.S. had visited Pago Pago Harbor on the Samoan island of Tutuila as early as 1839. In time, it proved to be a useful port for refueling in the Pacific during trade missions. Germany and the United Kingdom also had interest in the islands. In 1899, after a brief conflict, Germany and the U.S. effectively agreed to split up the islands, with the U.S. controlling the eastern five—including Tutuila. The United Kingdom relinquished any claims, but secured other German possessions in the Pacific. While the German portion would eventually move into New Zealand's hands in 1914 before becoming independent in 1962 (Samoa), American Samoa remains a U.S. territory today.[15]

In 1902, with its overseas empire expanding, the U.S. sought to purchase an archipelago of Caribbean islands from Denmark (the Danish West Indies). The territory consisted of three main islands—Saint Croix, Saint John, and Saint Thomas—as well as several minor islands. The harbor in Charlotte Amalie, located in Saint Thomas, was considered an excellent spot for a Naval base.[16] Despite U.S. interest, however, the Danish Parliament rejected the sale by just one vote. Ultimately, however, the two sides would reach a deal. In 1916, Denmark agreed to sell the islands—to be called the U.S. Virgin Islands—for $25 million. To date, the purchase marks the most money the U.S. has ever paid for foreign land.[17]

Of the six inhabited territories acquired between 1898 and 1917, only Hawaii has since become a U.S. state (in 1959). The others have met different fates. In a conflict that is often overlooked, the U.S. fought a bloody war with Philippine rebels in the four years that followed the Spanish-American War. Over 4,000 Americans were killed, along with at least 200,000 Filipino residents. While U.S. control of the Philippines was secured by 1902, violent skirmishes continued to erupt in the years that followed. Independence was granted to the Philippines after the Second World War, in 1946.

The other territories have not gained independence or statehood, an arrangement made possible by the Supreme Court. After the U.S. acquired Guam, the Philippines, and Puerto Rico, the Supreme Court heard nearly two dozen cases beginning in 1901—known as the Insular Cases—in an effort to clarify the constitutional status of the newly-acquired territories. In one important case, *Downes v. Bidwell* (1901), a tax on oranges shipped from Puerto Rico to New York was challenged on the grounds that taxation is banned on interstate commerce (i.e., commerce between U.S. states). A 5–4 Supreme Court majority ruled that while the territories belonged to the U.S., they were not entirely part of it. The ruling effectively created a new distinction between *incorporated* and *unincorporated* U.S. territories. Congress, the majority noted, was empowered to recognize incorporated territories, or those where all U.S. laws and constitutional rights applied. It could, however, choose to manage possessions as unincorporated territories; in these cases, Congress could determine which parts of federal law applied. In a statement that had clear racist overtones, the majority declared that placing the newly-acquired Spanish possessions on a statehood path (as territories historically were) would be "a false step that might be fatal to the development of ... the American empire.... If those possessions are inhabited by alien races, differing from us in religion, customs, laws, standards of taxation, and modes of thought, the administration of government and justice, according to the Anglo-Saxon principles, may for a time be impossible." The recently acquired Spanish possessions, the Court majority believed, should not be viewed the same as previous U.S. territories on the mainland. Here, the Court distinguished between "the annexation of distant and outlying possessions ... and earlier expansion within the contiguous territory inhabited only by people of the same race or by scattered bodies of Native Indians."[18] In *Hawaii v. Mankichi* (1903), the Supreme Court ruled that Congress had effectively already incorporated the Hawaii Territory in the Hawaii Organic Act of 1900, when Hawaiians were granted U.S. citizenship. No such designation, however, had yet been approved regarding Guam, the Philippines, and Puerto Rico. As they remained unincorporated territories, the application of U.S. law in the future would therefore be left to Congress.[19]

In *Dorr v. United States* (1904), the Supreme Court clarified that "fundamental rights," or "those that are the basis of all free government," still existed in the territories.[20] By contrast, "procedural" rights enumerated in the Constitution did not apply unless Congress explicitly said so. The definitions of "fundamental" and "procedural" are, of course, open to interpretation. Applying this doctrine, for example, the Court has found that the Sixth Amendment's right to a jury trial is a procedural right that does not apply in the territories. Again, racism was certainly a factor here; in the *Dorr* case, Justice William Day bluntly noted that it was unwise to confer jury trial rights to Puerto Rico given that it was "peopled by savages."[21]

Most of the Insular Cases dealt with territories acquired through the Treaty of Paris with Spain. However, the rulings would also apply to territories not yet incorporated (American Samoa) or added in the years that followed (the U.S. Virgin Islands and Northern Marianas Islands). While the U.S. Virgin Islands were acquired shortly after the Treaty of Paris (1917), the U.S. would not gain sovereignty over the Northern Marianas Islands until 1986. The story traces to the Second World War, when the U.S. liberated the Pacific islands from Japanese control. After the war concluded, the U.S. administered the 14 islands comprising the Northern Marianas Islands. A majority of residents on the islands supported integration with U.S.-controlled Guam, but Guam rejected this overture in a 1969 referendum. Afterwards, the Northern Marianas Islands pursued a permanent relationship with the U.S. Voters approved a territorial agreement with the U.S. in 1975; after a series of steps, the U.S. gained full sovereignty over the islands and its roughly 50,000 residents in 1986. Much like the other overseas territories held by the U.S., the Northern Marianas Islands was unincorporated.

Using its broad discretion, Congress and the federal courts have applied (and refused to apply) aspects of federal law to the territories over the years. Citizenship has been granted to those born in each territory except American Samoa. Territorial residents pay federal taxes for Social Security and Medicare, but do not pay federal income tax. Supplemental Security Income (SSI), a federal program that provides aid to the poor, is available to residents of the Northern Marianas Islands, but not the other territories. The Affordable Care Act, which expanded access to healthcare in all 50 states and D.C., has not been fully applied to the territories; residents are ineligible for federal subsidies to help them purchase insurance, while insurers are exempt from numerous coverage requirements.[22] For many years, the federal minimum wage ($7.25 an hour) did not apply in several territories; Congress only recently (in 2015) enacted legislation requiring it everywhere. The federal courts have generally applied Equal Protection Clause guarantees to citizens in the territories, but in the Northern Marianas Islands, they have not.[23]

Like the District of Columbia, the territories lack voting representation in Congress. This has always been true for territories, though given their diminished standing under federal law, it is perhaps more consequential for today's unincorporated territories. When Congress crafted an aid package for people and businesses during the Covid-19 outbreak in 2020, territorial residents could not assume that they would receive the same aid as their fellow Americans. With no voting representative in Congress to apply pressure on their behalf, it was perhaps no surprise that they were among the last Americans to receive aid checks during the crisis.[24] Furthermore, the inadequate Medicaid funding provided by Congress to the territories meant that each had a fragile healthcare infrastructure from which to manage the pandemic.[25]

Natural disaster relief has also lagged in the territories. In 2009, an earthquake and tsunami hit American Samoa, killing 34 people. Five years later, leveled buildings still remained in Pago Pago Harbor. In 2017, Hurricane Maria devastated Puerto Rico, killing nearly 3,000 people and leaving nearly the entire island without power. In 2018, an internal FEMA report found that the agency failed to prepare for the previous year's hurricane season and did not adequately support the affected regions.[26] Nearly three years after the hurricane, about 100 schools remained closed, and many roads and buildings were in disrepair. Congress allocated additional aid to Puerto Rico in 2018, but it was not dispersed until 2020 (and even then, only partially) due to disputes between the island and the Trump administration over repair costs.[27] U.S. House Representative Stephanie Murphy of Florida commented, "The hard truth is that Puerto Rico's lack of political power allows Washington to treat Puerto Rico like an afterthought."[28] Puerto Rico Governor Ricardo Rosselló added, "Because we don't have political power, because we don't have representatives, [no] senators, no vote for president, we are treated as an afterthought."[29] It is certainly not crazy to believe that had American Samoa or Puerto Rico had voting representatives in Congress at the time of their respective disasters, they may have been in stronger positions to receive aid in a timely manner.

And when crises hit the territories, local governments often lack the same tools to manage them internally as U.S. states do. For example, when a bad economy or natural disaster causes an economic downtown, states are able to file Chapter 9 bankruptcy to restructure their debt. This, however, is not an option for the territories. Instead, they are often forced to resort to other measures that further exacerbate fiscal problems—like drastic cuts to social programs or the sale of high-interest bonds.[30]

Any accounting of political equality in the U.S. must consider the territories. Today, there are nearly 4 million Americans without the full rights and privileges of citizenship. Many commentators have demanded that the situation change, calling for either independence or statehood for the territories. Statehood, of course, would place the territories fully on par with other U.S. states and render the Insular Cases null and void. Many progressives, in particular, have recently called for Puerto Rican statehood as a means to improving the Democratic Party's long-term prospects in the Senate. I believe a more deferential approach is needed. The political status of the territories should be determined by the residents of these respective communities. True respect for democracy demands that people control their political destinies. And while it may surprise some Americans, there are loud voices in the territories against both independence and statehood.

But why would residents of the territories prefer to have fewer rights or opportunities to choose elected officials? In some cases, there are fears that becoming fully subject to U.S. laws will threaten cultural norms and practices. In American Samoa, for example, the territorial senate is not elected but rather comprised of various island chiefs. This clearly conflicts with the U.S. Constitution, which requires a "republican form of government." In addition, a "roads-closed" prayer time practiced in some communities would appear at odds with the First Amendment's Establishment Clause. In the Virgin Islands, attempts to draft a new territorial constitution—which would be necessary for statehood—have repeatedly stalled because ancestral natives (whose families have lived on the islands for centuries) have demanded special rights and privileges (e.g., property tax exemptions, the exclusive right to serve as governor). Such exemptions would also likely be deemed incompatible with the Constitution. More generally, many Americans living in the territories are well aware that much of Native Hawaiian culture has been threatened and, in some cases, destroyed by the "Americanization" of the islands.[31]

Several of the territories have held referenda regarding their political status. Puerto Rico has held six plebiscites since 1967; in 2012, statehood was supported for the first time, though the structure of the ballot led some to argue that the results did not indicate a true mandate. Voters were asked two questions: (1) Do you support the current territorial arrangement with the U.S.? and (2) Would you support independence, statehood, or a free association agreement with the U.S. (i.e., an independent country still dependent on the U.S. for defense and other limited services). A majority voted "no" on the first question, while statehood secured majority support on the second question. In 2020, a slim majority expressed support for statehood in a referendum that more directly asked if voters backed it. Because the vote was both narrow and non-binding, however, many advocates acknowledge that additional action may be necessary before Congress votes to recognize Puerto Rico as a state. In 2021, House

Representative Darren Soto of Florida and Jennifer Gonzalez-Colón, Puerto Rico's non-voting House delegate, introduced the Puerto Rico Statehood Admissions Act. If approved, the bill would ask Puerto Ricans to vote again on statehood, but the vote would (for the first time) be federally binding. If a majority were to back statehood, Congress would be required to grant it. A separate measure, supported by House Representatives Alexandria Ocasio-Cortez and Nydia Velasquez of New York, calls for more deliberative steps. Their bill would authorize a status convention whereby Puerto Rican voters would select delegates to discuss an array of options regarding the island's political status. Ultimately, several options—potentially including both statehood and full independence—would be presented to voters. Congress would agree to respect the wishes of Puerto Rican voters as expressed through this referendum vote.

While many democracy reformers believe Puerto Rico should be granted statehood immediately, it is imperative that the island determine its own political future. Both of the above bills would authorize a *binding* way for island residents to do so, as Congress would be forced to accept any outcome. Either option would represent democratic progress. Should Puerto Rico ultimately choose statehood, the island's 3.2 million residents would finally become full participants in American democracy after over 120 years of relative neglect. With at least four representatives in the House, two senators, and six electoral votes (under the current rules), Puerto Ricans would be empowered to demand equal treatment in social services, infrastructure improvements, and rights before the law.

While it is (or at least should be) an entirely immaterial consideration, assumptions that Puerto Rican statehood would guarantee Democrats additional representatives in Congress are misguided. Puerto Rico had Republican governors from 2009 to 2013 and from 2019 to 2021. In fact, in 2020, Republican Governor Wanda Vázquez Garced endorsed Donald Trump's reelection for president. Jennifer Gonzalez-Colón, Puerto Rico's aforementioned non-voting House delegate, is also a Republican. Furthermore, it is always difficult to predict how a community will become integrated into a new partisan political environment. It is worth noting that at the time they were added as states in 1959, most assumed that Alaska would be a Democratic state and Hawaii would be a Republican one. Both assumptions, of course, were dead wrong. In short, it is impossible to know how Puerto Rican voters would identify with the two major U.S. political parties before the island becomes a state.

Several of the other territories have held referenda regarding their political status. In 1993, more than 80 percent of Virgin Islands residents supported maintaining territorial status, with only 13 percent supporting full integration with the U.S. (i.e., statehood). As of 2022, Guam is fighting to hold a new status referendum, but federal courts have ruled that voting eligibility for the proposed plebiscite is illegally race-based and therefore violates the U.S. Constitution. Guam's law would only allow native inhabitants of Guam, or those who became U.S. citizens because of the 1950 Organic Act and their descendants, to participate. Because most of the people who fit that definition are ethnically Chamorro, voter eligibility so closely parallels a racial classification that the courts consider it a proxy for race.[32]

As these examples demonstrate, statehood does not appear likely for the smaller four U.S. territories in the foreseeable future. Many territorial residents worry about the "Americanization" of their respective homelands, while cherished local customs sometimes conflict with the Constitution. Nevertheless, more can be done to provide a voice to the roughly 300,000 territorial residents of American Samoa, Guam, the Northern Marianas Islands, and the U.S. Virgin Islands. First, should residents desire it, American Samoans should be granted birthright citizenship, something already guaranteed in the other territories. Second, those of us in education must do a better job integrating the territories—their culture, history, and current events—into our discussions of American life and politics. Often, calls for increasing "awareness" are empty gestures designed to deflect action that one prefers to avoid. In this case, awareness is really needed! Most Americans are unaware that communities of fellow citizens live in distant places such as American Samoa, Guam, and the Northern Marianas Islands. They are equally unaware that these communities serve in the U.S. military at higher rates than any state. In Guam, for example, one in eight residents is a veteran. Like citizens living in Washington, D.C., many have given their lives in American conflicts abroad. While data is difficult to obtain for all territories and conflicts, at least 381 Puerto Ricans were killed in the Second World War. During the Korean War, 843 Americans from American Samoa, Guam, Puerto Rico, and the U.S. Virgin Islands perished. Another 434 from these territories died in the Vietnam War. Finally, during the post–9/11 wars in Afghanistan and Iraq, the five current U.S. territories have lost at least 98 service members in action. How many mainland citizens are aware that so many of their fellow Americans were willing to die to defend their country—even while they had no voice in authorizing the associated conflicts?

Third, in the interest of empowering all Americans to participate in their democracy, each territory should have voting representation (one seat) in the U.S. House of Representatives. This action should be taken without any requirement that the territories surrender additional autonomy. While non-voting members are currently sent from each territory to the House, only voting representation allows the territories to exercise true political power. Representatives will be able to gain influence on committees, leverage their votes to advance the needs of their people, and secure aid for their communities. Territorial residents will see that their national government values their input and views them as fully American.

I recognize that because their populations are smaller than all U.S. states, providing House seats to the territories increases malapportionment in the House. This admittedly contradicts my discussion in Chapter 3, which advocated the Wyoming Rule in order to ensure that all House districts throughout the U.S. contained more equal populations. While this is a fair criticism, remember that the territories' overrepresentation in the House would still be accompanied by a complete lack of Senate representation. Under these circumstances, it would be very difficult to argue that territorial residents would be *better* represented than those living in the 50 states. Adopting the Wyoming Rule for the House (based on the smallest state's population), while carving out an exception for the territories, seems reasonable.

Furthermore, should the Electoral College eventually be replaced by a national popular vote, each American citizen living in the territories should gain the ability to vote for president. If the president is to hold power over all U.S. citizens, there is no reason to exclude some citizens from the process of selecting one. Meanwhile, as I hinted above, because the Senate is designed to represent states (for better or worse), this feature of representation could be reasonably reserved for only those territories willing to take this leap.

The reality is that the situation concerning the territories is both complicated and path dependent. Decisions made over the past 125 years have shaped today's reality. As a result, today's solutions are bound to be messy and imperfect. The best course of action, in my view, is to follow the wishes of the people and err on the side of democracy. Providing the territories with *no* national representation—as is currently the case—is wholly undemocratic and at odds with the wishes and interests of most territorial residents. Granting full representation—including Senate seats— to communities that have *chosen* not to become full participants in the American political community (as states) seems unwise as well. A sensible middle position—one that grants voting rights in institutions representing the American *people*, but not those representing *states*—would both advance political equality and reserve benefits (Senate seats) for communities choosing to fully integrate with American politics and society.

Conclusion

When the U.S. House approved D.C. statehood for the first time in 2020, the country barely seemed to notice. The same scant attention was paid by the media and the country when Puerto Ricans opted for state-hood in a non-binding referendum several months later. Occurring with the backdrop of the Covid-19 pandemic, protests regarding systemic rac-ism and police brutality, and a presidential election between Republican Donald Trump and Democrat Joe Biden in 2020, there was simply little oxygen for these issues. When statehood *did* receive attention, it was gen-erally framed as a partisan matter. Democrats, the argument went, hoped to add both Washington, D.C., and Puerto Rico as states to help them win additional House and (especially) Senate seats. Conversely, Republi-cans were resistant because they feared such a Democratic advantage. As I discussed in Chapter 1, statehood has *always* been political. Recall that Republicans added Nevada to the Union in 1864 simply to help President Lincoln's reelection campaign, and that the Dakota Territory became two states in 1889 at least partially to ensure two additional Republican sena-tors. Politics will likely remain a factor in any debates regarding statehood or enhanced rights for the territories.

But even if partisan considerations cannot be eliminated, they could become somewhat neutralized by broad public support. If Americans are largely uninterested in (or unaware of) the plight of D.C. or territorial residents, then it is easy for elected officials to defer to partisan interests. Under these conditions, opponents have no reason to fear backlash for defeating measures designed to enhance the voice of marginalized Ameri-cans. But if the issue can galvanize the attention and passions of the Amer-ican people, then politicians (at least some of them) will need to weigh this when making decisions. Recall that the U.S. fought the Spanish-American War largely because a groundswell of public support demanded it; the same must happen to advance rights for those forgotten Americans liv-ing outside the 50 states. Those of us with a platform can help by bringing awareness to the issue. In my experience, I do not need to tell students (or other adults) that D.C. or territorial residents deserve congressional repre-sentation. Once I simply discuss the current situation, a majority of people express both shock and support for change.

Another way to build momentum for change is to address the obvi-ous racial and ethnic dimensions of this issue. As I discussed, the District of Columbia is almost 50 percent Black, a percentage nearly four times the national share. Each of the five territories are predominately non–white; in fact, Guam has the smallest share of non–Hispanic whites in the U.S. at just 6.9 percent of the population. Any movement to address biases against people of color should examine the gross political inequities facing these communities. In 2020, protests swept through American cities in protest of police brutality and systemic racism in the U.S. With graphic videos of unarmed Black men being killed by police, the movement appeared to attract support in new places. In the 2020 presidential exit poll, 57 percent of voters, including one-in-five Donald Trump supporters, said they supported the Black Lives Matter movement. Just a few years earlier, the movement was considered politically toxic. At a time when more Americans are challenging racial and ethnic biases in their hearts and laws, the needs of District and territorial residents could find a more receptive audience than in the past.

CHAPTER 5

Eighteen Years Is Enough

On February 14, 2016, I was sitting in a bar in Washington, D.C. (The Pig on 14th St.) with my wife and sister when I heard the news that Supreme Court Justice Antonin Scalia had died. Appointed by President Ronald Reagan in 1986, Scalia had been a stalwart conservative on the High Court for three decades. With the Roberts Court divided between five conservatives and four progressives, Scalia's death was a monumental event. It appeared that Democratic President Barack Obama would be able to appoint a progressive justice to replace him, decisively shifting the balance of the Court.

By the time I finished eating my barbeque sandwich and drinking my bourbon flight, Senate Majority Leader Mitch McConnell of Kentucky (interesting coincidence) had announced that the Senate would not consider *any* replacement made by Obama. Because it was Obama's final year in office, McConnell would simply leave the seat open and consider a nominee from the following president. Given that Obama still had 11 months remaining in his term, this move was viewed as a brazen partisan power grab at odds with Senate tradition. Even when Obama nominated Merrick Garland, a moderate judge for whom the Senate had previously confirmed to the U.S. Court of Appeals for the District of Columbia, McConnell did not relent. When the 2016 election was won by Donald Trump, the new Republican president appointed U.S. Appeals Court Judge Neil Gorsuch—a staunch conservative—to fill Scalia's seat.[1] Democrats, who were outnumbered in the Senate by a 52–48 majority, filibustered the nomination. In return, McConnell and his Republican colleagues changed the cloture rules so that simple majorities could move forward on Supreme Court nominees.[2] Gorsuch was confirmed, 54–45, in a mostly partisan vote.

Four years later, I was bathing my 23-month-old daughter when my wife yelled upstairs, "Justice Ginsburg died!" The news was not terribly surprising, as the 87-year-old liberal icon had been ill for years. It was, however, politically important because it occurred less than seven weeks before the 2020 presidential election. Within hours of Ginsburg's death,

Mitch McConnell announced that Republicans *would* consider Trump's replacement before the election. Given his actions in 2016, this seemed blatantly hypocritical. McConnell justified his decision by noting that the president and Senate were from the same party in 2020, unlike 2016. Democrats cried foul, but few voters appeared to change their minds in the 2020 election on the basis of McConnell's decision. Trump nominated U.S. Appeals Court Judge Amy Coney Barrett to the High Court[3]; by late October, she was confirmed in a 52–48 vote. Conservatives now had a solid 6–3 majority on the Supreme Court.

Democrats were (and remain) aghast at the series of events that delivered conservatives such commanding control of the Supreme Court. From their perspective, President Obama had the rightful ability to fill Scalia's seat in 2016, but was wrongfully denied. Then, after Hillary Clinton won the popular vote for president in 2016, she was defeated in the undemocratic Electoral College. Republicans won the White House, filled Scalia's seat, replaced retiring (and sometimes moderate) Justice Anthony Kennedy with a younger, more conservative justice (Brett Kavanaugh) in 2018, then managed to replace a progressive legend (Ginsburg) with a young conservative just weeks before a presidential election. Furthermore, each nomination was confirmed by a Senate that had a Republican majority largely because the chamber's bias towards small states currently benefits Republicans (see Chapter 1).

Democratic disillusionment was compounded by the fact that the Roberts Court had already stifled progressive priorities. Since 2010 alone, the Roberts Court has used its power of judicial review to weaken public sector unions,[4] limit Medicaid expansion and contraception access under the Affordable Care Act,[5] permit then–President Trump to ban travel from several majority Muslim countries,[6] end abortion rights, and restrict climate protections.[7] In fairness, the Roberts Court has sometimes ruled in ways consistent with progressive ideas. Most of the Affordable Care was upheld in 2012, 2015, and 2021,[8] same-sex marriage was legalized in 2015,[9] and the Court disallowed President Trump from ending the DACA program aimed at protecting children from deportation in 2020.[10]

The Roberts Court has also ruled on a number of cases pertaining to political equality. In general, its decisions have stifled and prevented progress. The Court permitted states to require photo identification at the polls in 2008. In 2010, a 5–4 majority allowed unlimited outside spending in elections in *Citizens United v. FEC.*[11] The same narrow majority gutted an important piece of the Voting Rights Act in 2013 (*Shelby County v. Holder*).[12] In *Rucho v. Common Cause* (2019), the High Court chose not to restrict partisan gerrymandering.[13] And in 2020, the Court allowed

Wisconsin to reject late-arriving ballots, even if the delay was not the fault of the voter. I believe that each of these rulings were deeply detrimental to the cause of political equality in the U.S.

Regardless of whether one agrees with me about the Court's recent actions, it is indisputable that the federal courts—especially the Supreme Court—play a tremendously important role in the U.S. political system. While unelected, the courts have the ability to shape and redefine the meaning of the Constitution through the power of judicial review. There is hardly a major policy area that has not been greatly affected by Supreme Court rulings. Labor law, taxes, environmental protection, healthcare, international relations, race, gender, sexuality, and more are subject to the constant mercy of black-robed judges and justices. There is every reason to believe the Court will remain active in these areas, as well as the democracy reform topics discussed in this book. The Court would likely demand a say in determining whether my proposed reforms regarding the Senate, the Electoral College, and D.C. statehood, for example, are acceptable under the Constitution. It is not an exaggeration to say that without supportive—and sometimes proactive—federal courts, many efforts to increase political equality will fail.

Given their awesome power to shape public policy and democratic institutions, it is essential to scrutinize the federal courts and their design. If the courts are designed and shaped in ways that violate political equality, then any inequities are spread like a virus onto every issue on which they rule. In this brief chapter, I address two fundamental questions regarding the federal courts and political equality. First, should unelected courts possess the aforementioned power that they currently do? And second, if so, how should those who exercise this power be selected? I conclude that while robust judicial power *is* consistent with political equality, the current appointment and confirmation process is not. Reform is needed to ease stress on the courts, reduce partisan drama, and guarantee that some citizens do not have disproportionate control over the judiciary.

The Courts and Political Equality

The Constitution is rather vague—*even by the Constitution's standards*—about the structure and power of the federal courts. Article III notes, "The judicial power of the United States, shall be vested in one Supreme Court, and in such inferior courts as the Congress may from time to time ordain and establish." Basically, while the Constitution created the highest federal court (the Supreme Court), it allowed Congress to create the lower court structure beneath it. While Congress swiftly exercised its authority in 1789, the organization of today's courts stems largely from the Judiciary Act of 1891. District courts (of which there are now 94) serve as trial courts where most federal cases begin. Appeals courts (of which there are now 13) hear challenges to district court rulings. Finally, the Supreme Court holds appellate jurisdiction over most federal matters; if its justices choose (today, four of nine must agree) to hear challenges to appeals court rulings, they can. In addition, the Supreme Court enjoys original jurisdiction over some matters, meaning that it may hear cases without them first going through federal district or appeals courts. In the Constitution, original jurisdiction is limited to "all cases affecting ambassadors, other public ministers and consuls, and those in which a state shall be party." In *United States v. Texas* (1892), the Supreme Court clarified that original jurisdiction also covers disputes between a state and the federal government.

While the Constitution does not explicitly empower the federal courts to exercise "judicial review," or the power to strike laws deemed at odds with the Constitution, many of the Framers believed that they would hold this power. At the Philadelphia Convention, James Madison commented, "A law violating a constitution established by the people themselves, would be considered by the Judges as null & void."[14] George Mason, Madison's fellow Virginia delegate, said that federal judges would be able to "declare an unconstitutional law void."[15] Madison and Mason were hardly alone. Delegates from a majority of the 13 states made comments supporting judicial review at the Convention. While the Supreme Court exercised judicial review as early as 1796 (*Hylton v. United States*) when it evaluated the constitutionality of a carriage tax,[16] it did not explicitly assert its power to strike unconstitutional laws until the 1803 case, *Marbury v. Madison*. As I have documented throughout the book, the federal courts are not limited to evaluating acts of the U.S. Congress. Because the Constitution's Supremacy Clause deems the document to be the nation's "supreme law of the land," the federal courts are also empowered to strike state acts if they violate it. It is through this power that the Supreme Court has blocked state death penalty laws, anti-miscegenation laws, and segregated schools, for example.

Given its power to eliminate or alter acts approved by elected legislatures and executives, some believe judicial review is an inherently undemocratic practice. In 1820, former President Thomas Jefferson noted, "Our judges are as honest as other men, and not more so. They have, with others, the same passions for party, for power, and the privilege of their corps. ... Their power [is] the more dangerous as they are ... not responsible, as the other functionaries are, to the elective control."[17] Indeed, federal judges are not elected. This is intentional, as they are intended to be insulated from politics. Without the need to satisfy a constituency or behave in the interests of reelection, judges are better suited to objectively evaluate matters from a legal perspective. In doing so, they serve as a check on majorities and their selected representatives. Free from retribution, the courts are able to protect rights, even when doing so is unpopular. The Supreme Court has done this on numerous occasions; it has, for example, protected flag burners, neo–Nazi marchers, and pornographers who majorities would have preferred to silence.

Could such unconstrained power be considered "dangerous"? Absolutely. But Jefferson omits some considerations that make the courts less limitless than his quote implies. First, as his one-time rival Alexander Hamilton commented in *Federalist No. 78*, the courts have "neither the sword nor the purse."[18] Because they have no power to enforce their rulings through force or appropriation, their decisions gain legitimacy only through their acceptance by Congress, the president, states, and, ultimately, the people. If the courts repeatedly stray too far from public opinion, then they risk being ignored. The Supreme Court has retained its legitimacy for much of U.S. history, but there are times when its rulings have been flouted. When Chief Justice Roger Taney ruled that President Lincoln had no right to suspend habeas corpus at the start of the Civil War in *Ex parte Merryman* (1861), Lincoln effectively ignored him.[19] Surely, judges and justices are aware of this risk. In recent years, Chief Justice Roberts—a reliable conservative for much of his career—has increasingly sided with progressive justices on cases ranging from abortion rights to immigration to healthcare. Roberts, it has been reported, is mindful of the Court's legitimacy if it is frequently at odds with the American people.

Second, while judges and justices are unelected, they are chosen by elected officials. Elected presidents nominate them, while an elected Senate confirms them. And while they are not subject to reappointment, Congress always has the power to impeach judges for the vague offense of "high crimes and misdemeanors." Furthermore, Congress has the power to limit the power of the Supreme Court. While Congress cannot restrict the Supreme Court's original jurisdiction, it can limit its appellate jurisdiction through the Constitution's Exceptions Clause. The clause, found in Article III, Section 2, reads "the supreme Court shall have appellate Jurisdiction, both as to Law and Fact, with such Exceptions, and under such Regulations as the Congress shall make." Congress could therefore restrict the Supreme Court's ability to review the constitutionality of a large swath of state and federal actions or laws. It is worth noting that over 90 percent of the cases heard by the Supreme Court are through its appellate jurisdiction.

So, while Jefferson and others are correct that the federal courts—

especially the Supreme Court—are both unelected and powerful, they are not without their own checks by elected branches.

Powerful courts can also help advance democracy reform. Through their power of judicial review, the federal courts have enormous space to modernize the Constitution. And because amending the Constitution is very difficult, courts offer more achievable means to democratizing the document. In recent years, the federal courts have not been stewards of political equality. Instead, recent courts—especially the Roberts Court— have created new obstacles. It is important to remember, however, that this has not always been true. During the twentieth century, the Supreme Court issued numerous rulings that redefined the Constitution's democratic identity in a positive way. The Court (belatedly) ended all-white primaries and grandfather clauses, ended malapportionment in state legislatures and the U.S. House, enhanced the reach of the Voting Rights Act, and took steps in the direction of ending partisan gerrymandering.[20] Most of these actions, at the time they were taken, were unlikely to happen at the hands of elected legislatures or chief executives. In fact, had it not been for *Baker, Reynolds*, and *Wesberry* (recall Chapter 3), it is almost certain that absurdly malapportioned legislatures—which badly discriminate against urban and non–white communities—would *still* be in place in many states. Make no mistake—a strong Supreme Court offers tremendous promise for democratic progress. And given the constraints that Congress and the amendment process face, it is not an avenue that should be dismissed by those who wish to make the U.S. a more politically equitable society.

Putting Judges on the Bench

Powerful courts that are shaped by democratically-elected actors are not inherently undemocratic. However, several factors regarding the current judicial appointment process do raise significant concerns. First, as Chapters 1 and 2 detail, neither the president nor (especially) U.S. senators are selected through an ideal democratic process. Because some citizens have more influence than others in both the Electoral College and Senate, those institutions are not always reliable indicators of the popular will at a given moment. It therefore follows that judges appointed by presidents and confirmed by senators are also not always aligned with public preferences. Moving to a national popular vote for president, along with reducing malapportionment in the Senate, would make judicial appointments more consistent with public sentiment and enhance democratic control over the courts.

The nature of lifetime appointments to the federal courts presents additional problems. Article III, Section 1 of the Constitution notes that federal judges "both of the supreme and inferior Courts, shall hold their Offices during good Behavior." More clearly, unless they are impeached and removed from office by Congress, federal judges may serve for as long as they wish. By serving indefinitely, judges are further insulated from political considerations when issuing decisions, as they need not worry about reappointment and confirmation by elected branches. In *Federalist No. 78*, Hamilton defends the "permanent tenure of judicial offices" as a means towards protecting judges from "legislative encroachments."[21]

While the above logic is fundamentally sound, there are multiple reasons why lifetime appointments are problematic today. First, given changes to U.S. life expectancy since the 1780s, federal judges can now routinely serve on the bench for multiple decades. As political scientist David Karol notes, Supreme Court justices from 1789 to 1970 served for an average of 15 years. In the 52 years since, the average has jumped to more than 25 years.[22] While each justice is still appointed and confirmed by elected officials, long tenures increase the likelihood that one will become out of touch with the population they serve. If someone is appointed in 1992, but remains on the High Court in 2022, did the country that currently exists ever really have a voice in selecting them?

Furthermore, while they often uphold legal principles that appear at odds with their personal views, judges *are* political actors. Even if they do not always act with a partisan agenda in mind, the way that a judge views the Constitution and the law carries political consequences. While it would be improper for Congress or the president to dictate how judges rule, it is sensible for elections to have predictable consequences over appointments to the judiciary. For example, if Democrats win four presidential elections over the course of 20 years, but Republicans win only one, then the demands of political equality dictate that Democratic presidents should have four times as much control over the federal judiciary during this span of time. Only then would the people's collective wishes— as expressed at the ballot box—be respected. When voting for president, voters deserve to know that the position will carry a tangible and predictable amount of influence over the judiciary. Under the current system, however, presidential equity is non-existent. Some presidents, as a result of dumb luck or strategic decisions made by judges, are able to fill more seats than others. Regarding the Supreme Court, President Jimmy Carter served one term (1977–1981), but had no opportunities to appoint Supreme Court justices because no vacancies arose. The next one term president, George H.W. Bush (1989–1993), was able to fill two seats. A generation later, Donald Trump, also a one-term president, was afforded three appointments. Had Ruth Bader Ginsburg lived an additional four months, President Joe

Biden would have appointed her replacement. A likely Biden appointment, when compared to Trump's pick of Amy Coney Barrett, would have had dramatically different consequences for the Supreme Court's ideological composition for decades.

Two-term presidents have also had varying opportunities to shape the Supreme Court. Bill Clinton, George W. Bush, and Barack Obama each made two replacements on the Court, though Obama would have had three if Mitch McConnell had considered his nomination of Merrick Garland to replace Antonin Scalia. Ronald Reagan and Richard Nixon were more fortunate; Reagan filled three seats and Richard Nixon filled four! Given the significant amount of power for long stretches of time granted to each Supreme Court justice, it is wrong (and undemocratic) that some elected presidents control the Court's fate much more than others.

The case of President Obama's nomination of Merrick Garland raises an additional issue. In an increasingly partisan environment, Senate judicial confirmations have become much more contentious. In light of Mitch McConnell's willingness to essentially ignore Obama's appointment, it is becoming difficult to imagine the Senate confirming many presidential Supreme Court appointments from the opposite party. Senate confirmations for lower court seats already lag terribly when the presidential party does not control the Senate. In 2007–2008, a Democratic-controlled Senate confirmed ten appeals and 58 district court appointments made by Republican President George W. Bush. Notably, 11 appeals court nominations made by Bush were left vacant. The situation worsened over the next decade. In 2015–2016, a Republican-controlled Senate confirmed just two appeals and 18 district court appointments made by President Obama. When Obama left office, 17 appointments he made to federal appeals courts were left vacant; all would be filled by President Trump and confirmed by the Republican-led Senate.

Even when the same party controls the presidency and the Senate, delays occur. The Senate has long practiced varying forms of a process known as *senatorial courtesy*. When a vacancy arises for an appeals or district court seat in a senator's home state, the two senators from the state are consulted. If they do not grant their approval to the nomination by returning a "blue slip," the nomination does not move forward. Between 2018–2020, the Republican-led Senate allowed the Senate Judiciary Committee to move forward with appeals court nominees that did not have two positive blue slips, but it retained the tradition for district court nominees.[23] The process of consulting senators, securing blue slips, and considering the large number of vacancies on the federal courts is time-consuming, leading to delays.

Vacancies on the federal courts create strains when it comes to managing caseloads. In 2014, the Brennan Center analyzed docket data and interviewed more than 20 chief judges on federal courts, ultimately concluding that vacancies "impact the ability of many courts to effectively and timely administer justice."[24]

Modernizing the Appointment Process

Given the realities of modern life expectancy and polarization, as well as an urgent need to advance political equality, the federal court appointment and confirmation process demands reform. Regarding the Supreme Court, one particular proposal has gained steam in recent years. Rather than allow justices to serve for life, each would instead serve for one non-renewable 18-year term. Terms would be staggered so that one of the Court's nine justices would see their term end every two years. Presidents could therefore rely on making two Supreme Court replacements during a 4-year term. When Representatives Ro Khanna of California and Don Beyer of Virginia introduced a version of this idea in the House, their bill—the Supreme Court Term Limits and Regular Appointments Act of 2021—also required the Senate to act on Supreme Court nominations within 120 days of their appointment. If the Senate failed to consider a nominee within this window, it would effectively waive its "advise and consent" privilege under the Constitution.[25]

This suggested reform raises various questions, even among some who believe it would improve the appointment process. First, many wonder whether this change can be achieved through simple legislation, as opposed to a constitutional amendment. Because federal judges may serve "in good behavior," the bill would be unable to end lifetime appointments; only an amendment could do that. However, future appointments to the Supreme Court could stipulate that after 18 years, a justice must leave the High Court and enter service on a federal district or appeals court if they wished. Appointments would still be for life, but not exclusively on the highest court. Whether the Supreme Court would accept this sort of change through legislation is unclear, though justices would risk appearing to deny the will of the people in favor of their own power if they blocked it. In doing so, they could threaten their own legitimacy.

The second question regards those nine justices currently serving on the Supreme Court. Each was promised a lifetime appointment to that particular court when selected and confirmed. Under the aforementioned House bill, the nine current justices would not be subject to the new 18-year terms. While all nine would continue serving on the Supreme Court "in good behavior," presidents would immediately begin making two appointments per four-year term. As a result, the Court would likely grow from nine members to a larger number for a period of time. There is nothing constitutionally problematic about temporarily (or permanently) expanding the Supreme Court; the Court originally had just six justices and has seen its size expand or shrink seven times since then. The Court has had nine members since 1869, but Congress has the power to adjust the number at any time. Under the bill, once the nine current members depart the Court through voluntary retirement, impeachment, or death, all future justices would serve fixed 18-year terms, and the Court's size would revert to nine. With very limited exceptions, no president (or the voters who selected them) would be more privileged than others in shaping the Court.

Third, let's address the exceptions I just referenced. Under this reform, what happens if a justice retires or dies before the end of their 18-year term? In this case, the sitting president would make the replacement, but the new justice would only serve until the original term ended. In these instances, some presidents will indeed be privileged to shape the Supreme Court more than others, as they will have had two of their own 18-year appointments plus a replacement appointment. Any advantage gained by a president, however, would be mitigated by the fact that replacement terms would generally be short.

Recently, there have been calls in progressive and Democratic Party circles to "pack the Supreme Court," or add permanent seats for the purpose of undoing the hypocritical actions of Senate Republicans in 2016 and 2020, respectively. Advocates argue that either *both* Merrick Garland and Amy Coney Barrett should have been considered in election years, or neither should have been. Because Republicans denied Garland, but confirmed Barrett, they effectively gained an unfair advantage on the High Court. Most Democratic court-packing proposals call for Congress to increase the number of Supreme Court seats from nine to either 11 or 13. As I mentioned earlier, this change can be accomplished through simple legislation, as it has in the past. Democrats' desire to increase the Court (at least to 11 seats) is entirely defensible, as the party was indeed denied a seat. Adding two seats to be appointed by a Democratic president would restore the partisan balance that would have existed if either (1) both Garland and Barrett had been confirmed or (2) neither had been. This change, however, would not come without risks. First, the overtly partisan nature of this act would lead to near certain retaliation from Republicans as soon as they gained control of Congress and the White House. Second, the Court's legitimacy could suffer if majority parties in Congress simply add seats in an effort to ensure the Court votes according to one party's desire.

A more promising solution, in my view, is to fix the underlying problem. By removing the advantage that any president has over the appointment process (as detailed above), both political equality and stability are best served in the long-run. While this reform is less immediately satisfying and fruitful for Democrats, presidents would still be able to shape the Court in the very near future. If either party were to win a disproportionate number of presidential elections in the next decade or so, its imprint on the Supreme Court would be both notable and consequential.

Regarding the lower federal courts, reform is needed to streamline the confirmation process. Backlogs cause unnecessary delays in both the administration of justice and the clarification of pressing constitutional matters. Recall that the aforementioned Khanna-Beyer Supreme Court bill gave the Senate a 120-day "advise and consent" window to consider Supreme Court nominations. Under the measure, if the Senate does not vote on a High Court nominee during this period, the appointment would become finalized. I see little reason why a comparable window should not be applied to federal district and appeals court nominees as well. In 2002, President George W. Bush suggested reforming the process so that the Senate Judiciary Committee held hearings on all federal court nominees no more than 90 days after their appointment. Then, within 180 days of the nomination, the Senate would be expected to hold a floor vote. Bush also suggested that federal judges who intend to retire (or enter senior status) provide notice at least one year in advance of leaving the bench.[26] While not all departures from the Court are planned, many are. If presidents had a longer period of time to identify replacements for most retiring justices, the process could move much faster. I believe Bush's proposals are sound ideas that could improve the process. Others have suggested that the Senate Judiciary Committee's budget be increased so that more staff can be hired, allowing the vetting process for nominations to move faster. This too would be a welcome reform. Contrary to what many Americans believe, most senators (and their staffs) are not lazy. Confirmation lags are mostly due to political considerations and legitimate constraints on time. By instituting some reforms that limit delay (mostly for political or ideological reasons) and increase staff support, the process could be greatly improved.

Conclusion

The federal courts play an important role in the American political system. In addition to protecting fundamental rights, they are well-positioned to help the Constitution evolve and become a more powerful democratic instrument. The Supreme Court has largely failed to advance political equality in recent decades; in fact, it has initiated numerous setbacks. Nevertheless, both the High Court and the lower federal courts hold this potential. As a result, democracy reformers should not seek to strip the courts of their important powers or take actions that will de-legitimize them. Rather, the focus should be on ensuring that judges and justices are appointed in a manner that best reflects public sentiment. By limiting Supreme Court service to 18 years and better regulating the Senate confirmation process for all judges, this end could be achieved.

CHAPTER 6

Let the People Vote!

Access to the polls has never been straightforward in the U.S. National standards are fairly limited, meaning state and local laws govern much of the electoral process. Because states predated the nation, many had their own distinct norms and laws before the Constitution was adopted. In colonial times, "virtually every substantive aspect of voting was under local control and varied considerably from one place to the next."[1] While many New England colonies permitted secret voting by the 1680s, voice voting was common across the South through the 1780s.[2] Voter eligibility also lacked uniformity. In South Carolina, a justice of the peace had to certify that citizens were naturalized before they could vote. In Pennsylvania, German immigrants both voted and served in government without naturalization.[3] Religious requirements were prevalent in the colonies, though Rhode Island promoted religious freedom and had fewer restrictions. While most colonies held elections on a single day, some states—New York and Virginia—were known to hold three or five-day elections. Many colonies lacked formal age, sex, or residency restrictions. These decisions were instead left to small towns and county governments, who set a wide variety of standards. Some towns allowed widows with property to vote, while others even allowed Native Americans and free Blacks to participate in elections.[4]

The Constitution allowed states to retain considerable autonomy with regard to their elections. As I have discussed, the Framers allowed state governments to draw their own U.S. House districts. State legislators were (until the Seventeenth Amendment) empowered to choose U.S. senators, while states could also determine how their presidential electors would be selected. When it came to electing individuals to these offices (and others), the Constitution set no explicit national standard regarding voting rights. The right to vote was left to be determined by each state individually. The Guarantee Clause of the Constitution required each state to have a "republican form of government," though states had considerable flexibility when it came to interpreting and implementing it. Finally, the Constitution left the responsibility of running and funding elections to state and local governments, allowing for a wide range of election administration practices.

In the early years of the U.S., no state employed anything resembling a modern democracy. Many states limited suffrage to property owners. All states—with the exception of New Jersey until 1807—limited suffrage to men. And most states—even those that had banned slavery—barred Black Americans from voting until the Civil War.[5]

Of course, access to the ballot box has since expanded considerably. The evolution of voting rights in the U.S. has been thoroughly researched and discussed in several recent texts. Alexander Keyssar's *The Right to Vote* (2009) and Michael Waldman's *The Fight to Vote* (2016) chronicle the early debates of the Framers, recent fights regarding voter suppression, and everything in between. Alec Ewald's *The Way We Vote* (2009) explores the intricacies of election administration in the U.S., emphasizing the high degree of autonomy that local governments have generally had in the voting process. In this more succinct chapter, I highlight the process through which voting rights have evolved from a privilege for the few to a right of the many. It is a history worth celebrating, but one that is surely incomplete. Political equality requires that *all* citizens have a reasonable opportunity to express their will regarding who leads their governing institutions. As recent elections have painfully revealed, this is not yet the case in the United States. Among other deficiencies, registration and ID requirements can be burdensome and confusing, lines are too long, and ballots are too often discarded for frivolous reasons. More generally, voting is treated by elected officials and judges as a privilege, rather than a fundamental right (as the Constitution demands). This must change. In the chapter's final pages, I discuss a series of achievable reforms that would broaden access to the polls and help ensure that American elections better reflect the popular will.

The Past is Prologue

The Framers of the Constitution spent considerably more time debating the institutional structure of the new national government than the right of citizens to participate in it. Lively debates centered on the nature of representation in Congress and the presidential selection process, but not access to the polls. The Framers' inaction on voting rights reflects both a willingness to defer to states and a vision of democracy that is incompatible with modernity.

The story of how the U.S. came to adopt a more inclusive system of voting rights is a long and complex one. In this section, I discuss the process through which particular groups—non–property owners, Blacks, women, and young voters—secured access to the ballot box. In doing so, several themes are apparent. First, change has often been frustratingly slow and non-linear. Second, state initiatives have commonly been a prelude to national action. And finally, as I have observed with other institutions covered in this book, major national reforms have generally emerged only when public demands are loud and unrelenting.

Democracy for All (White Men)

For a variety of reasons, the early 1800s saw a wave of pro-democracy momentum for white men. As settlers populated the frontier, the vote was seen as the rightful reward to those who formed "the hardworking backbone of society."[6] Furthermore, the War of 1812—a rematch with the United Kingdom primarily caused by the impressment of U.S. sailors, trade policy, and conflict with Native American tribes—produced a flurry of veterans who felt as though they deserved the franchise. In the South, expansion of white voting rights was also seen as a way to solidify the institution of slavery. In *The Fight to Vote*, Michael Waldman, president of the Brennan Center for Justice, quotes a Virginia lawmaker who noted, "We ought to spread wide the foundation of our government, that all White men have a direct interest in its protection."[7]

Calls for democracy escalated, leading to changes at the state level. In 1800, just three states (Kentucky, New Hampshire, and Vermont) had universal suffrage for white men. Between 1812–1821, six western states became part of the nation and gave the vote to every white male. During the same period, four older states with property requirements abolished them. As new working-class citizens populated the voting rolls, new political movements emerged. When the Democratic-Republican Party split in the early 1820s, many of these new "burly … tobacco-stained" voters lined up behind Andrew Jackson.[8] A war hero who had been born in a log-cabin, Jackson was the first of many presidential candidates to convince working-class voters that he was "like them." Jackson railed against banks, northeastern elites, and "the moneyed interests." He connected with voters who believed those in power used their influence to exploit the working-class and enlarge their pockets. While Jackson was defeated by John Quincy Adams in the 1824 presidential election, he returned in 1828 under the banner of the Democratic Party. This time, he bested Adams—a (brilliant) New England elitist with no interest in populism—in a landslide. Jackson's political rise, spearheaded by "ordinary" Americans who organized themselves in hundreds of communities across the U.S., was the direct product of an expanded electorate.

Democracy was not on the march for all Americans during this period. In fact, it retracted for both women and Blacks. Women had been able to vote in New Jersey but saw this right removed in 1807. And while six states—Maryland, Massachusetts, New York, North Carolina, Pennsylvania, and Vermont—permitted free Blacks to vote in 1790, every new state that joined the Union after 1819 explicitly denied Blacks the right to vote. In both Pennsylvania and New York, Black voting rights were rescinded. In 1826, only 16 Black New Yorkers were qualified to vote.[9] Progress does not always proceed in a perfectly linear fashion.

Race

The story of how slavery evolved from an issue that was "accommodated" to the cause of a full-blown civil war has been eloquently told by many historians. David Potter's *The Impending Crisis, 1848–1861* (1977) and James McPherson's *Battle Cry of Freedom* (2003) are outstanding, detail-oriented accounts. For our purposes in this book, the conflict evolved for two irrefutable reasons. First, in the years leading up to the 1860s, resistance to slavery (especially its expansion) grew in the North. The 1830s and 1840s saw significant change in the North, as industry expanded and the Second Great Awakening—a period of religious revival stressing the reform of individuals through discipline, order, and restraint—continued to flourish. Abolitionist papers such as William Lloyd Garrison's *The Liberator* reached American homes, while Frederick Douglass and others visited meeting halls throughout the North excoriating the evils of slavery. Moral and religious opposition to slavery increased. Other (less heroic) causes were important too; many Northerners increasingly feared that slave owners would buy frontier lands and populate them with slave labor, blocking opportunities for free white farmers to cultivate such ground.

Second, while the North became increasingly hostile to slavery, the South grew even more supportive. In the South, the development of the cotton gin by Eli Whitney in 1793 had made cotton production much more lucrative. As a result, the southern economy began to depend more heavily on it. As this economic reality developed, southerners such as South Carolina Senator John Calhoun increasingly defended slavery as "a positive good," arguing that slaves lived better lives in bondage than their intellectual capacities would allow if freed from it. The famous "Cornerstone Speech" delivered by Confederate Vice President Alexander Stephens echoed this idea. Speaking just a few weeks before the Civil War began, Stephens stated, "Our new government is founded upon exactly the opposite idea ... that the negro is not equal to the White man; that slavery—subordination to the superior race—is his natural and normal condition."[10]

As attitudes polarized and hardened, divisions could no longer be accommodated. Seven southern states seceded after Abraham Lincoln was elected president in 1860, months before he was even inaugurated. Four more southern states soon followed. Despite Lincoln's pledge that he had no intention of banning slavery in states where it already existed, neither he nor his new political party (the Republicans) were trusted in the South. War broke out and killed over 600,000 people between 1861 and 1865.

Lincoln's cautious, measured evolution on slavery during the war is widely considered to be an act of effective political pragmatism. Lincoln rarely led on the issue of slavery; he was willing, however, to evolve with the times, staying a step ahead of the country and perhaps a step behind the most ardent abolitionists. Depending on one's perspective, this posture can be seen as brilliant or timid, or perhaps even both. Lincoln began the conflict with the sole expressed goal of preserving the union. In August 1862, he bluntly declared, "If I could save the union without freeing any slaves I would do it; and if I could save it by freeing all the slaves I would do it; and if I could save it by freeing some and leaving others alone I would also do that."[11] But as the war continued, animosity towards the South and support for abolition both increased in the North. As a result, Lincoln gradually supported stronger action against slavery. Lincoln began by supporting plans to compensate slave owners for freeing their slaves. He also backed proposals to send freed slaves to new colonies in Africa. In the Emancipation Proclamation, announced in September 1862, Lincoln moved decidedly towards full abolition. He agreed to unconditionally free all slaves in areas in rebellion (without compensation for owners). The Emancipation Proclamation, however, did not end slavery in the U.S., as it remained permissible in states loyal to the union—Delaware, Maryland, Kentucky, and Missouri. Only the Thirteenth Amendment—which Congress approved in 1865 with Lincoln's blessing—achieved that.

After the Civil War, two additional amendments were added to the U.S. Constitution. The Fourteenth Amendment (1868) grants citizenship to anyone "born or naturalized in the United States" and guarantees every person due process and equal protection under the law; the Fifteenth Amendment (1870) provides that "[t]he right of citizens of the United States to vote shall not be denied or abridged by the United States or by any State on account of race, color, or previous condition of servitude." In each case, these amendments empower Congress to enforce their provisions through "appropriate legislation."

Initially, during the Reconstruction period after the Civil War, Congress acted to ensure that voting rights for Blacks were respected. The Enforcement Act of 1870 made it a federal crime to "deny the civil or political rights of any American." The law called for federal supervision of the voting process, including registration. By 1872, with Black citizens casting ballots across the South, there were 320 elected Black legislators in the region serving in the federal and state governments.[12] The leaders of the South Carolina House and Senate, the governor of Louisiana, and a U.S. senator from Mississippi were all Black men. But as memories of the Civil War faded and economic concerns grew in the 1870s, many lost interest in enforcing voting rights for southern Blacks. In 1876, the Supreme Court limited the power of the Enforcement Act, ruling (in *United States v. Reese*) that the Fifteenth Amendment did not grant any individual the right to vote, but rather restricted states from giving any citizen preferential treatment. In doing so, the Court effectively permitted states to design creative restrictions that could disproportionately prevent Blacks from voting.[13]

Followed the *Reese* decision, southern legislatures instituted poll taxes, knowing that many poor Black sharecroppers were unable to pay them. States also administered literacy tests, many of which were nearly impossible to pass. In order to protect white voters from taxes and difficult tests, many states adopted "grandfather clauses," whereby those citizens whose grandfathers had been permitted to vote were exempt from these requirements. Generally, this exempted white voters, but not Black voters, whose grandfathers had been slaves.

In the late 1800s and early 1900s, southern states also instituted "white primaries." In the South, the Democratic Party was dominant, meaning that the winner of primary elections generally won without much competition from the Republican Party. But because political parties are private organizations, they were permitted to set rules for voting in their primary elections. By restricting primary ballots to whites, southern states effectively banned Blacks from voting in the most meaningful elections.

For decades, the federal courts largely accepted these restrictive practices. In 1915, the Supreme Court did rule in *Guinn v. United States* that Oklahoma's grandfather clause (and therefore those in many other states) was an unconstitutional violation of the Fifteenth Amendment.[14] But when Oklahoma and other states creatively rewrote their laws to continue disenfranchising Blacks, the Court looked the other way. Oklahoma passed a law declaring that "all persons, except those who voted in 1914, who were qualified to vote in 1916 but who failed to register between April 30 and May 11, 1916, with some exceptions for sick and absent persons who were given an additional brief period to register, would be perpetually disenfranchised." In essence, Oklahoma was providing a narrow 12-day window for Blacks to register, while most whites were exempt from the window. The Supreme Court did not invalidate this absurd work-around until 1939 (in *Lane v. Wilson*).[15] Five years later, in 1944, the Court declared the white primary unconstitutional in *Smith v. Allwright*.[16] But Black participation

Civil rights leaders, including Dr. Martin Luther King, Jr., initially had reason to doubt that President Lyndon Johnson would be a willing partner in advancing racial equality. But in his time in office, Johnson would sign a series of civil rights laws that brought the U.S. much closer to its democratic promise. One of the most successful measures was undoubtedly the Voting Rights Act of 1965, which effectively ended Jim Crow voting laws in the U.S. (photograph by Yoichi R. Okamoto, U.S. Department of State, CC PDM 1.0: *https://creativecommons. org/publicdomain/mark/1.0/*).

in elections remained anemic, as violence, intimidation, and other forms of discrimination made registering and voting difficult. In many jurisdictions, despite the Court's ruling in *Lane*, white registrars required only Blacks to complete nearly impossible literacy tests.

At the height of the Civil Rights Movement in 1964, Congress passed and President Lyndon Johnson signed the Civil Rights Act. The law banned discrimination on the basis of "race, color, religion, sex, or national origin," ending racial discrimination and segregation in schools, employment, and public accommodations. Several months after the law's passage, various organizations—including the Southern Christian Leadership Conference (SCLC) and the Student Nonviolent Coordinating Committee (SNCC)—called for the federal government to protect the voting rights of Blacks. Voting protections had largely been omitted from the 1964 law. After peaceful marches in Selma, Alabama, led to violent confrontations with police, momentum for action on voting rights increased. In the summer of 1965, Congress passed and President Johnson signed the Voting

Rights Act, a powerful measure that would finally deliver the promise of the Fifteenth Amendment nearly 100 years later.

As I discussed in Chapter 3, the Voting Rights Act includes several sections designed to protect the ability of all persons—regardless of race—to vote. Notably, Section 2 prohibits any jurisdiction from implementing a "voting qualification or prerequisite to voting, or standard, practice, or procedure ... in a manner which results in a denial or abridgement of the right ... to vote on account of race, color, or language minority status." In 1982, Congress amended the law to add a "results" rest, which prohibits any voting law that has a discriminatory effect regardless of whether the law was *intentionally* enacted or maintained for a discriminatory purpose. Section 4 of the law includes a coverage formula whereby certain jurisdictions with a history of discrimination are forced to comply with special restrictions. The most recent coverage formula—updated in 1975—applied to the entire states of Alaska, Arizona, Texas, Louisiana, Mississippi, Alabama, Georgia, South Carolina, and Virginia. Additionally, certain jurisdictions in California, South Dakota, Michigan, Florida, North Carolina, and New Hampshire were covered as well. While the federal government would be charged with enforcing voting rights throughout the country, these particular jurisdictions—under Section 5 of the law—would be unable to make any changes to their voting laws without preclearance (or pre-approval) from the U.S. Justice Department.

The Voting Rights Act was a quick success. While only 29.3 percent of Blacks were registered to vote in jurisdictions subject to the Section 4 coverage formula before the law, this number jumped to 52.1 percent within two years of its passage. Between 1965 and 1985, the number of Blacks elected as state legislators in the 11 former Confederate states increased from three to 176.[17] Due to its quick and sustained success, many consider the Voting Rights Act to be the most effective civil rights law in U.S. history.

In 2013, however, the law was weakened by the Supreme Court in *Shelby Co. v. Holder.* In that case, the Supreme Court invalidated the coverage formula, ruling that it was no longer justified given changes in the covered jurisdictions since 1975. Preclearance was still permitted under the law, but only if a new formula was drafted and approved by Congress.[18] With Congress gridlocked and unable to act, preclearance was effectively dead. Discriminatory voting laws could now be challenged only *after* they were adopted. The result has been a confusing cluster of federal court decisions allowing, ending, and delaying the implementation of various state voting laws. And with the Supreme Court unable and unwilling to become involved in every specific case, lower courts have often had the final say regarding specific state laws, with varying results across the country. I will have more to say about the Voting Rights Act—and court interpretation of it—later in the chapter.

Sex

With the exception of New Jersey for a short time in the late 1700s and early 1800s, no U.S. state permitted women to vote before the Civil War. Before the conflict, many women's rights activists had been active in abolition movements aimed at ending slavery. Following the Thirteenth Amendment, these citizens were naturally encouraged and mobilized to push for full voting rights for women. The American Equal Rights Association (AERA) was formed in 1866 and hoped "to secure Equal Rights to all American citizens, especially the right of suffrage, irrespective of race, color or sex." The AERA quickly split, however, in 1869 over support for the Fifteenth Amendment. Activists like Susan B. Anthony and Elizabeth Cady Stanton did not support an amendment that would grant Blacks the right to vote, but continue to deny rights to women. They led the formation of the National Woman Suffrage Association (NWSA), which would advocate for a broad series of reforms to make women equal members of society. The NWSA was countered by the American Woman Suffrage Association (AWSA). AWSA supported the Fifteenth Amendment granting Black men the right to vote. More generally, AWSA focused solely on achieving voting rights for women. In doing so, they were generally more willing to pursue a state-by-state strategy rather than simply seek change in the Constitution.[19]

On November 1, 1872, Anthony sought to use the courts to advance the cause of voting rights. She walked with her sisters Guelma, Hannah, and Mary to a voter registration office in Rochester, New York, and asked to be added to the voter rolls. Anthony argued that the newly-approved Fourteenth Amendment, which stated, "No State shall make or enforce any law which shall abridge the privileges or immunities of citizens of the United States," stipulated that women could not be denied the right to vote. The registration officials consulted a local lawyer, John Van Voorhis, who advised them to register the women after they took a standard oath. Four days later, Anthony and 14 other women cast ballots in the 1872 election.

Any sense of victory, however, was short-lived. Several weeks later, each woman was arrested for violating the Enforcement Act of 1870, which made it a federal crime to vote in congressional elections if the voter was not qualified to vote under state law. The arrests were covered heavily in the newspapers, providing Anthony with an opportunity to generate publicity for the suffrage movement. The women were tried in the U.S. Circuit

Court for the Northern District of New York. Ultimately, Judge Ward Hunt ruled that the Fourteenth Amendment did not provide women the right to vote. He determined that Congress had been clear that the purpose of the amendment was to extend equal rights to freed slaves and Black men. There had been no indication that Congress had intended to apply voting rights to women. Judge Hunt stressed that voting is *not* a privilege of citizenship. Women were indeed citizens, but like children and the mentally ill, they were not necessarily entitled to voting rights.[20] The fight for women's suffrage was dealt an additional blow by the Supreme Court in 1875. In *Minor v. Happersett*, the justices affirmed that the right to vote was not one of the "privileges or immunities of citizens of the United States" when the Fourteenth Amendment was ratified. At the time, the High Court was not only unwilling to apply the Constitution to expand political equality; it was actively interested in finding narrow interpretations that restricted it.[21]

With the Supreme Court unwilling to apply post–Civil War amendments to the fight for women's suffrage, the movement focused on (1) building support for a constitutional amendment and (2) advancing the cause at the state level. At first, neither objective found much success. In 1878, Senator Aaron Sargent of California introduced the first women's suffrage amendment in Congress, the aptly-named Susan B. Anthony Amendment. While Sargent's bill did not receive a vote, the Senate did approve a resolution in 1882 to establish a Select Committee on Woman Suffrage. In 1886, the committee submitted a report to the full chamber supporting a suffrage amendment. However, when it finally received a vote in 1887, it was handily defeated, 16–34.[22]

As prospects for constitutional change appeared increasingly grim, the two leading women's rights organizations—NWSA and AWSA— finally merged to create the National American Woman Suffrage Association (NAWSA). Recognizing the futility of seeking constitutional change in the near future, the organization focused on achieving progress at the state and local level. Opportunities would quickly come in the West, as numerous states and territories continued to be settled and organized there during this time. Women's suffrage had already been granted in the Wyoming (1869) and Utah Territories (1870). When each became a state in the 1890s, suffrage continued. Idaho, another new western state, adopted full women's suffrage in 1896. The population of the these newly-established western states was small, however, meaning the vast majority of American women still had no voting rights. After no additional states approved women's suffrage during the next 14 years, one can imagine how hopeless the effort must have seemed. By 1910, it had been 38 years since Susan B. Anthony (who had since died) cast her vote in the 1872 election; since then, progress had been painfully slow.

Major social upheaval is often needed to raise awareness, change minds, and ultimately bring drastic changes to the U.S. political system. Social activism is a constant of American society. And while many movements die, go dormant, or remain limited in support, some intersect with ripe settings for change and transform society in durable ways. When this happens, success can come quickly; change that never seemed possible can suddenly become mainstream. The Voting Rights Act of 1965 was inconceivable only a decade earlier. But during that time, the Civil Rights Movement took major steps forward. Through non-violent resistance, skilled leaders exposed the cruelty of segregation and institutionalized white oppression in the South. And as a large, well-educated, younger generation came of age in the 1960s, the movement intersected with a broader social reaction against the traditional, conservative mores of the 1950s. The result was massive legal change (e.g., the Civil Rights Act of 1964, the Voting Rights Act of 1965, etc.) in a relatively short period of time.

The push for women's suffrage also benefited from broader momentum for societal change. By 1910, the Progressive Movement was in full swing. Americans from both major parties were organizing against poor working conditions, inequality, and the abuse of monopolies. A federal income tax was created, millions of acres of land was conserved, trusts were defeated, and labor unions were strengthened. Activists were also demanding democratic reforms, ultimately leading to the direct election of senators in the Seventeenth Amendment (1913) and the proliferation of party primaries to determine nominees for various offices. Within this context, a new generation of skilled women's rights activists would ultimately seize the momentum of the times to achieve their long-sought goal.

After a frustrating decade with little progress, state action on suffrage resumed in the 1910s, as Washington (1910), California (1911), Oregon (1912), Arizona (1912), Kansas (1912), Montana (1914), and Nevada (1914) all granted women the right to vote in all elections. With the movement regaining its footing, the NAWSA asked Alice Paul and Lucy Burns to chair the organization's Congressional Committee in 1912.[23] Paul and Burns were both battle-tested young activists who had returned from overseas after joining the fight for women's suffrage in England.[24] Their task was to ensure that the Susan B. Anthony Amendment continued to be introduced in each Congress, with the hope that it may one day be considered and passed. Paul and other activists planned a public march, believing that it may be an effective way to revitalize and build popular support for the movement. While there were only 5,000–10,000 attendees at the 1913 Woman Suffrage Procession, the marchers (and the hecklers they confronted) did bring some renewed attention.[25] For the first time in decades, the amendment was debated on the floors of Congress.

Grassroots activism continued. In 1915, Paul's committee presented a petition to Congress with the signatures of two million supporters. California activists organized a car trip whereby suffragettes rode across the country to Washington, D.C. Over a period of two years, thousands of picketers protested outside the White House.[26]

With momentum surging, a wave of new states approved full women's suffrage in the late 1910s. For the first time, these states included some in the East and Midwest where sizable populations resided. New York approved suffrage in 1917, while Oklahoma, South Dakota, and Michigan followed in 1918. Many other states, while continuing to deny full voting rights for women, began to permit limited participation in elections. States including New Mexico, New Hampshire, and New Jersey allowed women to vote in school, tax, or bond elections. In Florida, one small town (Fellsmere) allowed women to vote in municipal

After spending several years in England, Alice Paul returned to the U.S. in 1910 and immediately led efforts to advance voting rights for women. In 1913, she organized the Woman Suffrage Procession, a public march designed to generate new momentum for reform. In the years that followed—despite being jailed and abused—she would continue to picket, organize petition drives, and lobby Congress. By 1920, the efforts of Paul and other activists were vindicated, as the Nineteenth Amendment guaranteed women the right to vote in all U.S. elections (photograph by Underwood & Underwood, CC PDM 1.0: *https://creativecommons.org/publicdomain/zero/1.0/?ref=ccsearch&atype=rich*).

elections starting in 1915. Women were permitted to vote in local elections throughout Vermont beginning in 1917. Arkansas (1917) and Texas (1918) gave women the right to vote in primary elections only. Finally, a number of states allowed women to vote in presidential, but not all state, elections. Illinois was the first to permit this in 1913; ten others followed by 1919.[27]

By 1919, the U.S. was a tired country. It had just lost over 100,000 troops after entering the Great War (World War I) on the side of the Entente Powers. The Spanish Flu pandemic had killed at least 200,000 Americans in 1918 alone and was still wreaking havoc. The Progressive Era had radically transformed both economic and democratic life in the U.S. Many were beginning to yearn for what soon-to-be successful presidential candidate Warren Harding would call a "return to normalcy." Thankfully, the Progressive Era was able to deliver one final transformative achievement. President Woodrow Wilson, who had been preaching the gospel of democracy both during and after the war, finally supported women's suffrage in 1918. In 1919, both houses of Congress approved the Nineteenth Amendment, guaranteeing that no citizen could be denied the right to vote on behalf of their sex. Slightly over a year later, 35 of 48 states had approved the amendment, leaving just one needed for ratification. In Tennessee, the lower chamber was deadlocked at 48–48 when Representative Harry Burn, just 24 years old, received a letter from his mother. Readying for yet another vote on the measure, Burn read the letter. It stated, "Dear Son: Hurrah and vote for Suffrage and don't keep them in doubt ... be a good boy and help Mrs. Catt [now the president of NAWSA] put the 'rat' in ratification."[28] Burn listened to his mother and supported the amendment, extending the franchise to nearly 30 million American women.

Age

Efforts to expand voting rights to Blacks and women were advanced by effective social movements that capitalized on momentum for national change. Similarly, national events helped deliver voting rights to those aged 18–20. In the early 1940s, all U.S. states permitted only those aged 21 or older to vote. In 1941, Senator Harley Kilgore of West Virginia offered an amendment to lower the national voting age to 18. Kilgore argued that "nearly 90 percent of the approximately 7,000,000 Americans between 18 and 21 were already contributing to the war effort, either through military service or other forms of war work."[29] Supporters used the slogan, "Old enough to fight. Old enough to vote." Despite the support of First Lady Eleanor Roosevelt and President Dwight Eisenhower (in 1954), Congress was unable to agree on lowering the voting age. Several states, however, did take action. Georgia lowered its voting age to 18 during the Second World War (in 1943) and Kentucky followed in 1955. Alaska and Hawaii entered the union in 1959 with the voting ages of 19 and 20, respectively.

All but the aforementioned four states, however, continued to prohibit voting until the age of 21. Support for lowering the age, however, was clearly increasing. While Gallup found that just 17 percent of Americans supported lowering the voting age in 1939, 58 percent backed it by the late 1960s.[30] The primary catalyst for the change was the Vietnam War, which again saw thousands of young Americans serve (and die) in battle despite having no say in choosing the government that sent them. Furthermore, the broader momentum for social change in the 1960s and early 1970s presented a favorable environment for advancing the causes of democracy and rights for young people. In 1970, President Richard Nixon signed an extension of the Voting Rights Act that lowered the voting age to 18 for all federal, state, and local elections. In *Oregon v. Mitchell* (1970), however, a divided Supreme Court found that the federal government could not set the age requirement in state and local elections.[31] As a result, an amendment to the Constitution was needed. With support for lowering the voting age now widespread, the Twenty-Sixth Amendment passed by overwhelming majorities in both the House (401–19) and Senate (94–0) in March 1971. Less than four months later, it became part of the Constitution after 38 states quickly ratified it.[32]

The Age of Voter Convenience (and Voter Suppression)

By some measures, the Twenty-Sixth Amendment was the final battle in a nearly two-century struggle to extend the franchise to adult citizens. Since 1971, American citizens (at least without a felony conviction) aged 18 and older have had the legal right to register and vote. In the 51 years since, debates regarding voting rights have mostly shifted to the ease of access that citizens have to the polls. In some ways, voting has undoubtedly become more convenient in most states and localities during this time. Absentee voting is now available to most Americans, early in-person voting sites are plentiful in many states, and registration laws have been eased in states ranging from Idaho to Maryland.

At the same time, however, troubling new barriers to voting have also been erected. Polling places have been reduced, leading to longer lines in many jurisdictions. Voter identification laws effectively disenfranchise as many as one in ten Americans. Voter purges kick citizens off the registration rolls without their consent. Some of the aforementioned reforms regarding registration and early voting have recently been threatened with cuts. And the complicated web of federal, state, and local laws governing elections continues to make voting much more confusing and inefficient than necessary. A true democracy should expend the necessary resources to make it easy for all citizens to express their will at the polls. This is still not the reality of voting rights in the United States.

The unnecessary burdens to vote at least partly explain why the U.S. has one of the lowest turnout rates in the democratized world. Most presidential elections in the past half-century have seen turnout rates below 60 percent. Turnout in midterm elections generally hovers around 40 percent of eligible voters. Notably, turnout was unusually high in the recent midterm (49.3 percent) and presidential elections (66.7 percent).[33] This is great news! But even this heightened level of participation in 2018 and 2020, respectively, lags behind many democracies. In recent national elections, various nations—New Zealand, Israel, Netherlands, South Korea, Australia, Denmark, Sweden, Belgium—have seen turnout rates over 75 percent.[34]

Many other reasons have been suggested for the United States' chronically low turnout, including winner-take-all elections, uncompetitive contests, a high level of dissatisfaction with the political process, and the fact that the U.S. has a lot of elections (causing voter fatigue). There is merit to each of these claims, but the inconvenience of voting in the U.S. is a proven cause as well.

In this section, I review the mixed bag of voting changes that have emerged in recent decades. As I will demonstrate, many pro-voting reforms were initially backed by both Democrats and Republicans. In recent years, however, voting rights have become extremely contentious. With the issue becoming a partisan battleground, a plethora of new laws have been adopted since the early 2000s. Some have expanded voting rights, some have restricted them, and many have ended up in court. As a result, it is inaccurate to say that voting has gotten unambiguously harder during this time. It *is* accurate, however, to say that voting is still not easy enough.

Bipartisan Convenience Voting

When Congress first set a universal Election Day for presidential elections in 1845, it chose to hold such contests on the first Tuesday following the first Monday in November. The most accepted rationale is that November 1 was unappealing because it was the day that merchants typically did their books from the preceding month.[35] By setting the date as the first Tuesday that followed a Monday in November, possible dates would only include November 2 through November 8. As for the day of the week, Sunday was not an option because it is the Sabbath for Christians. Monday was difficult because it often took a full day for farmers to travel to town (where they would vote). Wednesday was market day (in town), when farmers would sell their crops. So, Tuesday made sense. Travelers could leave on Monday, vote on Tuesday,[36] and be in town for market day on Wednesday. This arrangement made sense in 1845, though it is obviously less applicable today. The durability of Tuesday as Election Day is a classic example of path dependency. Even when no longer optimal, old traditions can be very hard to break.

Because Tuesdays are often inconvenient for Americans—and because Election Day has never been a national holiday—voting by mail is attractive to many. Absentee voting was first employed in the U.S. during the Civil War, as troops were permitted to cast ballots in their home states. For most of U.S. history, absentee voting has been limited to those who have a valid reason (e.g., health, travel, work) that they cannot be present on Election Day. Simply being "busy" has not generally been considered an acceptable reason. In 1978, California became the first state to allow "no-excuse" absentee voting. Any registered voter could request a ballot through the mail several weeks before Election Day. During the 1980s, other states followed with liberalized absentee rules, including Oregon and Washington.[37]

As no-excuse absentee laws continued to proliferate, Texas became the first state to offer early in-person voting in 1987. Similar to California and other states, voters would no longer need to provide an excuse if they wished to vote before Election Day. The notable difference was that voters were offered *physical locations* whereby they could arrive during the weeks before Election Day and cast a vote. In response to its considerable popularity, Texas Governor Ann Richards signed a bipartisan measure in 1991 increasing the number of early voting locations required within each county. In some counties, including the populous Harris County (Houston), up to 25 early voting sites were mandated.

After observing early in-person voting's success in Texas, other states adopted their own programs. In Nevada, a 1993 law establishing physical locations throughout the state was approved by 21–0 and 42–0 margins in the state's assembly and senate, respectively. That same year, the Republican-led Colorado Legislature approved an early voting law on a bipartisan basis. All citizens would be permitted to vote either through the mail or at early in-person locations. Republican Donetta Davidson, chief elections officer in the Colorado Secretary of State's Office, helped convince the legislature to approve the law as a way of "making voting more convenient."[38] Within a few years, large bipartisan majorities in both Arizona and New Mexico adopted broad early voting laws as well.

Early voting—both through the mail and in-person—was generally popular with both voters and election administrators. Voters appreciated the opportunity to cast ballots at their convenience, while administrators often found that it reduced stress on Election Day.[39] Given its popularity, early voting laws continued to surge across the U.S. By the mid–2000s, a majority of U.S. states had adopted laws allowing any registered voter to cast a pre–Election Day ballot. Adopters included heavily populated states such as Florida, Georgia, Illinois, North Carolina, and Ohio.

A handful of states opted for a unique form of early voting. In 1998, Oregon eliminated physical voting and instead moved to an exclusively vote-by-mail (VBM) system. Registered voters would no longer need to request that a ballot be sent to them; instead, all voters would receive one in the mail in the weeks preceding an election. After years of observing Oregon's policy (and increased turnout), Washington became the second state to adopt universal VBM. The state gradually implemented the policy on a county-by-county basis during the 2000s before mandating it statewide in 2011. In 2013, Colorado approved universal VBM, but opted to complement mailed ballots with some early and Election Day polling sites. By the end of the 2010s, both Hawaii and Utah had joined the club by adopting their own universal VBM programs.

As options expanded, more Americans chose to cast early ballots. By 2008, over 30 percent of American voters were doing so before Election Day through the mail or at in-person early voting sites. The figure continued to rise, reaching 41 percent in 2016.

As the voting window expanded in many states, the process of registering to vote was also becoming easier in some states. Traditionally, states have required that citizens register to vote in advance of participating in elections.[40] Most states have generally stopped accepting registration requests about 15–30 days before an election. The U.S. is unique in this regard, as most democracies do not require advance registration for citizens at all. In 1973, Maine became the first state to allow same-day registration (SDR); Minnesota and Wisconsin followed in 1974 and 1975, respectively. Citizens could both register to vote and cast a ballot at the same time and place. While the programs were popular, they did not immediately spread. Registration reforms were quiet for two decades until Wyoming adopted SDR in 1993. Wyoming was quickly followed by Idaho (1994), North Carolina (1994), and New Hampshire (1996). By 2010, nine states and the District of Columbia allowed voters to register at a polling place during the early voting period or on Election Day (or both).

The registration process also received a boost from the federal government in 1993, when Congress and President Clinton approved the National Voter Registration Act. The law—commonly referred to as the "motor voter" law—required state officials to offer registration to anyone applying for a driver's license (or renewal) or seeking public assistance.

Convenience Voting Gets Political

It is common for a political party or group to oppose voting rights if they believe it will hurt their electoral interests. In 1800, Federalist-dominated legislatures in Massachusetts and New Hampshire repealed their laws allowing eligible citizens to choose their respective state's presidential electors. Both feared that the state's voters were turning towards the Democratic-Republican Party.[41] The National German-American Alliance opposed women's suffrage in the early 1900s because it believed women would support Prohibition.[42] And most notably, southern Democrats long opposed voting rights for Blacks in the South, a reflection of both racism and a fear that Black voters would threaten their power.

As I have repeatedly noted, I am not interested in judging the underlying political philosophies of the two major parties in this text. The efficacy of safety net programs, tax cuts, tariffs, education policy, the Affordable Care Act, carbon restrictions, and labor unions are beyond the scope of this work. In these chapters, I am focused on political equality alone. The actions of political parties and actors with regard to *this* subject are therefore fair game. And in commenting on them, I am not interested in creating false equivalencies or ensuring that both parties' actions are viewed favorably. I am guided only by the facts. As I noted in the Introduction, this sort of *nonpartisan* approach is distinctive from a *bipartisan* one. Sometimes the truth indicts one side more than the other; a nonpartisan approach acknowledges this, while a bipartisan approach often will not.

In the twenty-first century, there is simply no denying that the Republican Party has disproportionately sought to reduce voter convenience. I believe these actions are counter-productive not only to American democracy, but potentially to Republicans' own long-term political interests. The discussion that follows bluntly chronicles these efforts.

As the previous section demonstrated, efforts to make voting easier enjoyed bipartisan support for much of the late twentieth century and early twenty-first century. These issues generally became much more divisive, however, after Barack Obama's victory in the 2008 presidential election. Republican-led legislatures across the U.S. increasingly opposed new early voting and same-day registration (SDR) laws and sought to adopt new measures that restricted access to the polls. These included voter identification laws, voter registration purges, and the shuttering of polling places. I detailed many of these voter suppression efforts in my 2021 book on early voting, *Tuesday's Gone.* Here, I will highlight some of the most notable post–2008 restrictions pursued by states.

Without question, many Republicans believed that Barack Obama benefited from early voting laws in swing states such as Florida, North Carolina, and Ohio in 2008. And indeed, early voting had been an important part of Obama's strategy to mobilize his electoral base. In fact, Obama's national field director, Jon Carson, bluntly declared that "early voting didn't change our strategy. It was our strategy."[43] Obama's campaign, flush with over $700 million in fundraising, launched an effective operation to contact potential supporters and direct them to the nearest early voting location in the weeks preceding Election Day. The effort focused heavily on young people, as well as working-class voters who might find voting on Election Day to be most inconvenient. Republicans, who had largely supported early voting's adoption and expansion for decades, took notice. A featured *New York Times* editorial commented, "Republican lawmakers have taken a good look at voting patterns, realized that early voting might have played a role in Mr. Obama's 2008 victory, and now want to reduce that possibility in 2012."[44] Cynthia Tucker of the *Atlanta-Journal Constitution* noted the change in Republican thinking. She remarked, "I remember a time when Republicans liked early voting. They liked it because they thought it served their middle-class constituents. When did they become unhappy with early voting? After 2008. The Obama campaign was extremely well-organized. And one of the things they did was to encourage their voters to come to the polls early. They did. After Obama took advantage of early voting, Republicans said 'oops,' we need to cut back that early voting."[45]

After winning control of many state governments in 2011, Republicans sought to limit convenience voting options. Given that early voting has been demonstrated to increase turnout by several percentage points, this development was bad news for American democracy.[46] In May 2011, Florida Governor Rick Scott signed legislation that cut the state's early voting period from 14 to eight days. Republicans argued that opening the polls for fewer days would provide savings to counties at a time when budgets were tight. The bill made several other changes, including ending early voting on the Sunday before Election Day. Democrats and community leaders felt that this action was politically motivated, arguing that it hampered efforts to mobilize Black voters. The party had previously transported voters to early voting sites as they exited church on Sunday mornings, events known as "souls to the polls." Political scientists Michael Herron and Daniel Smith examined the effects of Florida's law, finding that the state's early voting cuts reduced the turnout of racial and ethnic minority groups in 2012.[47]

Electoral changes in Florida were not limited to early voting; the new law also included a provision preventing voters who had changed their address since the last election from updating their status at the polls. The address change restriction was expected to hurt college students in particular—a group that overwhelmingly supported Barack Obama in 2008.

North Carolina Republicans also acted to limit early voting options. Over 60 percent of North Carolina votes were cast early in 2008, one of the highest rates in the nation. In early 2011, the Republican-led legislature reduced the early voting period by a full week. Jim Davis, a Macon

County Republican, argued, "We were just trying to minimize the time early voting polls were open ... so the expense is not so great for local election boards."[48] But the North Carolina elections board and many county boards said the changes would actually cost *more* money because additional voting sites would be needed on Election Day. In addition to cutting early voting, the law eliminated high school registration drives for 16 and 17-year-olds, ended provisional voting for residents who arrived at the wrong precinct, and barred counties from extending voting hours in the event of long lines. Furthermore, the law required that all voters present photo identification at the polls in order to vote. Ultimately, Democratic Governor Beverly Perdue received and vetoed a version of the law. After Republican Governor Pat McCrory was elected, he signed the bill in 2013.

The voter identification requirement approved in North Carolina was part of a broader national push. Traditionally, after a citizen registers to vote in the U.S., they are listed in their precinct's book of registered voters. Then, when they appear at a polling place, they state their name. The poll worker finds their name and asks them to sign next to it, under penalty of electoral fraud (a felony) if they impersonate someone else. This system has worked well; in 2020, a 20-year voter fraud study conducted at the Massachusetts Institute of Technology (MIT) found voter impersonation to be "exceedingly rare," noting that it only occurs in 0.00006 percent of instances. For context, it is about five times less likely than getting struck by lightning.[49] Nevertheless, in the final decades of the twentieth century, some states began requesting voter identification at the polls. By 2000, 14 states had such laws. The laws had been passed and implemented by both Democratic and Republican-led legislatures. Concern among voting rights advocates was somewhat limited, however, because each of the 14 states had a procedure in place to allow citizens to vote even if they lacked an ID. This began to change in the 2000s, when both Georgia and Indiana approved the first "strict" photo identification laws that would turn away prospective voters who lacked a valid ID. In 2011, a wave of Republican-led legislatures began approving new strict ID measures. In addition to North Carolina, such laws were adopted in Arkansas, Kansas, Mississippi, North Dakota, Pennsylvania, Tennessee, Texas, Virginia, and Wisconsin by 2015.

These strict ID laws are highly troubling, as an estimated 11 percent of American adults lack a photo ID.[50] Now let's be honest—for most Americans, the idea of obtaining a photo ID does not seem burdensome at all. We need them to drive, buy alcohol, and even to get certain over-the-counter medicines at the drug store. But the reality is that for millions of citizens, there *are* significant barriers to obtaining an ID. Securing one requires a trip to a government office. For those without transportation, this alone is a challenge. According to a Brennan Center for Justice study, about 500,000 eligible voters do not have access to a vehicle and live more than ten miles from the nearest state ID-issuing office. Furthermore, many ID-issuing offices also have limited business hours. Obtaining an ID is also costly for low-income persons. A birth certificate is usually required in order to obtain an ID. These can cost around $10 to $25. For women who have changed their names at marriage, a marriage license (with equivalent costs) is often also required. And for those born in a different state, the time and financial costs may be even greater.[51] In my view, these costs are effectively poll taxes, which are banned by the Twenty-Fourth Amendment. The Supreme Court, however, has not (yet) adopted this interpretation.

Many Republicans cite the need to prevent voter fraud when advocating for strict ID laws. Some, however, have candidly acknowledged a political motive. The majority leader of the Pennsylvania House, Mike Turzai, bragged in June 2012 that the state's new voter identification law was "gonna allow Governor [Mitt] Romney to win the state of Pennsylvania, done."[52] In 2013, a North Carolina Republican Party official said on Comedy Central's *The Daily Show* that his state's voter ID law would "kick the Democrats in the butt."[53] In 2016, House Representative Glenn Grothman of Wisconsin declared, "I think Hillary Clinton is about the weakest candidate the Democrats have ever put up.... And now we (Wisconsin) have photo ID, and I think photo ID is going to make a little bit of a difference as well."[54] Confirming a political motive, political scientists Daniel Biggers and Michael Hanmer have found that a state's propensity to adopt identification laws increases when a Republican legislature and governor assume power and a state's Black and Latino populations (who tend to be heavily Democratic) are larger.[55] Additional research suggests that ID laws serve their political purpose. Examining county turnout data from 2012 to 2016, researcher John Kuk and his colleagues have found that strict photo ID laws effectively depress turnout in racially diverse counties, regardless of efforts taken to contact prospective voters or help them obtain IDs.[56]

In Ohio, Republicans did not adopt a strict ID law. They did, however, approve a 2011 law reducing early voting from 30 days before an election to 21 days by mail and 17 in person—eliminating a "golden week" when citizens could register and vote on the same day. The bill also prohibited counties and others from mailing absentee ballot applications to all registered voters. Some counties, including Cuyahoga County, had adopted the practice in an effort to improve turnout.

In Maine, Republicans voted to end the state's same-day registration (SDR) program in 2011, but it was restored in a ballot referendum later that year. Efforts to repeal SDR were also launched in other states, though it was only successfully eliminated in Montana (and not until 2021). This is good news for voter turnout, as researchers are perhaps most united in the belief that eased registration requirements boost participation. Barry Burden, a professor at the University of Wisconsin, and his colleagues have reported that SDR states are associated with an additional 2.5 points of turnout for every ten days of registration and voting that they allow.[57]

More successful were Republican efforts to reduce polling places in jurisdictions across the U.S. A 2019 report by the Leadership Conference on Civil and Human Rights found that over 1,200 polling places in the South were closed between 2013 and 2019. In Texas, one of the country's fastest growing states, more than one in ten polling places were closed during this time. In Arizona, closures were even more drastic; more than one in five had been shuttered. In Georgia, 214 precincts were closed between 2012 and 2018, even though the state's population increased by over one million residents. Notable closures also took place in Alabama and North Carolina during this time.[58] The results were predictable; voters were faced with longer lines at the polls.[59]

After Joe Biden defeated Donald Trump in the 2020 presidential election, Republicans across the U.S. reignited efforts to restrict voting access. By May 2021, at least 22 Republican-sponsored bills restricting voting access had been approved in state legislatures.[60] The bills sought to make it harder for citizens to register to vote, receive and return absentee ballots, vote early at in-person sites, and much more. In March 2021—after the state narrowly supported Biden and two new Democratic senators—Georgia approved a sweeping voting law that cut early voting, strengthened the state's photo ID requirement, and made it illegal for outside groups to provide water or food to citizens in long voting lines (of which Georgia has plenty). The law was considered so restrictive that Georgia-based firms such as Coca-Cola openly criticized it. Major League Baseball—which was slated to hold its 2021 All-Star Game in Atlanta—swiftly relocated the contest to Colorado.

The Voting Rights Act of 1965 has proven to be a formidable obstacle to some of the aforementioned voting restrictions. As I discussed in Chapter 3, the law restricts states from instituting voting changes that disproportionately hurt racial and ethnic minority groups. States cannot, however, be forced to adopt measures that make voting easier. For example, imagine that State A approves early voting, but State B does not. If State A wishes to later cut its early voting offerings, it can only legally do so if federal courts conclude that the changes do not disproportionately make voting harder for racial and ethnic minorities. If the cuts are determined to have this effect, they can be blocked. In this example, State A is required to continue its early voting program (without cuts), while State B is still allowed to have no early voting law. Under the Voting Rights Act, once you establish a new level of convenience, any changes cannot have a discriminatory impact on racial or ethnic minorities.[61]

Until 2013, no state with a history of voting discrimination based on race could change any voting laws without "preclearance" from the U.S. Justice Department. Recall that in *Shelby Co. v. Holder* (2013), the Supreme Court ruled that preclearance under the Voting Rights Act was still acceptable, but that the formula for determining which jurisdictions were covered would need to be updated. Because Congress has been unable to reach agreement on a new coverage formula, the federal government (and the federal courts) can now only challenge new election rules *after* they are adopted. Even with a weakened Voting Rights Act, federal courts have effectively limited some of the voting restrictions passed in recent years. Because the Supreme Court does not hear an appeal to every case decided in the federal courts, however, many final decisions have come from either federal district or appeals courts with jurisdiction over a particular area.

In Florida, a federal district court approved the state's early voting cuts in 2012, though the legislature gave counties the right to restore them in 2013. In 2016, a federal appeals court ruled that North Carolina's 2013 state law that cut early voting by a week, got rid of SDR, and adopted a strict voter ID law targeted Blacks with "surgical precision." As a result, it was inconsistent with the Voting Rights Act. A new voter ID law was approved by voters in a 2018 ballot referendum, but it too was blocked by the courts—this time at both the state and federal levels. While a final ruling was pending, the ID law could not take effect in 2020 as planned.[62] Meanwhile, the State Board of Elections ruled in 2020 that each county must have at least one early voting site for every 20,000 registered voters.

Some restrictions, however, were permitted to stand. While strict voter ID laws in Arkansas, Pennsylvania, and Texas were struck down by courts, eight states still had enforceable laws in effect by 2016. That year, the U.S. Court of Appeals for the Sixth Circuit permitted Ohio to implement a reduction in early voting days from 35 to 28, along with the termination of a week-long period when citizens could both register and vote early at the same time.[63]

Also in 2016, a U.S. district judge blocked a Wisconsin law that cut early voting by 18 days (from 30 to 12), limited early voting to weekdays, and allowed jurisdictions to have just one early voting site. Ruling that Black and Latino voters were more likely to use early voting, District Judge James Peterson ruled that the law "intentionally discriminates on the basis of race."[64] However, the U.S. Court of Appeals for the Seventh Circuit restored the cuts in 2020, as well as a ban on sending absentee ballots to most voters by fax or email.[65]

While most rulings on voting restrictions have been issued by federal district and appeals courts, the Supreme Court addressed the issue of "voter purges" in 2018. States have long made efforts to keep their registration rolls accurate. Those who move or die, for example, are generally removed from state registration lists. In fact, the 1993 "motor voter" law requires that states take steps to keep their lists accurate. Ohio, however, has unusually strict criteria regarding its voting rolls. In Ohio, the state is allowed to purge voters' names from the rolls if they have not voted in six years or responded to a postcard from the state informing them that a purge is imminent. In *Husted v. Philip Randolph Institute*, the High Court ruled 5–4 that this policy—also practiced in Georgia, Montana, Pennsylvania, Oklahoma, Oregon, and West Virginia—is acceptable.[66] The decision angered voting rights advocates. While most agree that states must try to remove registrations that are no longer valid, there is evidence that purges are often full of mistakes. The Brennan Center has reported that recent purges in Arkansas, Virginia, and New York, for example, erroneously purged thousands of valid voters from registration rolls.[67]

In sum, Republican-led efforts to reduce convenience voting since the late 2000s have had mixed success. While more Americans are required to present photo ID in order to vote, some ID laws have been overturned. And while voter purges have increased and polling sites have been reduced, cuts to early voting and SDR programs have often been blocked. Furthermore, the popularity of these programs has made it difficult for legislators in some states to even attempt to eliminate or cut them. Recall that some of the states with the most robust voter convenience programs are Republican-led states who adopted the programs in the 1980s and 1990s before they were politically divisive. Texas approved early voting in the late 1980s through a non-controversial voice vote. Idaho approved SDR with little controversy in the 1990s. While the politics in these states would likely not allow early voting or SDR to be adopted today, these programs have now become embedded in their respective states' political cultures. And because citizens like them, there is pressure on legislators not to disrupt them.

Not only have early voting and eased registration requirements survived most attempts to cut or eliminate them, but each reform is expanding to more states. Recent gains have mostly been in traditionally Democratic states that were initially slow to embrace voter convenience measures. In fact, Republican attempts to cut early voting and other programs have likely incentivized Democrats to adopt them in places where they had previously not. Since 2010, ten additional states and the District of Columbia have initiated early voting programs. Meanwhile, the number of SDR states has more than doubled—from nine (plus D.C.) to 20. Again, most of the new SDR states are Democratic-leaning; of the 12 new adopters, only Utah has voted Republican in a presidential election since 2004.[68]

On the subject of voter registration, a new reform has also emerged rapidly in recent years. Rather than simply allow citizens to register on the day in which they vote, 20 states have launched programs to automatically register adult citizens. Each program is designed to register a voter when they interact with their local department of motor vehicles (DMV) or (in some states) another government office. In three states—Alaska, Massachusetts, and Oregon—a citizen who is not registered to vote is sent a mailing informing them that they will be registered by a certain date unless they choose to opt out by signing and returning a postcard. In the other 16 states, customers provide information needed to register to vote as part of their transaction at the government office. Voters see a screen that tells them their information will be used for voter registration unless they choose to decline.[69]

Because automatic voter registration (AVR) is a new form of voter convenience, it will take some time to determine how effectively it can increase participation. Early indications, however, are promising. Researchers Jake Grumbach and Charlotte Hill report that individuals in AVR states are about one percentage-point more likely to vote, even when accounting for a range of demographic factors, election characteristics, and other voting laws that may affect turnout. Notably, the effect is much higher for younger voters. People between the ages of 18 and 24 who live in AVR states are 6.3 percentage points more likely to vote.[70]

Finally, the first few decades of the twenty-first century saw an expansion of voting rights for those with a felony conviction. As of 2018, more than six million Americans remain unable to vote because of a conviction; nearly five million of these citizens are not in prison, but remain ineligible because their state disenfranchises at least some of those on parole, probation, or with a past conviction. Nevertheless, states have moved decidedly in the direction of allowing felons to vote after completing their prison sentence. Since 1997, seven states have ended policies that permanently disenfranchised ex-felons, while six have expanded voting rights for those under community supervision. Seventeen states have eased the process through which ex-felons can seek to have their rights restored. Should reform efforts continue, millions of Americans could join the voter registration rolls in the coming years.[71]

Voting During a Pandemic

The Covid-19 pandemic has been a monumental crisis for the U.S. Many have lost their jobs, thousands of businesses have shuttered, and over a million Americans have perished. With the crisis landing during a presidential election year in 2020, the need for social distancing also greatly complicated the voting process. In an effort to preserve their health and prevent the spread of a deadly illness, an unprecedented number of Americans sought to cast ballots by mail. Hoping to avoid long Election Day lines (but preferring to vote in person), others opted to vote at early in-person sites. Much like the broader voting rights landscape since the late 2000s, citizen needs were both accommodated and stifled in 2020. On the positive side, many states and localities appropriately eased the process for casting early ballots. Before the pandemic, 16 states still required a valid excuse (e.g., health, travel, work) in order to receive an absentee ballot. After Covid-19 hit, three of these states—Massachusetts, Delaware, and South Carolina—eliminated the excuse requirement. Eight additional states allowed voters to cite the pandemic as a valid reason to vote absentee. Four states—California, Nevada, New Jersey, Vermont—and D.C. adopted universal VBM for 2020, sending mail ballots to all registered voters in advance of the election. In doing so, they joined Hawaii, Colorado, Oregon, Utah, and Washington, all of whom already had universal VBM laws. Meanwhile, in Nebraska, 11 lightly populated counties used VBM. Nine states did not automatically mail ballots, but did proactively send absentee ballot applications to all voters.[72] Three states—Georgia, Maryland, and New Jersey—established drop boxes where voters could safely leave their absentee ballots. Drop boxes had proven to be popular in the eight states that already employed them before the pandemic.[73] These accommodations undoubtedly made voting safer in 2020 and very possibly saved lives.

But voting in 2020 still involved unnecessary hurdles. In the months before the 2020 election, concerns emerged that the U.S. Postal Service would be unable to deliver mail-in ballots in a timely manner. The agency, run by Donald Trump appointee Louis DeJoy, had recently eliminated employees' ability to log overtime, barred workers from making extra trips to deliver late-arriving mail, and removed hundreds of mail sorting machines. The changes quickly led to mail delays. While DeJoy argued that the actions were needed due to budget shortfalls, some worried that they were designed to undermine faith in mail ballots and delay the arrival of ballots at elections offices. Before Covid-19, most states (32) only allowed mail-in ballots to count if they arrived by Election Day. Late-arriving ballots would be discarded. While some states eased this rule in 2020, state and federal courts were a bit uneven in accommodating these changes. In 2020, Kentucky and Massachusetts changed their policies to allow postmarked ballots arriving three days after Election Day to count; each change proceeded without much fanfare. In Michigan, a state court of claims judge ordered clerks to accept ballots that were postmarked by the day before Election Day, even if they were not received until November 17 (14 days after the election). Ultimately, however, the Michigan Supreme Court affirmed a lower court decision overturning the ruling; late-arriving ballots throughout the state would be tossed.[74]

In Wisconsin, a U.S. district judge ruled that ballots postmarked by Election Day (November 3) should count if they arrived by November 9. But the decision was appealed and ultimately struck down by the U.S. Supreme Court in a 5–3 ruling. The High Court, however, did not block a Pennsylvania Supreme Court ruling allowing postmarked ballots to be counted if they arrived up to three days after Election Day. In explaining the conflicting rulings, Chief Justice John Roberts noted that federal courts had improperly intervened in a state matter in Wisconsin, while in Pennsylvania, a state supreme court was rightfully applying the state's own constitution.[75]

The situation regarding mail-in ballots was a bit chaotic in Minnesota. The secretary of state's office initially approved a seven-day extension for mail-in ballots, allowing them to count if they were received by November 10. Just five days before the election, however, the U.S. Court of Appeals for the Seventh Circuit ordered all ballots received after Election Day to be segregated. The ruling implied that a later challenge to the state's new policy regarding mail-in ballots could deem late-arriving ballots invalid. With the ruling coming after many voters had already mailed their ballots, there was understandable anxiety about whether they would arrive on time.[76]

Some Pennsylvania voters were concerned that their ballots may not count for an entirely different reason. In September 2020, a state supreme court ruling declared that if voters simply placed their absentee ballots into return envelopes before mailing them back, they would be rejected. Instead, the state mandated that the ballot first be placed in an enclosed "secrecy envelope," which could then be inserted into the return envelope. The reasoning was that once election officials received mail-in ballots, they used the outer envelope to verify that the person (1) was registered and (2) had not already voted *without* being able to see the person's vote choices.[77] The ruling, which came after some ballots had already been returned, was a change from how the state handled absentee ballots in the past, including in the 2020 primaries. Given the late change and possibility for confusion, there were reasonable concerns that the number of rejected ballots could be massive. In the 2019 municipal elections in Philadelphia, 6.4 percent of absentee ballots had been "naked." Ultimately, in the 2020 general election, at least 4,000 general election ballots in Philadelphia alone were discarded for arriving "naked." The statewide number was undoubtedly much greater.[78]

Voters faced additional burdens. In 31 states, officials discarded ballots if they determined that an absentee voter's signature did not match that found on their voter registration form or driver's license application. Obviously, a signature mismatch is not indicative of fraud. Do you sign your name the same way every time? Over the course of several years? I certainly do not! And even though research has determined that voter fraud via absentee ballots is exceptionally rare, such requirements had led to over 318,000 ballot disqualifications in 2016. According to *The Atlantic*'s David Graham, "Rejections disproportionately hit certain demographic groups, including elderly voters, young voters, and voters of color."[79]

Many states do not even provide voters with an opportunity to challenge their ballot rejection. Only 18 states mandate a ballot "curing" process, which usually entails a phone call from an elections official or a mailed notice. But if voters cannot be reached or fail to take the (sometimes onerous) steps necessary to prove their ballot is legitimate, their votes are simply tossed. This is shameful. Hannah Fried, the national campaign director of All Voting Is Local, a non-profit group committed to expanding voting access, recently commented, "If you're an eligible voter and you voted, your ballot should not be rejected for a highly technical reason out of your control—because the signature was sloppy, or you cannot write in the same way you used to be able to write. There's something fundamentally unfair about it."[80] I could not agree more.

Given concerns about the mail in 2020, many voters preferred to physically drop off their completed absentee ballots to ensure timely delivery. In Texas, both Harris and Travis County sought to establish multiple drop-off locations for voters to deliver ballots. But Governor Greg Abbott intervened, allowing all counties to have only one drop-off site. In Ohio, Secretary of State Frank LaRose similarly blocked six major Ohio cities who hoped to provide drop box locations across their respective counties. Instead, his directive allowed voters to only drop ballots at their county elections office. Given that Ohio's largest counties have over one million residents, this made the process very inconvenient for some.[81]

Meanwhile, many of those who did vote in person in 2020 waited in exceptionally long lines. In some parts of Georgia, wait times were as long as 11 hours during the early voting period.[82] Media accounts praised voters for being willing to wait so long to exercise their civic duties. While such praise is deserving, no one should ever need to stand in line for hours—especially during a pandemic—to cast a vote. Surely, the unique circumstances of 2020 contributed to the long lines seen in some places. Localities struggled to know how many voters to expect in person given the unusually large number of absentee ballot requests. Furthermore, a large number of voters arrived at the polls with absentee ballots in hand (that had been mailed to them) and declared that they wished to vote in-person instead. The additional administrative step resulted in slower lines in many places.

But the reality is that long lines existed before Covid-19. The problem is not new, and we should not expect it to magically go away when the virus is controlled. Long lines, like so many of the voting obstacles discussed in this chapter, are a product of more durable problems with American elections. Solutions are within our grasp, but they will require bold action by the federal government.

Reform

Writing just one day after the 2020 elections, scholars Lee Drutman and Charlotte Hill offered the following blunt assessment of voting in the United States (2020):

> Fair, secure, and straightforward voting is the foundation of a functioning democracy. But a lethal combination of partisan politics, longstanding neglect, and sheer cheapness has caused our electoral system to fall into disrepair. To fix it, we need to give America's democratic infrastructure the same attention and resources we give other national priorities.[83]

As Drutman and Hill note, politics are part of the problem. As I have detailed in this chapter, Republicans have repeatedly sought to make voting harder over the past decade or so. After winning majorities in many state houses after the 2010 elections, Republican legislators and governors pursued voter ID laws, early voting cuts, tougher registration requirements, and other burdensome restrictions on the franchise. Clearly, many in the party came to believe that easier voting access was disadvantageous to their electoral viability. Democrats hardly have a perfect record when it comes to voting rights either; heavily Democratic states such as Massachusetts and New York only recently adopted early voting, long after much of the country already had. And despite having full control of Congress (with large majorities) and the presidency in 2009–10, Democrats did not seriously pursue needed national voting reforms. Without question, some of the Democrats' renewed enthusiasm for voting rights in the years since is owed simply to their belief that such policies might be electorally beneficial.

Contrary to assumptions made by both parties, I am not convinced that voting burdens universally hurt Democrats (or that reforms would universally help them). Surely, racist policies and those that create hassle for college students will generally affect Democrats more than Republicans. And long lines in urban areas, which tend to be heavily Democratic, should also have disproportionate partisan effects. But more generally, both parties now have large bases of working-class voters who undoubtedly yearn for more convenient voting processes. Democrats perform well with non–white, working-class voters, but Republicans have become quite strong with white, working-class voters. Meanwhile, Democrats now have a large base of well-educated urban and suburban voters who are well-suited to overcome any electoral barriers. The 2020 elections may be instructive here. Before 2020, the running assumption was that if turnout ever rose dramatically, it would undoubtedly help the Democratic Party. It was widely believed that the population of non-voters was much more Democratic-leaning than Republican-leaning. In 2020, however, the electorate expanded considerably, as turnout was the highest it had been in over 100 years. Millions of new voters entered the electorate, with *both* parties gaining new supporters. In fact, the presidential margin may have been closer than expected because many low-propensity voters came to the polls and voted Republican. Writing in *The Washington Post*, David Weigel wrote, "Democrats [in 2020] won the White House and lost a myth about turnout."[84] Weigel quoted Faiz Shakir, a former campaign manager for Senator Bernie Sanders, as saying, "If you asked me before the election, 'What does this higher turnout across the country mean?' I'd have suspected it was a verdict against Trump…. I'd have said they were coming out for the first time because they were frustrated by the way this country is going. But there were a fair number of people coming out for the first time who wanted more of it."[85] It turns out that there were plenty of Democratic and Republican voters who had been sitting on the sidelines before 2020. In a future election where passions do not run quite as deep as in 2020 (most elections!), burdensome voting restrictions could keep some of these new voters from participating again. I see no reason to assume that only the low-propensity Democrats would be deterred by registration hassles, inconvenient early voting policies, or polling place closures. Most likely, burdens would keep low-propensity supporters of both parties at home.

Of course, even when voter suppression *does* confer a partisan advantage (and sometimes it does), it is still at odds with democracy and modern conceptions of equality. A fair system of voting is not simply a means to an end in a democratic society; it is an end itself. A government "of, by, and for the people" must strive to represent *all* of its people. By doing so, it not only achieves its promise, but also gives itself the greatest chance at maintaining legitimacy. When the people are able to speak, the voice of government will better reflect their collective voices. We should not expect political parties to advocate for policies that they find disadvantageous on their own. Parties are in business to win elections, gain power, and exercise their will. But those Americans who believe that every citizen deserves an equal voice in choosing their representatives *must* speak up for this cause. And as history teaches us, when people speak loudly enough, those in power—in both parties—have no choice but to listen.

But what sorts of changes should democracy advocates demand? First, there are important steps that Congress can take to ease the voting process for all citizens. While most voting reforms have traditionally been initiated by states, Congress has broad authority to regulate federal elections under the Constitution. As we have seen, Congress has used this authority to standardize Election Day for federal elections (1845), approve the sweeping Voting Rights Act (1965), and require that citizens be given the opportunity to register to vote at the DMV (1993). Now it must do more. First, Congress can update the Voting Rights Act with a new preclearance formula. Recall that in *Shelby County v. Holder* (2013), the Supreme Court said that the federal government may still require states with a history of voting discrimination (on the basis of race) to receive preclearance from the Justice Department before changing voting laws. The 5–4 majority ruled that the existing formula was outdated, but that Congress could create and implement a new one. The Voting Rights Advancement Act, which passed the House (but not the Senate) in 2019 and 2021, adopts this new formula. The bill would subject states to preclearance if repeated voting rights violations are found within the previous 25-year period. Because the 25-year window "rolls," it constantly updates, allowing states to become free from preclearance if they steer clear of discriminatory voting practices. The bill also permits the attorney general to place federal observers in any state where a serious threat of racial discrimination in voting exists.[86] Alternatively, Congress could simply—as Senator Joe Manchin of West Virginia has proposed—make all 50 states subject to preclearance. If it were to do so, the Justice Department could strike any discriminatory voting laws in the U.S. before they take effect.[87]

In both 2019 and 2021, the House also approved the For the People Act, a comprehensive voting rights measure. The bill, whose gerrymandering reforms I discussed in Chapter 3 (and whose campaign finance reforms I will discuss in Chapter 7), would *require* that states take the following steps to ease the voting process[88]:

- Adopt automatic voter registration (AVR).
- Adopt same-day registration (SDR) for those for whom the AVR system missed.
- Add new safeguards to ensure that properly registered voters are not purged from the voter rolls.
- Allow 16-year-olds to pre-register to vote.

- Improve accommodations for voters with disabilities.
- End disenfranchisement for felons who have completed their sentences.
- Require all jurisdictions to use paper ballots.
- Provide at least two weeks of early voting.
- Allow any eligible voter to request and submit an absentee ballot.
- Provide voters with ample opportunities to cure discrepancies raised through signature match checks.
- Provide funding for poll worker recruitment and training.
- Designate Election Day as a federal holiday.
- Require states with voter identification requirements to permit voters who lack identification to vote if they complete a sworn written statement attesting to their identity (unless the individual is a first-time voter who registered by mail).
- Provide free postage for absentee ballots.

Should it eventually be passed and signed into law, the For the People Act could make voting considerably easier for millions of Americans. In addition to removing registration burdens and expanding opportunities to cast ballots, the bill would provide needed consistency to voting rights across the U.S. Citizens could move to new counties and states without finding that opportunities to vote are considerably different.

In their aforementioned article, Drutman and Hill advocate for the bill's passage, but also caution that more must be done. They note that while the bill mandates that states comply with a variety of new requirements, the federal enforcement mechanisms are not particularly strong. The authors advocate for a new Federal Elections Agency that can ensure that states follow the law's requirements, investigate claims of voter suppression, and disperse funds to states and localities for election administration. Furthermore, the agency would be empowered to centralize voter registration records and (if the Voting Rights Enhancement Act is approved) perhaps assume the responsibility of providing preclearance to states seeking changes to their election laws.

Whether the U.S. establishes a new Federal Elections Agency or not (I like the idea!), it is clear that more money is needed to administer elections. Recall that more than 1,200 polling sites have been shuttered in the South since 2013 (the year of the *Shelby County* decision) alone. In Georgia, there are more than 2 million more registered voters than there were in 2013. Remarkably, however, the state's polling locations have been cut by nearly ten percent during this time. Today, nine counties—Fulton, Gwinnett, Forsyth, DeKalb, Cobb, Hall, Cherokee, Henry, and Clayton—have nearly half of the state's active voters but only 38 percent of the polling places.[89] Some of these closures, along with the other troubling barriers to voting discussed in this chapter, are clearly the product of voter suppression. But the problem is also a financial one in many jurisdictions. I have spoken to dozens of election administrators over the past decade who have expressed a desire to expand polling sites and ease other burdens of voting, but simply lack the necessary resources. Surveys of election administrators across the U.S. confirm this sentiment. Even if states and localities continue to run their elections, we should ensure that they have the resources to carry out their duties.

For context, the U.S. currently spends about $2 billion annually on elections, or about $8 a voter. Most democracies spend considerably more. In Canada, a recent national election cost the country about $13.50 per voter.[90] For a tiny fraction of the annual discretionary budget, the U.S. could infuse states and localities with the funds needed to support programs that have been proven to expand participation. This includes more polling places on Election Day, more early voting sites, more staff, better staff training, and more public service messages to communities regarding voter options. All of these things would increase convenience, streamline processes, and make voting less confusing and frustrating for so many citizens.

Finally, beyond legislative fixes, the federal courts need to think about voting differently. In a democratic republic, there is no right more important than the ability to freely choose elected representatives. A right to vote was not included in the original Constitution, but through various amendments, the document now recognizes the right in five different places. Voting is *not* something that American citizens must earn or work to achieve. It is not something bestowed in return for skills, education, or expertise. It is an entitlement of citizenship. It is a recognition that in a free society, no citizen should be asked to submit to the authority of a government that they did not have an equal opportunity to shape.

Because voting is a sacred right, the government has a responsibility to protect it. But too often, our courts still approach voting as though it were a privilege or a limited right that can be shoved aside for arbitrary reasons. For example, courts should never permit states to toss ballots because the mail arrived slowly. If a signature mismatch raises concerns about voter fraud, then states and localities should ensure that voters have ample opportunities to prove their vote is legitimate. Any other restriction on the right to vote, such as ID laws and voter purges, should be viewed by courts with great suspicion. If states and localities cannot credibly justify these actions from an election security perspective (and they have not yet), then these laws have no place in a democratic society. At the very least, the courts should require that states with voter ID laws develop exceptionally convenient ways for all citizens to obtain necessary documents free of charge.

If we believe in robust voting rights, then the government must assume the burden of ensuring that citizens can register and cast ballots in a convenient manner. Citizens should not be asked to navigate confusing websites, wait on hold endlessly, or stand in line for hours to vote. Moving to a new precinct, county, or state should not necessitate hours of labor in order for a citizen to remain a registered voter.

Because members of Congress and the president have electoral interests, the courts must play a central role in upholding voting rights. But in recent years, they have not. The sort of voting barriers allowed by the federal courts—a prior felony conviction, lack of photo identification, and excessive wait times—would never be accepted for most other rights protected in the Constitution. Imagine if free speech rights were conditioned on having a clean criminal record. Or if only those who had a photo ID could avoid an unreasonable search or seizure. Suppose that suspects could be detained for weeks without being charged because lines were moving slowly. As Omar Epps wrote in *The Atlantic* in 2013, "The right to vote of citizens of the United States remains a kind of stepchild in the family of American rights."[91]

But this has not always been the case. We have seen the power of assertive courts committed to democracy in the past. In the early and mid-twentieth century, the Supreme Court acted (not quickly enough) to ban grandfather clauses and all-white primaries. The Warren Court demanded an end to malapportioned legislatures (except the U.S. Senate) in the 1960s; several decades later, a series of cases stopped abusive forms of racial gerrymandering. The Constitution protects the right to vote in the Fourteenth, Fifteenth, Nineteenth, Twenty-Fourth, and Twenty-Sixth Amendments. A broad interpretation of this right could make it very difficult for any level of government to adopt burdensome voting regulations. But much like past courts, future ones are not likely to shift their interpretations without public pressure. It is up to citizens to demand that their sacred right to vote be rigorously protected.

Let this be our mission.

CHAPTER 7

"If You've Got the Money, Honey…"

It should surprise no one that money has always been a major factor in American politics. When a 23-year-old George Washington first ran for a seat in the Virginia House of Burgesses in 1755, he reportedly lost 271–40 because his opponent bribed voters with alcohol. Three years later, an older and wiser Washington ran again. This time, he supplied his own liquor and earned 331 votes, enough to win the seat.[1] More than a century later, during the Gilded Age, state and local political parties routinely funded political campaigns by "assessing" the salaries of government employees. Basically, employees funded the parties, who backed politicians and candidates who protected their jobs while in office. At the height of this era, Mark Hanna, a wealthy Ohio businessman, set up an unprecedented fundraising operation for 1896 Republican presidential nominee William McKinley. Hanna demanded that banks and businesses pledge a percentage of their profits to McKinley's campaign with the understanding that if elected, the candidate would be favorable to their interests. Hanna's effort helped McKinley raise $16 million against just $600,000 for the Democratic nominee, William Jennings Bryan. McKinley was elected in a landslide and dutifully supported corporate interests as president. Hanna was unapologetic about this effort, quipping, "All questions in a democracy [are] questions of money."[2]

During the twentieth century, Congress made several attempts to limit money in federal political campaigns. While these efforts were not entirely unsuccessful, loopholes in the laws and (especially) hostile court decisions have limited their effects. Today, the campaign finance system in the U.S. is littered with both large spenders and dark (or anonymous) money. While some restrictions remain, wealthy citizens, businesses, and other groups can generally spend without limit to influence who gets elected. The vast majority of citizens, of course, do not have this ability. Campaign spending does not always determine winners and losers, but it often plays a role. Furthermore, money has the ability to discredit ideas and deter those seeking office from pursuing sound policies.

Campaign finance is central to the idea of political equality. Even if all citizens are able to vote and have their votes count the same (neither is the case), equality cannot be truly achieved if some citizens can accompany their votes with massive amounts of supplemental influence. Similar to the other issues discussed in this book, campaign finance is complicated, and there is no perfect approach to it. And given existing barriers, improving the current system is undoubtedly a long-term project. Congress can take important steps now by ending dark money and emboldening small contributions to candidates. More substantial reform, however, can only be achieved if the federal courts view campaign spending as an issue of equal protection under the law, rather than simply freedom of speech and expression (as is currently the case). The Fourteenth Amendment must have a seat at the table, along with the First Amendment.

Money and Political Equality

Why do political campaigns need money? While this may seem obvious, it is a useful place to begin a conversation on this issue. Money that is donated to campaigns is mostly spent on communications with potential voters, including advertising via television, radio, the internet, and the mail, as well as door-to-door canvassing. Campaign money also allows each of these operations to be refined through the use of complicated targeting models. For example, when a campaign runs an advertisement in a community, it does so because its data suggest that the ad's messaging fits the population who will view it. In the twenty-first century, this sort of targeting is now done on an individual level. Through consumer marketing data, voter files, polls, and other available data sources, campaigns now have access to personal profiles of nearly all U.S. voters. This information is used to predict citizen attitudes, which informs the messages that prospective voters hear when canvassed, as well as the ads that they see on Facebook, YouTube, and other online sites.[3]

Donors and candidates (and their campaigns) view money as important because they believe the above interactions matter. If they did not believe money was important, donors would not bother giving it, and candidates would not spend time raising it. Because they *do* believe money matters, candidates may be inclined to alter their behavior in the hopes of obtaining or maintaining the support of donors. And if citizens gain more power by virtue of having more capacity to donate to campaigns, this is political inequality.

Research suggests that donors do affect the behavior of officeholders. While numerous studies have reported that the link between campaign contributions and roll call votes in Congress is unclear or non-existent, money works in less apparent (but equally important) ways. Consider the following example. In 2009–2010, Democrats had majorities in both the House and Senate, while Democratic President Barack Obama occupied the White House. The time was ripe to advance a major priority for the party—universal healthcare. It would be a challenge, however, because the healthcare industry—doctors, hospitals, drug companies, and health insurers—would fight every aspect of reform believed to hurt their bottom lines. They had previously helped sink healthcare reform pursued by President Bill Clinton in 1993–94 through a high-priced advertising campaign.

In 2009, Amy McKay was working as an APSA congressional research fellow on Capitol Hill.[4] As healthcare bills were being developed in the House and Senate, McKay tracked official public comments about the bill.[5] Comments are formal statements made by citizens regarding what they would prefer to see in (or out) of a bill under congressional consideration. McKay collected the letters and ultimately found that if a person hosted a fundraiser for a candidate, they became four times as likely to have their preferred policy offered as an amendment to the bill (introduced by a member of Congress). Democrats ultimately passed a major healthcare bill—the Affordable Care Act—with few defections in the House and none in the Senate. If one was simply analyzing roll call votes, it would appear as though Democrats refused to cave to powerful interests. After all, the bill contained hundreds of new regulations on the healthcare industry and committed billions to expanding care to the uninsured. The truth, however, is more complicated. It is clear that certain reforms were added or removed from the bill to suit the demands of well-funded interests. It was widely reported that President Obama and congressional Democrats made deals with various healthcare industry lobbyists in order to secure their support (or at least lessen their hostility) for the bill.[6] Some of these deals changed the legislation significantly. A public option, which would have created a government-sponsored insurance plan to compete with private insurers, was removed. Private insurers knew that if they had to compete with a non-profit government plan, they would need to lower prices to remain competitive. Measures to control drug prices were also trimmed to accommodate the pharmaceutical industry.

It is easy to conclude that Obama and congressional Democrats failed to act in the public interest by making deals with powerful interests. The reality, however, is that these interests had the ability to kill public support for the bill through aggressive, well-funded public campaigns. Obama and his allies had to decide whether getting most of what they wanted in the bill was better than possibly getting nothing. The problem is not that Democrats made these deals. Rather, the problem is that interests have the power (through money) to put politicians from both parties in these sorts of compromised positions.

In a separate research project, Christopher Witko and his colleagues agreed that campaign finance studies focused solely on "observable outcomes of the political process—bills passed, roll call votes, etc." often miss the point about money's effect on politics.[7] In their study, the authors examine congressional floor speeches as an indicator of what legislators prefer to discuss and hope to achieve. Focusing on economic policy, they report that members of Congress who receive more funding from "upper class interests" talk more about upper class economic priorities in the subsequent legislative session. The findings hold even when the authors control for other important variables that shape priorities, such as a member's partisanship. Again, money may not always affect roll call votes, but it likely affects the issues that receive votes in the first place.

Research has also found that campaign donors have an easier time gaining access to those in power. One study, conducted by political scientists Joshua Kalla and David Broockman, featured an experiment whereby a political organization attempted to schedule meetings between 191 House members and constituents from their districts.[8] The organization created treatment and control groups, informing House offices that some constituents (but not all) had contributed to their respective member's campaign. Ultimately, senior policymakers in the offices made themselves available between three and four times more often to those revealed as donors.

Arguably, the surest way to confirm that money affects elected officials is to capture the latter in moments of candor. Thankfully, officials sometimes oblige. Former Congressman Mick Mulvaney of South Carolina, who later served as President Trump's chief of staff in 2019–2020, once remarked, "We had a hierarchy in my office in Congress.... If you're a lobbyist who never gave us money, I didn't talk to you. If you're a lobbyist who gave us money, I might talk to you."[9] Former Congressman Barney Frank of Massachusetts once conceded, "We would be the only human beings in the history of the world who, on a regular basis, took significant amounts of money from perfect strangers and made sure it had no effect on our behavior."[10] Finally, President Joe Biden, who served in the Senate for 36 years, acknowledged in 2015, "It's awful hard to take a whole lot of money from a group you know has a particular position then you conclude they're wrong [and] vote no."[11]

A Brief History of Campaign Finance Law

Congress has acted to limit campaign fundraising and spending on numerous occasions. The first campaign finance regulations came during the Progressive Era. In 1907, Congress approved the Tillman Act, a measure that restricted corporations from making campaign contributions to candidates or political parties. The ban was later extended to public utility companies (1935) and labor unions (1943). Each of these restrictions remain in effect as of 2022, but the legal landscape has become much more complicated.

In 1971 and 1974, Congress took a more comprehensive approach to regulating campaign finance in the Federal Election Campaign Act (FECA). The law effectively created three sets of regulations. The first centered on candidates and their official campaign committees. The second pertained to political party organizations. The third addressed "outside groups," which include businesses, labor unions, and any other interest groups that advocate for political outcomes. The latter category includes prominent organizations such as the National Rifle Association, Planned Parenthood, and the Sierra Club, for example.

Regarding candidates and parties, FECA marked the first time that either were limited in terms of how much money they could raise from individual citizens. In fact, presidential candidates were encouraged not to raise or spend *any* money in general elections. Instead, major party nominees would each receive a grant of money from the federal government for use between the party nominating conventions and the general election. While accepting these public funds was voluntary, those who did so agreed not to raise or spend *any* additional money during this time. Because the grants were generous, every major party candidate accepted them between 1976 and 2004. Meanwhile, candidates seeking their party's presidential nomination were eligible to receive federal matching funds (up to $250 per donation) for their contributions if they agreed to limit their total fundraising until their party's nominating convention. This program was also successful, as every major party candidate between 1976 and 1996 opted into it.

Both general election grants and matching funds are still in place as of 2022. However, because candidates can now raise much more than the programs provide, candidates see participation as self-defeating. No candidate has accepted the general election grant since Republican John McCain in 2008, while no serious contender for a party nomination has opted into the matching funds program since 2004.

FECA did not create a public funding system for congressional candidates. Instead, candidates were expected to continue raising private contributions. In order to prevent the wealthy from having too much influence, the law only allowed federal candidates to accept $1,000 (or less) from individuals during their campaigns. Furthermore, independently wealthy candidates were severely limited from using their own money to

fund their campaigns. Meanwhile, the national political party committees, who provide support to candidates running for all federal offices
across the country, were permitted to raise substantially more ($20,000)
from individuals during an election cycle.

Regarding outside organizations, FECA gave corporations, unions,
and other interest groups the ability to form political action committees
(PACs). These PACs could solicit contributions of up to $5,000 from indi-
vidual donors for the purposes of election spending. With the accumu-
lated funds, PACs could then either contribute to candidate campaigns
(up to $5,000 each) or fund independent expenditures. An independent
expenditure is when an organization conducts its own election activities
(rather than donating money), which may include television advertisements or direct mail to voters. In conducting these expenditures, PACs
were permitted to directly advocate for or against candidates running for
office, but could not "coordinate" their efforts with candidate campaigns.[12]

Not surprisingly, the FECA law was challenged in federal court. In
Buckley v. Valeo (1976), the Supreme Court ruled that campaign spending
restrictions are limitations on free speech and expression. And because
the First Amendment "affords the broadest protection to such political
expression in order 'to assure (the) unfettered interchange of ideas,'" the
majority noted that the standards for restricting campaign spending are
high. Nevertheless, the Court was convinced that restrictions on this form
of expression were justified by the government's interest in "the prevention of corruption and the appearance of corruption spawned by the real
or imagined coercive influence of large financial contributions on candidates' positions and on their actions if elected to office."[13] FECA's contribution limits on candidates, parties, and PACs were therefore permitted
to remain.[14] However, because spending restrictions could only be justified if reasonably aimed to prevent corruption, limits on self-financing
were eliminated. The Court reasoned that a wealthy candidate spending
millions of their own dollars could not corrupt themselves. The Court's
decision in *Buckley* focused entirely on the First Amendment, paying
no attention to how campaign contributions and spending could raise
important "equal protection" issues under the Fourteenth Amendment.

While the FECA kept very large donors out of candidate campaigns,
a loophole established by the Federal Election Commission (FEC) in 1978
allowed big donors, corporations, labor unions, and other groups to give
unlimited money to political parties for the purposes of "party-building."
While these "soft money" funds could not be used by parties to actively
promote their candidates, the distinction was often trivial. Advertisements could, for example, praise the efforts of a particular candidate without formally endorsing their campaign. In 2002, the Bipartisan Campaign

Finance Reform Act (BCRA) finally banned soft money. In addition, it added a new restriction by banning any advertising funded by corporate or special interest money that even mentioned the name of a federal candidate 60 days before a general election (or 30 days before a primary).

As early as 2007, there were indications that the Supreme Court was moving in a more hostile direction regarding campaign finance law. That year, in *Wisconsin Right to Life v. FEC*, a 5–4 majority weakened BCRA's aforementioned 60-day prohibition on outside spending that mentioned a federal candidate. The ruling allowed the regulation to continue but stipulated that if an advertisement could be reasonably deemed to be "something other" than an express advocacy ad, it *could* mention the name of a candidate up until the election. *Wisconsin Right to Life*, however, was only a preview.[15]

In 2008, a conservative group, Citizens United, made a critical film about then-Democratic presidential candidate Hillary Clinton. The group hoped to air the ad shortly before the 2008 presidential primaries and caucuses began. Because Clinton was a candidate, however, the film (or a preview for it) would effectively be a corporate-funded ad less than 30 days before a primary. While the FEC had issued exemptions to BCRA rules for films in the past, it refused to do so in this case because Citizens United was not a "bona fide" filmmaker. Citizens United sued the FEC, with the case landing in the Supreme Court in 2009. Originally, Chief Justice Roberts intended to author an opinion (with 5–4 backing) simply declaring that Citizens United (and more importantly, future non-profit groups wishing to air films) should be exempted from the BCRA rules. Associate Justice Anthony Kennedy, however, wrote a concurrence that made a much broader statement about political spending in U.S. elections. Roberts asked the parties to reargue the case in September 2009, which they did. In January 2010, the Court issued a landmark ruling. The 5–4 majority ruled that independent political spending is not inherently corrupting and therefore cannot be restricted by Congress. So long as an individual, corporation, union, or other interest group is not directly contributing to a candidate or party, they may spend unlimited sums advocating for or against candidates. Justice Kennedy's opinion viewed corruption through the narrow lens of a "quid pro quo" transaction. In other words, unless a donor is giving a candidate or party a contribution with the understanding that a deed will be delivered in return, corruption has not occurred.[16]

Citizens United led to the creation of "SuperPACs," which are basically PACs that can only engage in independent expenditures. By doing so, they can raise and spend unlimited amounts for the purposes of express advocacy towards candidates and parties. The ruling also permitted 501c4 groups—public advocacy organizations whose primary purpose is *not* electoral advocacy—to raise and spend unlimited sums in elections. Unlike SuperPACs, 501c4 groups must spend a majority of their funds on non-electoral activities. In addition, they are not required to disclose their donors to the FEC. This loophole has essentially allowed millions in "dark money" to enter U.S. elections, as there is no formal mechanism for tracking donors or how much they give.

The effects of *Citizens United* on election spending have been enormous. In 2008, the final cycle before the ruling, about $330 million was spent by outside groups on federal elections. In 2020, with SuperPACs and 501c4s now flourishing, the figure was over $2.9 billion. Interestingly, spending by businesses, unions, and other groups has not increased as much as anticipated.[17] Instead, SuperPACs have largely become a vehicle for wealthy individuals to pour massive sums into elections. By 2018, just 11 individuals had already given over $1 billion combined to Super-PACs since 2010. The list was led by conservative Sheldon Adelson, who gave $287 million to SuperPACs during this time. He was followed by two liberal donors—Tom Steyer ($213 million) and Michael Bloomberg ($123 million). In 2018 alone, $822 million was spent by SuperPACs.[18] Of this amount, over $295 million (36 percent) was given by the top ten individual donors. The largest 100 SuperPAC donors gave almost as much as millions of small donors, *combined.*

Of course, every candidate supported by large SuperPAC spending has not won. But as we have seen, contributions can set the agenda. They influence the issues that are debated, the details included in policy proposals, and the sorts of programs that are omitted from consideration.

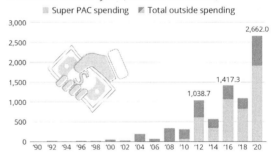

Outside Spending Takes Leap up in 2020 Election Cycle

Money spent by all outside groups* and Super PACs in federal election cycles (in million U.S. dollars)

■ Super PAC spending ⧄ Total outside spending

2,662.0
1,417.3
1,038.7

'90 '92 '94 '96 '98 '00 '02 '04 '06 '08 '10 '12 '14 '16 '18 '20

* Excluding party committees
Source: Opensecrets.org

ⓒⓕⓔ

statista ◪

Since the Supreme Court's 2010 ruling in *Citizens United v. FEC* (2010), outside spending has significantly increased in federal elections. Only a constitutional amendment or a new court decision could reverse the trend (Statista, CC BY-ND 3.0. To view the chart online, visit *http://www.statista. com/chart/17036/outside-spending-super-pac-spending-in-us-elections/*).

As Idrees Kahloon commented in *Harvard Magazine* in 2016, "Economic elites did not suddenly acquire political influence in 2010—but they may have further tightened their grip on it."[19]

Reform

A large majority of Americans support campaign finance limits. A May 2018 Pew survey revealed that 70 percent of respondents believed both individuals and groups should be limited in their ability to spend in elections.[20] So why is change so elusive? First, the Supreme Court has spoken loudly on the issue (in favor of unlimited spending). Unless the Court reverses itself or the Constitution is amended, any reform efforts will need to abide by its current rules. Second, it is always difficult to persuade Congress to adopt campaign finance reform because each member was elected through the current system. Third, while Americans largely support additional limits, the issue—like so many pertaining to political equality—is not particularly salient. Elected officials are therefore able to largely ignore it without fear of consequences. Finally, while Americans in all parties support reform, the issue has become politically polarized among elites. Democrats tend to support campaign finance reform, while Republicans are more lukewarm or opposed to it. The division is mostly ideological, as it is unclear that Republicans are advantaged by unlimited outside spending. While Republicans have received more outside support than Democrats since *Citizens United*, the 2012 election is responsible for much of the gap. During the 2018 midterm elections, pro–Democratic outside groups outspent their Republican counterparts.[21] In 2020, they did so again, outpacing pro–Republican groups by about $300 million ($1.6 billion to $1.3 billion).[22] And given that well-educated, wealthy citizens have voted Democratic in higher numbers in recent election cycles, this trend may not disappear anytime soon.

Ultimately, reform efforts must address two current problems with campaign finance law. Some changes are achievable by Congress, while others will eventually require a Supreme Court that recognizes the "equal protection" implications of campaign finance.

First, while contributions to federal candidates are now capped at $2,900 per election (as of 2022), research indicates that large donors still receive disproportionate influence and access to elected officials. One option is a new matching funds program. Recall that the voluntary public funding program for presidential candidates worked well until the cap became too low to entice candidates to join the program. Between 1976 and 1996, every major party candidate accepted matching funds during the nomination process; between 1976 and 2004, every candidate accepted the general election grant. The solution here is simple. The federal government needs to eliminate the cap on allowable spending for those opting into the program. In 2020, the cap during the nomination process was $51.85 million. For the general election, it was $103.7 million. Neither President Trump nor any Democrat accepted the funds because they all knew that they would be able to raise substantially more than those amounts on their own.

The aforementioned For the People Act, passed by the House in both 2019 and 2021, would reform the presidential matching funds program and create a new one for congressional elections. Once presidential or congressional candidates reached certain minimum thresholds in their fundraising, they would be eligible to receive matching funds for *all* contributions of $200 or less. The federal match would be six to one, meaning that a person's $10 contribution would actually provide $70 to the candidate. Candidates who opt into the program would need to agree not to accept any contributions over $1,000 for their campaigns. For both presidential nominating and general election campaigns, the maximum amount of federal funds received would be $250 million, though this number would rise as the cost of campaigns (presumably) grows in the future. As long as candidates followed these stipulations, there would be no limit on their overall fundraising during the nomination or general election stages.

In congressional elections, a new matching program would provide the same six to one match to candidates that meet minimum fundraising criteria. Participating candidates would again need to limit individual contributions to $1,000, but would not need to cap total spending. The maximum amount of federal funds any candidate could receive would be $5 million. Similar to the presidential program, this number would rise as campaign expenses increase. By amplifying the value of small contributions and capping larger ones, both the presidential and congressional matching programs would effectively decrease the difference between the size of donations received by candidates. If we believe that larger donors have greater influence on candidates (as research clearly indicates), then this reform should lessen these effects.[23]

The For the People Act's matching funds initiatives would be a major step towards reducing the power of donors in federal elections. Addressing the unlimited power of independent expenditures by SuperPACs and 501c4 groups will be more difficult, as the Supreme Court has effectively banned Congress from enacting meaningful limits. In my view, Congress should have the power to fully regulate outside groups and their election spending. But barring any major changes to the court's composition in the near future, the precedent set by *Citizens United* is unlikely to change. Congress can, however, pass the DISCLOSE Act, which would require 501c4 groups to reveal their donors as SuperPACs do. The *Citizens United* ruling gave its blessing to transparency efforts, meaning that this could be achieved through simple legislation. The bill fell one vote short of passage in the Senate in 2010, but has not come this close to approval since.

Regarding the broader issue of unlimited outside spending, citizens and activists must continue to voice their displeasure with the current state of affairs. Meanwhile, researchers should continue to gather evidence that it can indeed corrupt the process. With these efforts, a future Supreme Court may recognize the need to reassess the *Citizens United* ruling. Furthermore, when openings arise, we must all demand judges who are willing to apply more than the First Amendment to campaign finance questions. Political spending is also an "equal protection" issue, as those with more resources may gain disproportionate influence over our government. In *Harper v. Virginia Board of Elections* (1966), the Supreme Court majority struck down Virginia's poll tax for state elections, remarking, "A State violates the Equal Protection Clause of the Fourteenth Amendment to the U.S. Constitution whenever it makes the affluence of the voter or payment of any fee an electoral standard. Voter qualifications have no relation to wealth...."[24] It is hard to argue that the current rules do not confer an advantage to the wealthy. And if denying access to the polls on the basis of wealth is a violation of the Fourteenth Amendment's Equal Protection Clause, why should it be permissible to allow wealth to determine political influence more generally?

The federal courts *can* make the Constitution an asset—not an impediment—to political equality. Doing so does not require any more legal creativity than the courts often apply when interpreting other parts of the Constitution. Justices and judges must simply have the will to do it. Such initiative has existed in the past. In the *Harper* ruling, Justice William O. Douglas wrote, "The Equal Protection Clause is not shackled to the political theory of a particular era. In determining what lines are unconstitutionally discriminatory, we have never been confined to historic notions of equality, any more than we have restricted due process to a fixed catalogue of what was at a given time deemed to be the limits of fundamental rights. Notions of what constitutes equal treatment for purposes of the Equal Protection Clause do change."[25] This sort of thinking, if more widely shared by federal judges and justices today, could cure so many democratic ills in our system. It will not happen overnight, but it is essential that we prioritize the nomination and confirmation of judges with a willingness to view issues such as campaign finance as issues of inequality that have constitutional remedies. Given the monumental barriers to amending the Constitution, it may be our only hope.

CHAPTER 8

Growing Pains

In the preceding chapters, I have highlighted ways in which U.S. political institutions fail to embody the principle of political equality. I have placed particular emphasis on House and (especially) Senate malapportionment, the undemocratic Electoral College, disenfranchisement in D.C. and the territories, problems with Supreme Court appointments, voter suppression, and the excessive influence of wealthy donors. In each instance, the underlying issue is that electoral and governing institutions value some Americans over others. My proposed solutions to said problems have generally involved concrete changes to institutional structures or procedures—all of which would be achieved through laws, amendments, or court rulings. In this chapter, the problems I address are a bit different. Here, the focus is not the degree to which votes convert to power or the ease with which citizens can access the polls. Rather, Chapter 8 is devoted to the manner through which citizens obtain information to evaluate the political environment and participate in their democracy. While the right to vote is indeed sacred, citizens must also be able to collect and process objective facts in order to cast *informed* votes. If people operate with a distorted set of "truths," then the collective will they exercise at the polls will likely be a poor reflection of the country's needs and desires.

Anyone who even casually follows the news knows that political discourse in the U.S. has become entirely dysfunctional. Disagreements between the two major parties have been expanding for decades, while disgust with opposing opinions (and those who hold them) has multiplied. This "negative partisanship" has its roots in the social-cultural battles of the 1960s and 1970s.[1] As political scientist Lilliana Mason explains in *Uncivil Agreement* (2018), today's divisions are much deeper than policy disagreements; rather, they are embedded in racial, religious, and cultural identities that define how Americans see both themselves and their perceived opponents.[2] While it may not be the original source of this growing tribalism, political media has undoubtedly exacerbated pre-existing animosities between Democrats and Republicans. Many media companies, particularly those operating on the radio, internet, and cable news, advance biased, misleading, and entirely false information on a daily basis. Meanwhile, social media, which was once seen as a pro-democratic instrument, has become a tool for disseminating misinformation (false information) and disinformation (*deliberately* false information). On Twitter, Facebook, YouTube, and lesser-known sites across the web, messages often target vulnerable citizens at very low costs without attribution. Citizens already inclined to support a particular party or candidate can now satisfy their confirmation biases and opt into media realities that reinforce and harden their preexisting views. Comforted and reassured by affirmative coverage, citizens become less willing to consider alternative perspectives. Worse, information that demonstrates facts at odds with one's view is often discarded as fake or biased. The result is temporary reassurance, but also a deepening of rage and disillusionment towards alternative viewpoints.

Even those citizens who desire objective information about politics increasingly struggle to find it (or identify it when they do). Without reliable sources of facts, they become susceptible to misinformation and disinformation that bends, misleads, or fabricates political realities. In turn, conspiracy theories take hold, institutions (and their legitimacy) are more broadly questioned, and actual public policy discourse becomes buried behind mountains of nonsense.

Of course, there *are* objective truths. There *are* ideas that work. There *are* qualified candidates and effective policymakers. And there *are* some views at odds with reality. But in a world of confusion, distortion, and tribalism, citizens are struggling to recognize and accept basic facts that inform healthy debates. The result is that precious time is wasted on dispelling mistruths, officeholders are not held accountable, and, most importantly, political discourse is not generating positive change that tangibly improves the lives of Americans.

Tribalism Rising

It is difficult to understate the tectonic shift in American life that developed from social movements that emerged or gained steam during the 1960s and early 1970s. The Civil Rights Movement ended segregation and miscegenation bans, expanded voting rights, and even saw the federal government proactively seek to address past racial wrongs (e.g., through affirmative action). The Women's Liberation Movement led to a multitude of reforms that ended (legal) sex discrimination in the workplace, increased the rights of women in marriage and education, and legalized contraception and abortion. More generally, the movement fundamentally altered the way that many Americans viewed gender roles. During this same era, immigration was expanded, environmental awareness spiked, and LGBTQ+ Americans began to demand legal acceptance. Obscenity and pornography laws were loosened; the rights of the accused were expanded. The Supreme Court's ruling in *Engle v. Vitale* (1962), which banned prayer in public schools, highlighted broader changes in society regarding the separation of church and state.[3] And all of these changes occurred with the backdrop of the Vietnam War, a long, tragic conflict that led to years of protest across the country.

These developments, while sufficiently popular to produce change, were not accepted by everyone. Racism, of course, did not disappear. In fact, as rights for people of color expanded, many whites felt burdened and threatened. Consider the example of desegregation busing. Years after the Supreme Court banned segregated public schools in *Brown v. Board* (1954), many school districts in the U.S. continued to lack racial diversity.[4] As long as communities remained segregated, their neighborhood schools did as well. And because of systemic racism and economic inequality between the races, heavily white schools generally had more resources. Educational inequities between the races therefore continued. As the Civil Rights Movement advanced, many cities began instituting busing programs whereby Black students were driven to predominantly white schools in neighboring communities in order to create diverse schools. In *Swann v. Charlotte-Mecklenburg Board of Education* (1971), the Supreme Court upheld this practice.[5] Furthermore, federal courts began mandating that cities and towns institute busing as a remedy for continued segregation in their school systems. Many whites, including some who professed support for the Civil Rights Movement, vehemently opposed having their children attend integrated schools. Undoubtedly, some opposed busing plans because they were burdensome. Many students saw their school commute increase and were separated from their friends. For others, however, busing exposed latent feelings of racial hostility or anxiety (some would just call this *racism*). More white Americans began to feel as though the law was now geared towards addressing Black grievances without regard to their own.

Busing was not the only issue that generated backlash. Those with traditional attitudes regarding gender, religion, patriotism, abortion, and sexuality increasingly felt like strangers in their own country. During the mid–late 1970s, this angst became increasingly visible. Social conservatives organized against LGBTQ+ rights. Phyllis Schlafly's STOP ERA campaign helped defeat the once-popular Equal Rights Amendment, which would have enshrined equality for the sexes into the Constitution. Groups organized to ban controversial books, close pornographic theaters, and decry abortion. In 1979, with momentum for traditionalism growing, Jerry Falwell formed the Moral Majority, an influential interest group that would advocate for the views of religious conservatives. By the late 1970s, it was clear that the U.S. had entered what Republican presidential candidate Pat Buchanan later deemed a "culture war."[6]

Disagreements over cultural issues did not immediately overwhelm the party system in the U.S. The Democratic Party, while generally sympathetic to the progressive social causes of the 1960s and early 1970s, initially retained a large faction of southern conservatives and northern, working-class, white (often union) voters with more traditional social views. The Republican Party successfully consolidated the emergent Christian Right in the 1980 presidential election, though it also retained some northern and western social progressives with conservative economic views. The parties were big tents with plenty of crossover voters depending on the issue. Over the course of several decades, as cultural issues became more entrenched in the country's political discourse, social conservatives grew more favorable towards the Republican Party. Meanwhile, Democrats gained the support of many social progressives who had once identified as Republicans. The 2016 election has been called a "realigning" election, but this is misleading. The changes in partisan voting behavior that were observed in that election—mainly the movement of well-educated white voters towards Democrats and working-class white voters towards Republicans—had been gradually occurring since 1968. The 2016 race accelerated these changes, but things continued to move in the direction they had already been heading.

Today, the Democratic coalition consists of most non–whites, as well as urban and suburban whites with high levels of education. The Republican coalition is dominated by whites living in outer suburbs and rural communities. Democrats are highly progressive on both economic and cultural issues, while Republicans are decidedly conservative. Few pro-life, pro-gun Democrats remain, while Republicans in favor of government action to stem climate change are increasingly few. Some have defined this evolution of the parties as "sorting." It is not that society's divisions have changed, the theory goes, but rather that the parties now represent society's divisions more clearly.

Cultural issues are, by their nature, extremely divisive. They involve questions of identity, rights, faith, and morality—matters that are existential to the human experience. As such, disagreements about these issues tend to be passionate; compromises can be harder to reach than on economic questions. Imagine that two parties disagree about the minimum wage. One side believes it should be $20 an hour, while the other believes it should be $6 an hour. While it is easier said than done, a compromise can conceivably be reached somewhere in the middle. If it cannot be reached, the two sides need not hate one another over it. But now consider abortion policy. If one side believes abortion is a question of an individual's right to control her body, but the other believes a fetus is a human being entitled to the full rights of citizenship, there is not an obvious middle ground here. It is not hard to imagine why (1) the issue cannot be settled and (2) opposing sides can have animosity towards those who disagree. The same passionate debates (with little room for compromise) also surround issues such as LGBTQ+ rights, the role of prayer in school, the rights of women to serve in combat, and racial justice.

A Changing Media Landscape

The emergence of new media technology has helped the aforementioned differences develop into political tribalism. While it is not my intention to fully document the history of political media over the past several decades, it is worthwhile to highlight some notable developments.

Between 1949–1987, the federal government enforced the Fairness Doctrine, a policy that required any network using the national broadcast spectrum (e.g., network television, radio) to present news in a manner free of partisan or ideological bias. For much of this period, television was limited to three major broadcast networks—NBC, ABC, and CBS. The news that Americans received through these networks was comparatively dry by today's standards, but generally informative and not designed to inflame tensions or bias one's position. Americans learned about the Kennedy assassination, the Vietnam War, the Civil Rights Movement, and most of the Cold War via outlets regulated by objectivity standards. In 1987, however, the Fairness Doctrine was terminated; by this time, cable television (which does not use the broadcast spectrum) had emerged, making the regulation increasingly obsolete.

Without objectivity requirements, talk radio emerged as a major source of political commentary. Launching in 1988, *The Rush Limbaugh Show* would have 20 million weekly listeners by the 1990s. The program was light on news, but heavy on conservative talk. Limbaugh blasted Gulf War protesters in 1991 and, during and after the 1992 election, President Bill Clinton on a daily basis. Until his death in 2021, he routinely portrayed progressives as unpatriotic fools who hate freedom and the military, but love nothing more than undocumented immigrants and political correctness. He called those interested in women's rights "feminazis,"[7] while former Secretary of State Hillary Clinton was the "Hilldebeast." Racist stereotypes were advanced; Black basketball players were called "thugs,"[8] while former President Barack Obama was once referred to as "Barack, the magic negro."[9] Limbaugh's radio program, like others that followed, appealed to the worst instincts of its listeners. It inflamed emotions and directed listeners to blame politicians, the media, political correctness, multiculturalism, and coastal elites for all of their problems (and perhaps some they did not know existed).

Progressive talk radio programs are also polarizing, but they have never been as popular as *The Rush Limbaugh Show* or others featuring prominent conservative hosts (such as Glenn Beck and Laura Ingraham). Air America Radio experienced a surge in popularity at the height of the George W. Bush administration in the mid–2000s, helping to launch the careers of future MSNBC host Rachel Maddow and Senator Al Franken of Minnesota. But its success was short-lived. Political talk radio has always been most popular with older, white citizens, a population more inclined to share conservative viewpoints.

The era of cable news began with the launch of CNN in 1980, but the medium arguably did not become a force in political media until the 1990s. During that decade, CNN's popularity surged after its unparalleled coverage of the Persian Gulf War. By the end of the decade, more cable channels devoted to news had emerged. Both MSNBC and Fox News launched in 1996; before long, each would play central roles in the emerging culture war.

Fox News, which launched in 1998 as a "fair and balanced" alternative to a supposed "liberal media," positioned itself as a defender of conservative values and politicians. By the 2010s, the network's principal function was to degrade progressives, incite and exploit social divisions, and (after his 2016 election) blindly defend the statements and actions of President Donald Trump. Through creative headlines, scary graphics, and misleading soundbites, the day's news is typically framed to present Democrats as evil, incompetent, and unpatriotic; meanwhile, Republicans are treated as soldiers in the battle to defend traditional values and social structures. Studies have repeatedly shown that Fox viewers are disproportionately likely to believe empirical falsehoods. In 2003, a study by the Program on International Policy Attitudes (PIPA) at the University of Maryland's School of Public Affairs found that 67 percent of Fox News Channel viewers believed that the "U.S. has found clear evidence in Iraq that Saddam Hussein was working closely with the al Qaeda terrorist organization." By comparison, just 48 percent of CNN viewers and 16 percent of NPR/PBS viewers believed this false statement.[10] A 2010 Stanford

University survey found that "more exposure to Fox News was associated with more rejection of mainstream scientists' claims about global warming, [and] with less trust in scientists."[11] With regard to the Covid-19 outbreak, a 2020 study found that those who relied on Fox News and radio hosts such as Rush Limbaugh were more likely to believe in conspiracy theories or unfounded rumors. These included the beliefs that taking vitamin C could prevent the infection, that the Chinese government had created the virus, and that the U.S. Centers for Disease Control and Prevention (CDC) exaggerated the pandemic's threat "to damage the Trump presidency."[12]

Since the mid–2000s, MSNBC has functioned as a counter to Fox News on cable television. Programs such as *Countdown with Keith Olbermann* (2003–2011), *The Rachel Maddow Show*, and *The Last Word with Lawrence O'Donnell* have a notable progressive bias. Those who tune into these programs already inclined to oppose Republican positions only see their anger, frustration, and bewilderment increase.

Research indicates that MSNBC and CNN viewers, much like Fox viewers, have an underwhelming degree of political knowledge. A 2012 Fairleigh Dickinson survey found that when respondents were asked to answer five objective questions about the previous week's domestic news, MSNBC and CNN viewers were able to answer just 1.26 questions (on average) correctly. This was higher than the 1.04 questions that the average Fox viewer successfully answered, but less than NPR (1.51), Sunday talk show (1.47), or even *The Daily Show* (1.42) loyalists did. Notably, Fox viewers had even less knowledge than those who watched "no news" (1.22), while MSNBC and CNN viewers barely eclipsed this group. The study controlled for education and other demographic variables, lending confidence that the results were indeed due to exposure to particular networks.[13]

There is no more consequential recent change to the American media landscape, or perhaps simply American society, than the internet. Much has been said and written about the internet's effect on our lives. For our purposes, I simply wish to highlight some of its most notable effects on the political information environment. Given its conveniences, most Americans now obtain news online. According to a 2019 Pew study, 89 percent of adults get "at least some" news online; a majority get some news from social media sites specifically.[14] The numbers are, predictably, even higher among younger Americans. *News*, of course, is in the eye of the beholder. For some, *news* may refer to CNN.com or Yahoo.com stories. To others, it may mean posts from a political organization such as the League of Conservation Voters or the National Rifle Association. *News* can be tweets from a popular (or even not-so-popular) Twitter handle, or even political advertisements appearing before YouTube videos. The internet is not a monolithic news source; it is different for everyone.

The internet has fundamentally changed how most Americans consume information. While its effects are many, there are some particularly obvious ones. First, there is infinitely more information available. In the early 1990s, Americans had access to limited television news, their local newspapers, perhaps a few national newspapers, and magazines to which they subscribed. The internet provides access to nearly anything published anywhere by anyone. Second, information is now immediately available. The idea of a "news cycle" is basically obsolete. News is constantly flowing and changing. Third, the internet is far more anarchic than traditional media. Through a blog, a Twitter handle, or a phone camera, anyone can effectively be a political reporter and attract large audiences. Relatedly, the internet has almost no standards for credibility. While traditional media outlets generally wish to maintain legitimacy so that they can continue credibly reporting in the future, many online sources operate either anonymously or without much overhead. On the internet, the consequences of poor reporting are often minimal or even non-existent.[15]

Getting news from social media sites is an increasingly common experience

% of U.S. adults who get news on social media sites ...

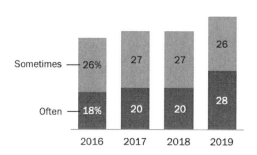

Sometimes — 26% | 27 | 27 | 26
Often — 18% | 20 | 20 | 28

2016 2017 2018 2019

A July 2019 study from the Pew Research Center found that over half (54 percent) of Americans now receive news from social media websites (see "Americans Are Wary of the Role Social Media Sites Play in Delivering the News," Pew Research Center, Washington, D.C. [Oct. 2, 2019]. *https://www.journalism.org/2019/10/02/americans-are-wary-of-the-role-social-media-sites-play-in-delivering-the-news/*).

So, what does the internet's emergence mean for Americans consuming political information? First, many traditional outlets—particularly newspapers—have been forced to close. Since 2004, at least 1,800 newspapers have been shuttered in the U.S.[16] In 2018, newspaper circulation fell to its lowest level since 1940.[17] While nearly all newspapers place their content online, many were slow to require paywalls on their websites. Advertising dollars online could not match the loss in subscription fees at most papers, causing a revenue crisis. And while many newspapers now have online paywalls, many Americans are not eager to pay when so much content remains online at no cost. The results are unfortunate for democracy. Newspapers were once the primary source of investigative journalism— the sort of reporting that is best able to monitor those in power. As newspapers close, or reduce their investigative budgets and staffs, this essential democratic tool is lost. One technology developer commented in 2020, "The decline of newspapers … has had a quantifiable effect on governmental oversight."[18]

As Americans turn to the internet for news, they enter the digital equivalent of a stereotypical Wall Street scene from so many 1980s films— lots of screaming voices, pushing and shoving, and a sense that no one is in charge. Make no mistake—excellent reporting and analysis *can* be found online. Traditional outlets that have survived the changing media landscape, such as *The New York Times, The Washington Post, The Wall Street Journal, The Economist, The Financial Times,* and *The Atlantic,* routinely produce objective, well-researched content. Online-only outlets such as *Vox, Slate,* and *The American Prospect* uphold traditional journalistic standards and offer thoughtful commentary. The speed and volume of online information, however, makes it difficult for the most thorough, objective content to emerge and be digested. As freelance writer and meditation teacher Michael Taft remarked, "In a normal working day in modern America, there's a sense of so much coming at you at once, so much to process that you just can't deal with it all."[19]

The proliferation of fake content on the web exacerbates this problem. Stories that appear in search results or on social media sites can look credible, but simply be the creation of domestic or foreign actors interested in spreading disinformation. Russian efforts during the 2016 presidential election are well-documented. Before, during, and after the election, Russia's Internet Research Agency created thousands of social media accounts designed to discredit Hillary Clinton and boost Donald Trump's candidacy. In doing so, they reached at least 126 million Americans on Facebook, 20 million on Instagram, and 1.4 million on Twitter.[20] Russia, who continued its efforts during the 2018 and 2020 elections, is not the only source of false or misleading information on the web. Countries like China and Iran have also sought to influence American politics through disinformation online, while domestic sources of fake news are also prevalent. In 2020, U.S. social media users spread various conspiracy theories and incorrect claims regarding vote-by-mail (VBM) options. Experts have noted that hostile foreign actors do not need to create their own fake information, but rather can simply amplify that developed within the U.S.[21]

One troubling example of domestic disinformation—further

promulgated by Russia—is the QAnon conspiracy. In October 2017, an anonymous post appeared on 4chan, an online imageboard site. The poster, Q Clearance Patriot (or later simply Q), claimed to be a high-level government official with Q clearance—a U.S. Department of Energy clearance required to access information on nuclear weapons. Over time, Q's posts spouted various conspiracy theories. Notably, Q alleged that powerful Democrats and other global elites were Satan-worshipping cannibals involved in a worldwide sex-trafficking ring.[22] Q claimed that those involved included (but were not limited to) President Joe Biden, former President Barack Obama, and former Secretary of State Hillary Clinton, as well as Hollywood celebrities such as Oprah Winfrey, Tom Hanks, and Ellen DeGeneres. According to the discredited conspiracy, former President Donald Trump was recruited by top military generals to run for president in 2016 in order to expose and end the aforementioned sex-trafficking ring.

Beginning in November 2017, just one month after Q first posted, Russia began actively spreading the conspiracy on the internet in an effort to build legitimacy for it. It appears as though its efforts may have worked. While the QAnon conspiracy strikes most Americans as absurd and reckless, it has gained millions of supporters. In fact, a December 2020 poll revealed that 17 percent of Americans believed that "a group of Satan-worshiping elites who run a child sex ring are trying to control our politics and media."[23] And when insurrectionists stormed the U.S. Capitol on January 6, 2021, in protest of Donald Trump's defeat in the 2020 election, a common theme emerged among those arrested—loyalty to QAnon.

Beyond QAnon, the internet is responsible for the spread of countless falsehoods. In a sobering 2018 study, three MIT researchers found that false stories are 70 percent more likely to be retweeted on Twitter than true stories. Moreover, they discovered that true stories take about six times(!) as long to reach 1,500 people as false stories do.[24] It is perhaps not surprising that a 2020 Pew study found that just 17 percent of those who primarily obtain their news from social media have "high political knowledge," compared to 45 percent of those who rely on traditional news websites and 35 percent of those who rely mostly on cable television.[25] James S. O'Rourke IV, a University of Notre Dame professor, blames citizens for not being more discerning information consumers online. He writes, "People will simply not seek out, read or take time to understand positions they do not understand…. A sizeable majority now live with a thin collection of facts, distorted information and an insufficient cognitive base from which to make a thoughtful decision. Accurate information is no longer driving out false ideas, propaganda, innuendo or deceit."[26] Larry Rosen, a professor emeritus of psychology at California State University-Dominguez Hills, agrees, writing, "I worry that many in the public ... do not have the skills to determine truth from fiction, and twisted truth can and does lead to misunderstanding the content."[27] These are valid criticisms, but *why* do so many citizens fall victim to misleading information online? I would argue that there are two fundamental reasons. First, given the nature of polarization in U.S. politics, some *want* to hear information that validates their passionately held views. Second, citizens often lack the necessary skills to find and distill accurate information on the web. Both causes are worthy of deeper investigation.

Many citizens fail to navigate the complex information environment because they have political biases that make agreeable content appealing, regardless of whether it is accurate. More bluntly, not all Americans are interested in seeking out the truth. Confirmation bias, or the tendency to search for, interpret, favor, and recall information in a way that confirms or supports one's prior beliefs or values, is not new. However, the internet offers unprecedented opportunities to satisfy such cravings. And in a nation where polarization was already an emerging reality before the internet, the temptation is often too strong to resist. Much like talk radio and cable news, the internet allows us to choose our own realities. We can follow a particular set of people on Twitter who will report the news in the manner we prefer. We can block opinions we detest. We can choose the blogs we read, the organizations that send us email updates, and the groups that we "like" on Facebook. In doing so, citizens can spend hours online each day absorbing a perspective of the world entirely different from someone down the street, or even down the hall. Rey Junco, director of research at CIRCLE at Tufts University, notes, "Individuals who get their news online choose media outlets that are ideologically similar and rarely read news from the opposing side."[28]

Junco notes that this sorting is exacerbated by the "algorithmic curation of feeds that promote ideological separation." Online marketing, including that by political groups and candidates, relies on individual data to target messages to web users. Everyone knows that when you search for a product online, you suddenly see banner ads and YouTube ads for similar products. The same data mechanisms are in place regarding politics. Those who are identified as potential supporters of a candidate or group are targeted with ads reinforcing these positions and advocating for related causes. Doing so helps raise money, enthusiasm, and political engagement for campaigns, causes, and groups. If someone visits the NRA's website or purchases a firearm, for example, it makes sense for Republican candidates to target this person with online ads. By doing so, however, citizens become further entrenched into their information silos. As Richard Forno, assistant director of the Center for Cybersecurity at the University of Maryland–Baltimore County, writes, "[Technology] … will continue to reinforce echo chambers that disallow acknowledgment of, let alone tolerance of, alternative views, new discoveries, facts and/or realities. This will contribute to further tribalism among citizens and also be reflected in the views/actions of their elected officials."[29] Yaakov J. Stein of RAD Data Communications agrees, adding "…advertising (and disinformation) is targeted at and tailored to people according to their preexisting views. This strengthens these preexisting views, reinforces disparagement of those with opposing views and weakens the possibility of being exposed to opposing views." Stein offers a sobering conclusion for democracy, noting, "The result is that free press no longer encourages democracy by enabling people to select from a marketplace of ideas." Not only does the internet fail to encourage the collection and distillation of competing ideas, but because it is fast, voluminous, and free, it also reduces the amount of traditional media that citizens consume. The result, as we have discussed, is often the "bankruptcy of traditional news outlets that spend resources on fact-checking" and the proliferation of biased sources that incite political righteousness and polarization.[30]

While polarization is a powerful deterrent to seeking objective truth, many Americans who seek accurate information are unable to find it. It would be easy to conclude that these citizens are merely gullible or lacking in intellectual curiosity. In some cases, this may be true. But the reality is more complicated. First, many Americans who believe that they are unaffected by biased news are fooling themselves. In fact, it is often the people with the narrowest information networks that are most self-righteous about knowing the truth. Second, it is worth noting that the internet age is still relatively young. Many Americans were not raised in a world where they were required to distill news for accuracy. Doing so is not a skill easily acquired, particularly when dealing with a medium that one learned in (sometimes late) adulthood. And even for younger Americans who cannot recall a time before the internet, navigating the web for accurate, objective reporting is very difficult.

Reform

When I teach the now-defunct Fairness Doctrine to undergraduates, many are simply amazed that such a thing ever existed. The idea that media objectivity was once enforced by the federal government seems so at odds with modern society. When I ask students if they believe some version of the Fairness Doctrine should be reinstated (and applied to the internet), opinions vary. Some express concerns about restricting free speech, but a majority of the class usually supports the idea in theory. Their reasoning is consistent and clear. Students yearn for objective information about politics and government—something that has been hard to find during their lifetimes (and most of mine).

Truthfully, it is not likely that the Fairness Doctrine will be reinstated or applied to the internet. In upholding its constitutionality in *Red Lion Broadcasting Co., Inc. v. FCC* (1969), the Supreme Court made it clear that the policy was acceptable because the broadcast spectrum—used by radio and television networks—was "scarce." As a result, it was acceptable for the federal government to require "suitable time and attention to matters of great public concern," as well as a fair discussion of various viewpoints.[31] Today, no such scarcity exists. There are no longer significant barriers to expressing an idea through television, radio, or the internet. A new Fairness Doctrine would likely be struck down as a violation of the First Amendment. While the policy served its time well, the challenges caused by the twenty-first-century information environment require new solutions.

Of those challenges, the internet is certainly the most vexing, as its troubling features are likely to persist. In the years to come, the internet will continue to present us with overwhelming volumes of content, making it difficult to sort through noise and find clarity. It is unlikely that online content will ever be free of biased, misleading, or even false information. Users will retain the power to enter and remain within information silos that promote confirmation bias. There is no use decrying these realities or fooling ourselves to believe otherwise. The internet—and social media in particular—is here to stay. The challenge is not deemphasizing these platforms; rather, it is finding ways to improve the information environment in light of them. This task is both formidable and critical. Citizens cannot be qualified democratic participants without easy means to accurate information about public affairs.

Removing all politically or ideologically biased content is not a realistic (or even desirable) option. People have a right to express, read, and share opinions. But there are steps that Congress could take to better regulate the information environment. First, Congress should demand that foreign governments seeking to influence U.S. politics be banned from social media platforms. Second, using its power to regulate interstate commerce, Congress can require far greater transparency regarding the collection and monetization of user data, as well as suspected violations of state and federal law on internet platforms. Finally, lawmakers must hold online companies accountable for the content appearing on their platforms. Under U.S. law, television and radio stations must abide by FCC restrictions regarding obscene, indecent, or slanderous material. Social media firms, however, claim that because they do not create their own content (as television and radio stations do), they are not responsible for what appears on their sites. In their view, companies such as Twitter, Facebook, and Google are merely "platforms for free speech" and are therefore exempt from regulations that govern traditional media outlets. Federal law actually codifies this exemption; under Section 230 of the Communications Decency Act (CDA), private online service providers are free from liability for content posted on their sites, with some notable exceptions (e.g., child pornography, human trafficking).

Of course, social media companies *do* effectively create content because they decide what individual users see on their sites. Through complicated algorithms, online firms collect personal data and determine which ads or posts we can view. Even though they are automated, these decisions are editorial in nature. Designing an algorithm that connects a story to a user is comparable to deciding whether to run an op-ed in Sunday's newspaper or lead a television newscast with a story. The difference is that online decisions are "narrowcasted," or made on an individual level, rather than for all consumers at once—so-called "broadcasting."

Given their power to bring content to users, social media companies should be subject to regulations similar to those governing other forms of media. Obviously, any new regulatory framework will need to accommodate the realities of the internet. No company can be expected to immediately flag every single post that violates the rules. But the law should require that firms have an effective process in place to swiftly find and remove illegal content. The Platform Accountability and Consumer Transparency (PACT) Act—a bipartisan bill sponsored by Senators Brian Schatz of Hawaii and John Thune of South Dakota in 2021—would (among other provisions) strip Section 230 protections from tech companies that fail to remove content after a judicial order finds it illegal. A more ambitious bill, the SAFE TECH Act—introduced by Senators Mark Warner of Virginia, Amy Klobuchar of Minnesota, and Mazie Hirono of Hawaii in 2021— would ensure that Section 230 protections do not extend to advertisements or other paid content. A tech company would therefore be fully liable for any content for which it is receiving compensation. In addition, the bill would subject tech companies to some civil liability in court. Victims of cyberstalking, harassment, and discrimination on a platform would have the right to sue for damages, while families could bring actions if a platform's content contributed to a relative's death.[32]

It is important, however, to be realistic regarding the power of regulation. Even if Congress takes the above actions—which I believe are sensible—we are not returning to the days of Walter Cronkite telling Americans "the way it is." Information overload is here to stay. Politically-biased content will continue to have a place on a multitude of radio stations, cable television channels, internet blogs, and social media platforms. If users wish to find political content that confirms their preexisting biases, they will be able to locate it. Social media sites will continue to allow (actually, encourage) like-minded people to interact, build networks, and share ideas. No law will be able to (or should) require people to seek objective information or engage with those for whom they disagree.

If the information environment is to be improved in the twenty-first century, change will mostly need to be driven by citizens themselves. First, citizens must demand that tech companies voluntarily adopt better measures to police their platforms. The First Amendment sets a high bar when it comes to government policing of media companies. While the government could better regulate criminal activity on social media sites (as discussed above), most content—even biased content—cannot be censored. But if customers demand that companies take proactive steps to improve the quality of information on their platforms—through flagging biased content, removing unverified accounts, or performing fact-checking—tech firms will be forced to oblige on their own. This is not entirely hypothetical. Over the past few years, major platforms have already improved their processes in response to public demands. Twitter banned all political ads, began flagging (though not removing) inaccurate statements tweeted by President Trump and others, and deleted billions of tweets (via its artificial intelligence censors) that violated site policy. And in 2021, after he instigated the January 6 storming of the U.S. Capitol, Trump was banned from Twitter entirely. Meanwhile, Facebook has given users the option to block political ads, while YouTube has changed its algorithm so that authoritative sources are more likely to appear in searches. These tech firms did not take these initial actions out of the goodness of their hearts. They are businesses—just like oil, pharmaceutical, and airline companies. They took these steps because there was clear dissatisfaction with the status quo. A 2019 survey indicated that 57 percent of Americans agree that social media sites "do more to divide the country," while 55 percent believe they "do more to spread lies and falsehoods."[33] In a separate survey, 72 percent of U.S. adults said social media companies have "too much power and influence in politics," while 47 percent thought the government "should be regulating major technology companies more than it is now."[34] It is this sort of public awareness that has pressured—and must continue to pressure—social media firms to regulate the worst excesses of their content.

Second, we (citizens) must all challenge ourselves to become more effective consumers of political information. It is not enough to follow politics and news. We need to know where to find accurate information, how to discern opinion from fact, and always challenge conclusions presented to us. We must treat "media literacy," or the ability to critically evaluate the information we encounter, as a fundamental tenet of twenty-first-century democratic citizenship.

While media literacy is essential for all citizens, education can play a vital role in addressing this challenge for today's youth. When I was in school, there was little focus on digesting and evaluating news. Instead, we were simply encouraged to "be informed." We were asked to watch prominent speeches, read a newspaper, and substitute an occasional sitcom with a half-hour television news broadcast. In those days, doing so was assumed to provide a certain level of civic awareness. And to a large extent, this was true. Today, this will not cut it. "Being informed" in the twenty-first century requires a broader set of tools.

First, it is more important than ever that students learn the basics of how their system of government operates, as well as the rights and responsibilities of citizenship (i.e., civics). When civic education is absent, misinformation is more easily able to infiltrate minds. According to a 2016 survey conducted by the Annenberg Public Policy Center, only 26 percent of Americans can name the three branches of government (down from 38 percent as recently as 2011). That same year, only 23 percent of eighth-graders were deemed proficient on the National Assessment of Educational Progress (NAEP) civics exam, a level unchanged since 1998.[35] It is notable that despite nearly two decades of the internet (and the vast information it offers), no improvement in civics scores has been observed. Kathleen Hall Jamieson, director of the Annenberg Center, commented, "Lack of basic civics knowledge is worrisome and an argument for an increased focus on civics education in the schools."[36] I agree! Today, only nine states and the District of Columbia require one year of U.S. government or civics. Thirty-one states require a half-year, while ten states have no civics requirement. In recent decades, federal education policy has focused disproportionately on improving academic achievement in reading and math, often at the expense of subjects like civics.

When citizens have a baseline of civics knowledge stored away, new information can be more easily and quickly digested, bias can be detected, and disinformation can be discarded. Conversely, conspiracy theories thrive when people are unaware of how institutions operate. For example, once someone knows the nature of presidential power, it is easier to ignore stories claiming that the president can unilaterally raise taxes, end Social Security, or institute Sharia Law. Once someone understands the role of the Supreme Court in affecting policy, news about a pending case or judicial opinion can be more easily distilled. Understanding the main ideological differences between the political parties helps one comprehend how and why each advances particular policies when in power.

When I reflect on my K–12 experience, I generally had committed, talented instructors. However, I must say that little time was spent on basic civics. I actually never took a course on American government until college! In both middle-school and high-school, history was prioritized over government or civics. I learned more about explorers, pyramids, and wars than the separation of powers, federalism, or constitutional law. I surely knew more about Civil War generals and battle casualties than presidential emergency powers, the filibuster, or malapportionment. In my case and many others, civics was simply something that was incorporated into our history courses. I believe this is unwise. The demands of twenty-first-century citizenship require a sound understanding of the foundations and processes of government. Civics education must be required at *both* the middle-school and secondary education levels. Finding instructors for such courses should not be difficult; today there are a multitude of high-quality political scientists who cannot find jobs in an increasingly tight higher education market.

Colorado is one state that has prioritized civics education in its schools. All Colorado high schools must teach one year of civics. According to a report by the Center for American Progress, "teachers are expected to cover the origins of democracy, the structure of American government, methods of public participation, a comparison to foreign governments, and the responsibilities of citizenship."[37] Other states would be wise to consider this impressive model.

Of course, it is not enough to simply require classes. Instruction at all levels must meet today's demands. In addition to understanding the functions and processes of government, students must learn how citizens can actively participate in the process. High schools should prepare students to register to vote, as well as embed civic activities into their curricula. By attending local town meetings, public demonstrations, and candidate debates, students can gain a more direct and objective understanding of government than Fox News or MSNBC will provide. Finally, all American government instruction should explicitly include discussions about the modern information environment, noting the sorts of challenges discussed in this chapter. Simple awareness of the problem (and its causes) can make students more alert to bias and misinformation when consuming political news. Today's students desperately seek guidance on where and how to find quality, objective information. Instructors can help by providing lists of sources that have been evaluated by independent media observers and deemed to be fair and informative.

Instructors at all levels can also develop exercises to build media literacy skills. When I first began teaching undergraduates, I would often assign readings about current events to make political science concepts relatable to students. In recent years, I have begun assigning multiple readings (and videos) covering particular events—all from distinct sources with different frames. Doing so ensures that students will be exposed to a diverse set of perspectives. In addition, rather than simply asking students to read and recall content from the assigned material, I challenge them to evaluate each source in an effort to identify its biases. In particular, I ask students to consider the following five questions (or sets of questions) after reading or viewing each story:

- Who wrote this story? If we can tell, what is their professional background? Do they have a history of advocating for certain sorts of positions?
- How is the author trying to attract our attention? Does it appear that the piece is designed to scare, confuse, amuse, or anger us?
- Why was this story written? Does it appear that the creator is seeking to advance particular positions?
- What conclusions does the story reach? What supporting evidence is being used to persuade us that these positions are correct?
- Is any important information missing from the story? Would (or could) someone else tell the same story differently?

The purpose of this exercise is not to dissuade students from reading or viewing any particular media sources. There is nothing wrong with consuming political opinion pieces or commentary; I read and view plenty of this material. I *do believe* it is important, however, to understand the nature of the media one is ingesting. The assignment above is designed to provide students with a model for evaluating the information they encounter. By no means is this the only set of questions that can achieve this goal. But in the years that I have challenged students to actively evaluate news sources, they have responded exceptionally well. Many have commented that they now approach information with more apprehensive eyes, with some noting that they now try to find several articles from credible sources when reading about a topic. Students will not remember all of the content we cover in class. But if exercises such as this can help them discern bias from news stories, then they will have acquired an invaluable skill for the duration of their lives as democratic citizens.

Of course, democratic education need not be limited to classroom settings. In ways big and small, we can all play a role in restoring truth and objectivity to our political debates. We can force ourselves to read high-quality news sources that we know are not designed to confirm biases. We can challenge our family and friends to do the same. We can consult sites like FactCheck.org to verify claims made by a candidate or officeholder. And we can take some time to consider the details and nuances of public policy issues—*even just one issue*—rather than spending hours reading and writing snarky political comments on Twitter or our other favorite social media sites.

The stakes are high. Functioning democracies require informed citizens to deliberate and reach conclusions on collective challenges. But if we are unable (or unwilling) to acquire the basic objective facts needed to engage political debates, then it becomes very difficult for public deliberations (and their outcomes) to reflect our collective will.

Conclusion

It is certainly not a revelation that the government created at the Philadelphia Convention in 1787 was not particularly democratic. While genuinely advanced for its time, it disenfranchised most Americans and empowered just a relative few. Slavery was permitted and accommodated, while voting rights were left unprotected. States choosing to deny the vote to free Blacks, women, and non-landowners were allowed to do so. While the House would be popularly elected, neither the malapportioned Senate—the more powerful of the two congressional chambers—nor the president would be. In the 1796 election—the first contested presidential contest in U.S. history—as few as 67,000 Americans cast ballots in a country of over 4 million people.[1] In an age before dinosaur science, the combustible engine, or general anesthetics, it should not surprise us that the Framers created a government incompatible with modern conceptions of human or political equality.

Arguably, the Constitution has retained its legitimacy for two reasons. First, despite its notable flaws, the document *did* articulate a bold democratic vision. This has allowed reformers to credibly claim that their pro-democratic stances and actions are consistent with the Constitution. Second, the Constitution has proven able to accommodate new demands through both formal amendments and new interpretations. While some in the legal community lament this fact, the Constitution has always been a "living" document.

Regarding its democratic vision, the Constitution famously begins with the following preamble:

> We the People of the United States, in Order to form a more perfect Union, establish Justice, insure domestic Tranquility, provide for the common defence, promote the general Welfare, and secure the Blessings of Liberty to ourselves and our Posterity, do ordain and establish this Constitution for the United States of America.

The Preamble is clear that "the people" are clearly in the driver's seat. The Constitution does not deem that *wealthy* people, *white* people, *educated* people, *kind* people, or *pretty* people are privileged in their capacity to choose a government. The term "the people" most logically means *all* people, much like "the teachers," "the farmers," and "the children" refers to all members of these respective groups unless otherwise noted.

The Constitution is not the only founding document with ambitious democratic assertions. The Declaration of Independence, drafted 11 years earlier, consists mostly of grievances against the British Crown. But it also boldly advances the notion of popular sovereignty. In asserting that "all men are created equal" and that "governments are instituted among Men, deriving their just powers from the consent of the governed," Thomas Jefferson laid the groundwork for a democratic society in 1776. Accepting the antiquated use of "men" rather than "people," the Declaration asserts that citizens have an equal right to choose a government that will—through the acquisition and exercise of power—represent their collective interests.

Of course, let's not kid ourselves. The Framers did not *intend* for the Declaration or the Constitution to confer political equality to all (or even most) adults. Many owned slaves, few believed that the voting rolls should include Blacks or women, and most had misgivings about citizens—even white men—directly choosing representatives. But because the documents reference the idea of a more inclusive, egalitarian democracy, they have consistently served as a north star for forward-looking citizens willing to challenge their country to better meet its lofty ideals. The examples are plentiful. At the 1848 Seneca Falls Convention, the first organized effort to advance equality for American women, the second paragraph of the Declaration of Sentiments merely added the words "and women" to the Constitution's Preamble. The Constitution, the attendees determined, was not flawed in its wisdom that citizens are entitled to "ordain and establish" any government that holds power over them; it just needed tweaks to apply to women.

Three years later, writing in *The North Star*, Frederick Douglass argued that the Constitution has "anti-slavery implications." Citing the Preamble, he noted that—despite its Three-Fifths Clause and implicit endorsement of bondage—the Constitution was not an impediment to freedom. Rather, it was a powerful "instrument" that could be "wielded on behalf of emancipation." Douglass also argued that the Article I clause terminating the slave trade in 1808 "showed that the intentions of the framers of the Constitution were good, not bad." The Framers, he believed, "looked to the abolition of slavery rather than to its perpetuity."[2] Douglass's argument was rather charitable to the Framers, but the Constitution included enough hints at equality to make his position credible.

On November 19, 1863, Abraham Lincoln delivered his famous Gettysburg Address at the site of the bloody Civil War battle that had taken place just four months earlier. Beginning his remarks with the iconic phrase, "Four score and seven years ago" (a reference to the Declaration), he noted that the nation was "conceived in Liberty, and dedicated to the proposition that all men are created equal." The Civil War, Lincoln argued, was not a refutation of the Declaration, but rather a test of whether the nation would rise to the occasion and move closer to its essential vision. He continued, "this nation, under God, shall have a new birth of freedom," pledging that "government of the people, by the people, for the people, shall not perish from the earth." The abolition of slavery did not defy our founding principles, Lincoln argued; rather, it helped to actualize them.

A century later, Supreme Court Chief Justice Earl Warren drafted the majority opinion in *Reynolds v. Sims* (1964), one of the most pro-democracy opinions ever written by the High Court. While the ruling declared that malapportioned legislatures were at odds with the Fourteenth Amendment's Equal Protection Clause, Warren went a step further in justifying the decision. He wrote, "The concept of 'we the people' under the Constitution visualizes no preferred class of voters, but equality among those who meet the basic qualifications. The idea that every voter is equal to every other voter in his State, when he casts his ballot in favor of one of several competing candidates, underlies many of our decisions."[3] It was not simply the Fourteenth Amendment, ratified in 1868, that deemed malapportionment at odds with the Constitution; rather, it was the preamble of the original document itself. In the sentences that followed, Warren doubled down. He added that, "The conception of political equality from the Declaration of Independence, to Lincoln's Gettysburg Address, to the Fifteenth, Seventeenth, and Nineteenth Amendments can mean only one thing—one person, one vote." For Warren and the Court's majority, granting disproportionate power to some citizens was at odds with various amendments to the Constitution, as well as the vision expressed in documents as old as the Declaration.

The Constitution has also proven durable because of its capacity for change. While it is extremely hard to amend, many of the Constitution's worst democratic defects have been corrected through the amendment process. The Thirteenth Amendment banned slavery, while the Fourteenth Amendment guaranteed "equal protection" under the law. The Fifteenth, Nineteenth, and Twenty-Sixth Amendments barred voting rights from being denied on the basis of race, sex, or age (for those at least 18 years of age), respectively. The Seventeenth Amendment provided for the direct election of senators, while the Twenty-Third Amendment gave the District of Columbia voting rights in presidential elections. In some cases, most notably voting rights for Blacks, additional congressional action—sanctioned by the Constitution—has been needed to fortify essential protections.

Because the amendment process is often insurmountable, the Constitution has also relied on evolving interpretations of its words to remain legitimate. Driven by courageous advocates, the Warren Court (in 1954) could read the same Constitution as the Fuller Court (in 1896) and determine that segregated schools are actually at odds with it. The Court, recognizing in the late 1930s that more government regulation of business was necessary, could apply the Interstate Commerce Clause more broadly than previous courts. And when the Women's Liberation Movement became a political force in the late 1960s and early 1970s, the Constitution provided leeway for courts to broaden the Equal Protection Clause to restrict (though not yet eliminate) gender discrimination.

After escaping slavery in Maryland, Frederick Douglass became a leading figure in the abolitionist movement. In advocating for change, Douglass believed that the Constitution could be a positive force for both liberation and equality (U.S. Department of State, CC PDM 1.0: *https://creativecommons. org/publicdomain/mark/1.0/*).

Unfinished Business

Through formal constitutional amendments, legislative acts, and court interpretations, the U.S. has gradually—if painfully slowly—moved closer to political equality. But as I have documented in the preceding chapters, much work remains. Malapportionment in the Senate gives some citizens nearly 70 times as much influence in the upper chamber as others. The Electoral College weighs small state residents almost four times as much as large state residents; as a result, the country occasionally gets presidents that it does not want. Worse, malapportionment in both the Senate and the Electoral College is growing, owing to the expanding population disparity between large and small states. Partisan gerrymandering in the House—currently allowed by the federal courts—has also worsened considerably in the twenty-first century, providing a clear advantage to Republican voters in shaping the lower chamber.

While voting has become easier for many citizens due to expanded early voting and eased registration rules in many states, citizens remain burdened by unnecessary photo identification requirements, voter purges, long lines, and confusing procedures. Disenfranchisement is even worse in the District of Columbia and the U.S. territories, where millions of citizens have no congressional representation or (in the case of the territories) say in choosing the president.

Other institutional designs are at odds with egalitarianism. The random nature of federal court appointments and the exceptionally long tenure of judges means that some presidents (and Senates) have disproportionate capacity to shape courts. Given the outsized role that the federal courts now play in setting public policy, this is deeply problematic. On the matter of money in politics, the Supreme Court's (hardly intuitive) interpretation of the First Amendment currently allows wealthy citizens to disproportionately fund political campaigns and shape electoral outcomes. Finally, as I discussed in Chapter 8, American democracy is also threatened by the rise of bias, misinformation, and disinformation in political media. Without the ability to acquire and distill basic information about current events, citizens cannot hold elected leaders accountable. How can the public exercise its democratic will if it lacks the tools to form informed opinions?

The Path Forward

The Constitution provides the necessary tools to address each of the above problems and bring the U.S. government into better alignment with "the people." In this book, I have offered dozens of suggestions designed to improve political equality among Americans. In some cases, the reform path is straightforward and key steps have already been taken. In both 2019 and 2021, respectively, the House passed the For the People Act (H.R. 1), a measure that would expand early voting, mandate automatic voter registration (AVR) across the U.S., mostly eliminate photo ID requirements for voting, end partisan gerrymandering, and increase public funding of elections (among other reforms). The House also approved the Washington,

D.C. Admission Act in both 2020 and 2021, a bill which would grant statehood to the District. The greatest remaining impediment to both the For the People Act and statehood for D.C. (and potentially Puerto Rico) is likely the Senate filibuster, as neither of these measures currently enjoy Republican support. As I discussed in Chapter 1, if ending the filibuster is necessary to allow majorities to advance democracy reform, then doing so is a no-brainer. There is also the possibility that a hostile Supreme Court would strike some of these reforms if they became law; most legal scholars, however, believe that each action stands on strong constitutional footing.

Other initiatives face greater obstacles. The National Popular Vote Interstate Compact (NPVIC) is the most achievable plan for reforming the Electoral College. Just to recap, if enough states agree to grant their electors to the winner of the national popular vote, then they can guarantee that this candidate will always win the presidency. Currently, states with 195 electoral votes have joined the compact; if states holding at least 75 more electors enter, the compact will become official. Obtaining support in the remaining states will be a formidable challenge. Furthermore, both Congress and the Supreme Court will likely need to approve the compact before it takes effect. Given both partisan divisions and constitutional concerns regarding this reform, such approval is far from guaranteed.

The U.S. House has not increased in size since 1911, despite the fact that the U.S. population has grown by 171 percent during this time! Increasing the House chamber by about 140 seats—by implementing the Wyoming Rule—would have several positive effects for political equality. First, it would reduce the disparity between the number of residents represented in House districts across U.S. states. Second, it would make representation more manageable for members and decrease, if only slightly, the cost of campaigning. Finally, as long as the Electoral College picks presidents (hopefully not much longer), an expanded House makes each state's electoral vote tally more proportional to its population, increasing political equality at least marginally. While Congress has the power to expand its own membership, this sort of institutional reform has not yet generated much momentum. If it were pursued, it could face some resistance from members fearing that their relative power would be reduced in a larger chamber. Small states would also likely resist a dilution of their influence in the House.

While statehood is a distinct possibility for Puerto Rico, the other four inhabited U.S. territories—American Samoa, Guam, the Northern Marianas Islands, and the U.S. Virgin Islands—do not appear likely to pursue it soon. Nevertheless, Americans living in the territories deserve representation in the U.S. House—the people's chamber. Only through voting representatives can territorial residents effectively compel the national government to be responsive to their needs. While House districts in the territories would contain smaller populations than districts representing residents of U.S. states—and seem to violate the spirit of the aforementioned Wyoming Rule—I believe an exception is warranted in this special case. Recall that the territories receive no representation in the U.S. Senate, meaning that any overrepresentation that they might receive in the House would be more than canceled out.

While the aforementioned For the People Act would help small donors achieve some parity with larger donors when contributing to presidential and congressional campaigns, the changes would still allow wealthy donors to enjoy some disproportionate influence over candidates. Furthermore, the bill would do nothing to stop the growing flood of independent expenditures in campaigns. Without a reversal of the Supreme Court's ruling in *Citizens United*, comprehensive reform on these fronts is impossible. Electing presidents and senators committed to controlling money in elections is the best way to ensure that the federal courts will eventually be comprised of judges and justices committed to doing the same. Given the lifetime nature of judicial appointments, however, this is likely a generational project.

On the topic of the federal courts, the current appointment and confirmation process is far too random and subject to chance. While Supreme Court justices should be shielded from politics, we know that the Court's decisions have political consequences. Nearly every major issue—abortion, LGBTQ+ rights, labor rights, healthcare, taxation, immigration, religious freedom, climate change, and more—has been affected by recent Court opinions. It is only logical that every president—over the course of his or her term—have the same opportunity (along with the Senate) to shape the Court. By allowing justices to serve for one non-renewable 18-year span, each presidential term would include two appointments to the Court. Voters would know the stakes when choosing presidents and senators, and the Court's composition would accurately reflect the will of the people as expressed at the ballot box. There is growing support for Supreme Court term limits in academic and political circles, but it remains unclear whether such a reform could be achieved through simple legislation. If a constitutional amendment were required, a much greater consensus would be needed.

The Senate, with its equal representation for all states, undoubtedly poses the most difficult political equality problem. To say the upper chamber is an entrenched part of the Constitution would be an understatement. Its existence is the result of the Constitution's principal compromise between large and small states. The Constitution even affirms that "no State, without its Consent, shall be deprived of its equal Suffrage in the Senate." Most interpret the Equal Suffrage Clause to mean that all 50 states would need to approve any changes to the Senate's apportionment structure. But not all hope is lost. As I discussed in Chapter 1, a sympathetic Supreme Court could allow reform to move forward without unanimous consent of the states. Many legal scholars believe the Equal Suffrage Clause itself could simply be repealed, allowing Senate apportionment changes to proceed through the normal amendment process. Others, including Professor Eric Orts of the University of Pennsylvania, believe that no additional amendments are necessary. Rather, they argue that various voting rights amendments to the Constitution—the Fifteenth, Nineteenth, Twenty-Fourth, and Twenty-Sixth—already empower Congress to address the Senate's malapportionment.[4] If this interpretation was ever accepted, Congress could change the Senate's apportionment structure through simple legislation. Admittedly, this path is ambitious and would require a Supreme Court committed to fulfilling the Constitution's egalitarian vision above all else; surely, this is not currently the case.

One Senate reform, however, is undoubtedly constitutional. As Professor Bert Neuborne of New York University has proposed, Congress could establish a formula whereby larger states are automatically permitted to split into two or more states if their population is a certain degree greater than the smallest state. While states already have the right to partition with the blessing of Congress, the law would effectively grant advance approval to any state meeting certain criteria. This would ensure that Congress did not simply allow partitions for some large states (and not others) for political reasons. If Congress, for example, stipulated that states with at least 10 times as many residents as the smallest state could split, up to 43 new states could be created and the Senate would be considerably less malapportioned than it is today. While this reform could be adopted by Congress through simple legislation, this would only be the first step in a long and uncertain process. States must also *wish* to be partitioned in order for it to succeed. And while doing so makes sense from a political equality perspective, many other factors—culture, history, economics— would likely be impediments to action. The cause of political equality will need to become much more ubiquitous across the U.S. before something of this magnitude becomes realistic.

Barriers to Progress

I am not naïve about the agenda discussed above. Achieving progress in the U.S. is inherently difficult because there are so many veto points. The House may support changes, but the Senate may not. Congress may approve bills only to see them vetoed by the president. Even if changes do become law, legal challenges can emerge, and the courts could defeat them. Without effective advocacy, public support for any measure can wane over time, especially if hostile, well-funded actors promulgate misleading messages about it (which always happens). Ultimately, however, if public awareness and support for democracy reform does grow in a sustained way, major progress is achievable. While there are many barriers to building public momentum for these efforts, I discuss three particularly notable challenges—federalism, the Framers, and partisan politics—in this next section. In addition to highlighting the role that each consideration plays in stifling democratic progress, I offer some thoughts regarding how each may be confronted.

Federalism

In mid–August 2020, with the Covid-19 pandemic killing about one thousand Americans each day, the Democratic National Convention was held remotely. Much like every national party convention in presidential years, the event would include a formal roll call whereby delegates from the fifty states, D.C., and the territories would cast their votes for the party's presidential nominee. Seeking a creative way to make the unprecedented (and potentially awkward) event work in 2020, the Democrats had each delegate slate record a short video showcasing their respective homeland while declaring their support for candidates. What resulted was one of the most poignant depictions of the United States that I can recall. Congresswoman Terri Sewell cast Alabama's votes from the Edmund Pettus Bridge, the site where courageous protesters were beaten in 1965 for demanding voting rights. Farmers spoke in front of cornstalks in Iowa, while a bricklayer in Missouri cast the state's votes with the famous Gateway Arch behind him. In South Dakota, a member of the Standing Rock Sioux Tribe discussed his ancestral homeland. Rhode Island delegates boasted of the state's calamari industry, while Michigan delegates proudly cast their votes in front of locally-made automobiles. Viewers were treated to ocean cliffs in California, Montana cattle, and the "Welcome to Fabulous Las Vegas" sign in Nevada.[5] Over the course of 30 minutes, millions were reminded of America's vast diversity, both in terms of people and their settings. The "Roll Call Across America" also served as a reminder that in the United States, *states* remain important political entities. States not only have power over a wide variety of policy areas, but they also remain legitimate sources of both legal and cultural autonomy in people's perceptions. When U.S. citizens hear that some laws differ across state lines, their response is generally not bewilderment, but rather simple acknowledgment. Of course laws vary by state, Americans reason, because states are distinctive, and they have power. This is the country we have always known.

The notion that states (and colonies before them) matter predates the Constitution. Unlike most of the world's democracies, states created the national government in the U.S. By the time of the American Revolution, the thirteen colonies had distinct cultures, religious and ethnic backgrounds, and governments. It was not surprising that each was hesitant to relinquish power to a new national government in the 1780s. The first effort to create such a government, the Articles of Confederation, reflected this reticence. The U.S. government was extremely weak, with no executive branch to enforce laws, no ability to raise revenue or regulate commerce, and unrealistic supermajorities needed to pass legislation. Delegates acknowledged the need to strengthen the national government at the Philadelphia Convention, but fears of granting too much power were still considerable. In fact, these fears were ultimately sufficient to secure approval of the Tenth Amendment—the last of the Bill of Rights amendments—which declares that all powers not given to the federal government shall remain the domain of the states (and the people).

While the federal government has undoubtedly become more powerful since the 1780s, the notion of state's rights has been durable. Southern states used the justification to secede from the Union in 1860 and 1861 over the issue of slavery. A century later, the same states rehashed the argument in defense of segregation. These are notable historical examples, but there are thousands of others. Today, states argue for the right to determine their own Medicaid rules, environmental regulations, marijuana laws, workplace regulations, abortion limits, and much more. When it came time to distribute Covid-19 vaccines in 2021, the federal government did not simply provide the vaccine to citizens; they provided supply to states, who were able to distribute it as they saw fit. Many defend state autonomy on the grounds that state governments operate "closer" to their populations, meaning that their laws will be a better reflection of the popular will. In addition, by allowing states to act as laboratories, states can test new policies before they are implemented nationwide.

The extent to which states *should* be empowered to determine their own economic and social policies—a very important question—is not the focus of this book. Other scholars and texts have astutely debated whether Lansing, Albany, and Cheyenne, as opposed to Washington, D.C., should take the lead in setting driving laws, the minimum wage, and criminal justice procedures. Federalism, however, can become a problem for political equality, which *is* my focus here. First, when states deny basic political rights to citizens, this is an American problem, not just a state problem.

Jim Crow laws, malapportioned legislatures, and voter ID laws all diminish the influence that some Americans have on democratic outcomes. When states empower some citizens over others, the level of democracy in the U.S. is diminished. Second, the prominent role of states in determining federal representation is at the heart of the national government's malapportionment problem. Perhaps Idaho should have the right to set its own land use policies or seat belt laws. To some, this is a fundamental aspect of American federalism. But even if one believes Idaho and other states deserve some autonomy, it is quite a logical leap to argue that citizens in Idaho—simply by virtue of living in a lightly populated state—should have disproportionate say over *national laws* enacted by Congress and the president.

Proponents of over-representing small states argue that without the extra boost, large states would trample over them. This argument is as old as the Philadelphia Convention, when small states were also unwilling to agree to any changes in representation that reduced their influence in the new national government. States each had one vote in both the Continental Congresses and the Articles of Confederation; lightly populated states were unwilling to forfeit this privilege in the Constitution, leading to the creation of the Senate. Because the Electoral College would be based on a state's House and Senate members, the malapportioned Senate would also grant small state voters disproportionate influence over choosing the nation's chief executive. Given that states would ultimately need to ratify the new Constitution—and grant it legitimacy—they held all of the cards.

When reforms to these vastly unfair institutions are suggested today, the same flawed arguments tend to reappear. Small states need protection! We cannot let California and New York dictate everything! As I discussed in Chapters 1 and 2, these arguments are mistaken and, in some cases, disingenuous. Heavily-populated states could never push their interests on smaller states because *there are no inherently large or small state interests.* Large states like California and New York include urban interests, but also substantial agricultural economies. Small states like Rhode Island still have sizable cities and all of their associated needs. Across small states, differences in climate, wealth, education, ethnicity, and partisanship are notable. In truth, the idea that "states have interests" is a fundamentally flawed notion. More accurately, citizens within states have interests. Malapportionment does not protect small states because there are no exclusively small state interests to protect. The only thing that Senate and Electoral College malapportionment achieves is valuing some Americans over others on the arbitrary basis of their address. This does not advance federalism at all. It only advances political inequality.

Opponents of democracy reform sometimes argue that more equally-apportioned institutions would diminish the important role that states play in our society. They would do no such thing. Americans can continue to value the distinctiveness of their states and territories, while still demanding equality in our collective national government. An Oklahoma rancher, a Pennsylvania school teacher, and a California web designer can all be proud of their home states—and believe they should enjoy some autonomy from Washington, D.C.—while still demanding that the national government hears the voices of all citizens equally. Given that the national government makes binding life-and-death decisions affecting *us all*, this is just basic fairness and common sense.

The Framers

"Never before or since was there a collection of men who...."

How many times have we heard this sentence—or beginning of a sentence—from political commentators, teachers, parents, and neighbors when discussing the Framers of the Constitution? As I have noted, I view the Framers' work in 1787 to be impressive for its time. And I will reiterate that the Constitution's underlying vision and malleability have allowed for great democratic advancements over the last 235 years. With that said, the Framers were people, not gods. They were politicians, not angels. And they were limited in many important ways. First, the Framers were constrained by the common prejudices—regarding race, sex, and class—of their time. Second, they were hampered by the novelty of their political experiment. At the time, there were no examples of large, pluralist democracies in the world from which to draw knowledge. In many ways, the Framers were "winging it" when designing institutions. While deliberations were generally sophisticated and thoughtful, without examples of even quasi-democratic societies from which to draw, the Framers' estimations were constrained.

Finally, the Framers were limited by the politics of their time. And yes, much like today's governors and members of Congress, the Framers *were* politicians! Much like Barack Obama had to abandon elements of his healthcare plan to get a bill approved in 2010, the Framers responded to political demands. Some delegates at the Philadelphia Convention, such as James Wilson of Pennsylvania, pushed for a popular vote for president. Some, like Ben Franklin, supported the abolition of slavery. But in an effort to build a national government out of 13 distinct states, consensus was needed, and compromises were made. Without protections for slavery and a malapportioned Senate, for example, many states simply would not have supported the ratification of the Constitution. Whether the more democratic-minded Framers secured the best compromises possible under the circumstances is a debatable question, but there was no possibility of a truly egalitarian national government emerging in 1787. As Otto von Bismarck once commented, "politics is the art of the possible."[6] This was true for Madison, Hamilton, and Wilson, much as it is today for Mitch McConnell, Nancy Pelosi, and Joe Biden.

It can be difficult to see the Framers in a non-glamorous light. As symbols of American civil religion, they are often depicted as something greater than human. Their faces adorn our money, while their names can be found on countless bridges, schools, roads, and awards. But to the extent that these symbols make it difficult for Americans to critically analyze undemocratic features of the Constitution, this god-like treatment is problematic. My view is that it is logically consistent to deem the Framers *both* impressive for their time and—as a result of their various limitations—ill-equipped to design governing institutions for the twenty-first century. The greatest gift that the Framers gave today's citizens is a Constitution with a bold vision and a capacity to grow and change. To resist pro-democratic reforms is not to honor the Framers' legacy; it is to stifle it.

Partisan Politics

Politics have always played a role in democracy reform. During the early 1800s, the admission of states was delicately balanced to ensure that neither pro nor anti-slave states dominated the Union. In 1864, Nevada was admitted as a state—despite a population of barely 6,000 people—to boost the Republican Party and President Lincoln's reelection chances.[7] Decades later, Republicans split the Dakota Territory into two states at least partially to create four reliably Republican Senate seats (rather than two).[8] It is important to remember that political parties exist for the sole purposes of acquiring and exercising power. It should surprise no one that they generally support or oppose reforms on the basis of their effect on electoral prospects.

Given the nature of political parties, there are two ways that democracy reformers can advance needed changes. First, reforms have generally succeeded when they acquire intense support in the electorate. Abolition, women's suffrage, the direct election of senators, and other changes all spent decades flailing in the political wind. Each of these ideas was, for some time, considered unachievable in the United States. But in each case, public support gradually—with some ebbs and flows—increased. And once voices for reform were sufficiently loud, the political class took action. In some cases, partisans initially opposed to action came to recognize that supporting a reform was less politically risky than continuing to block it.

In the twenty-first century, some needed efforts to advance political equality will require action from various levels of government. Even if enough states approve the National Popular Vote Interstate Compact (NPVIC), for example, both Congress and the federal courts will likely need to grant their consent. While adding states could be achieved through congressional legislation, structural changes to the Senate may require constitutional amendments. Efforts to severely limit money in elections are at odds with existing Supreme Court interpretations; this is only likely to change if public sentiment demands it or if more sympathetic justices join the High Court. The key to progress on these formidable fronts is building broad-based awareness and support among the citizenry. Only then will elected officials in both parties feel the necessary pressure to take action.

High-profile movements such as these generally take time. Thankfully, they need not start from scratch. Over the past few years, democracy reform has received greater attention. It has become increasingly common to see op-eds and books on the topic. Political candidates are raising issues in their platforms and speeches. And a growing number of non-profit organizations—such as the Brennan Center for Justice, Common Cause, DC Vote, and FairVote—are working to build awareness on matters pertaining to political equality. In a late 2018 article in *The American Prospect*, Miles Rapoport and Cecily Hines noted a slew of gerrymandering and voting rights reforms approved across the states, commenting "it looks like Fixing Our Democracy is officially Cool ... putting democracy reform front and center is not just 'good government'; it is good politics."[9] Momentum is indeed building; now we must keep our foot on the gas.

Second, in a world where politics matter, change will often be led by one political party. For example, the aforementioned For the People Act (H.R. 1) is overwhelmingly supported by Democrats, as Republicans have come to believe that the bill will disadvantage them at the ballot box. This critique, however, requires clarification. The bill would *not* create advantages for Democrats. Rather, it would make voting easier, ban Republicans *and* Democrats from engaging in partisan gerrymandering, and reduce the influence of powerful donors in both parties. Republicans may be correct that the reforms could hurt them in the short term (though see below), but if so, this is only because the bill would end advantages that the party currently enjoys. *Removing* an unfair advantage is very different from *creating* a new, unfair advantage. If a child steals a toy on the playground, the confiscation of such toy by an adult represents a net loss for the thief. But was it unfair to take the stolen toy and return it to her rightful owner? Of course not. Ending partisan gerrymandering, expanding voting rights, and reducing the disproportionate say that the wealthy enjoy in elections does not unfairly help Democrats; if anything, it stops existing advantages for Republicans.

Simply put, no one should assume that a reform effort is at odds with political equality solely because it has disproportionate support among the parties. If a measure seeks to correct an existing inequity, it should be objectively evaluated on its merits.

Furthermore, while democracy reform efforts could improve Democrats' electoral prospects in the near future—simply by creating a level playing field—the two-party system tends to be a self-correcting mechanism. The Republican Party would not simply disappear or become irrelevant. Rather, it would adjust to the new partisan equilibrium. Republicans would need to nominate presidential candidates who could win a majority (or at least a plurality) of presidential votes—something the party has done only once since 1988. Rather than win control of the House and Senate by dominating efficiently-drawn districts and lightly populated states, Republicans would be forced to offer an agenda that appeals to a wider share of the American population. The result would likely be a center-right party that advances conservative principles such as limited government, fiscal responsibility, and local autonomy. The party would likely need to more forcefully discourage extreme elements from gaining control of its message or leadership. While I can only speculate, over time the Republican Party could look much more like Ben Sasse and Lisa Murkowski than Ted Cruz and Josh Hawley. Many conservatives would likely welcome this development.

Final Thought

In this book, I have argued that the U.S. suffers from glaring, but correctable, political inequities. Despite the lofty vision espoused by the Framers and considerable progress over the years, Americans continue to have unequal voices in their democracy. Rather than focus only on problems and reform ideas, I have sought to carefully and objectively explain both how and why U.S. institutions developed into their current forms. Through an understanding of these historical processes, two facts become clear. One, institutions and arrangements are created in response to the norms, values, and politics of their time. Two, institutions can and do change in response to the people's changing demands. In the end, the United States is always subject to (and shaped by) "the consent of the governed."

Let them hear your voices.

Chapter Notes

Supreme Court opinions are officially published in a set of case books called the *United States Reports*. Because some recent cases have not yet been assigned to a specific volume in the *United States Reports*, an underscore (___) marks the spot where the volume number will ultimately be noted.

Introduction

1. President George W. Bush appointed Associate Justice Samuel Alito and Chief Justice John Roberts to the Supreme Court in 2005. While Bush did win the national popular vote in his 2004 reelection campaign, he lost it by over 500,000 votes in the election that initially brought him to office (in 2000).

2. Candidates win *majority* support when they secure the votes of more than half of all voters. Those who win *plurality* support simply secure more votes than any other candidate, regardless of whether their support represents more than 50 percent of the total votes cast.

3. By "representative," I am strictly referring to the ratio of residents to senators across the states. Of course, groups that lacked voting rights (e.g., Blacks, women) have more power in choosing senators today than they did in 1790.

4. Robert A. Dahl, *On Political Equality* (New Haven: Yale University Press, 2006), 39.

5. Sarah F. Brosnan and Frans B.M. de Waal, "Monkeys reject unequal pay," *Nature* 425 (2003), 297–299.

6. John Rawls, *A Theory of Justice* (Cambridge: The Belknap Press of Harvard University Press, 1971), 12.

7. Edmund Burke, "Speeches on Ar-

rival at Bristol and at the Conclusion of the Poll," *The Works of the Right Honorable Edmund Burke* (Boston: Little Brown, 1889), 95.

8. Hanna Pitkin, *The Concept of Representation* (Los Angeles: University of California Press, 1967), 126.

9. See John R. Hibbing and Elizabeth Theiss-Morse, *Stealth Democracy: Americans' Beliefs about How Government Should Work* (Cambridge: Cambridge University Press, 2002); Bo Rothstein, "Creating political legitimacy electoral democracy versus quality of government," *American Behavioral Scientist* 53 (2009), 311–330.

10. See David Estlund, *Democratic Authority: A Philosophical Framework* (Princeton: Princeton University Press, 2009); Stefan Dahlberg, Jonas Linde, and Stefan Holmberg, "Democratic discontent in old and new democracies: Assessing the importance of democratic input and governmental output," *Political Studies* 63, no. S1 (2015), 18–37; Sveinung Arnesan and Yvette Peters, "The Legitimacy of Representation: How Descriptive, Formal, and Responsiveness Representation Affect the Acceptability of Political Decisions," *Comparative Political Studies* 51, no. 7 (2018), 868–899.

11. Quoted in Fiachra Gibbons, "Bruce Springsteen: 'What was done to my country

was un–American,'" *The Guardian*, Feb. 17, 2012, https://www.theguardian.com/music/2012/feb/17/bruce-springsteen-wrecking-ball.

Chapter 1

1. The Philadelphia Convention, the meeting that produced the U.S. Constitution, is also known as the Constitutional Convention, the Federal Convention, and the Grand Convention at Philadelphia.

2. In order to serve in the House, a person must (1) be 25 years old, (2) have been a U.S. citizen for seven years, and (3) reside in the state in which they are seeking election. In order to serve in the Senate, a person must (1) be 30 years old, (2) have been a U.S. citizen for nine years, and (3) reside in the state in which they are seeking election.

3. Taeko Hiroi and Pedro Neiva, "Malapportionment and Geographical Bases of Electoral Support in the Brazilian Senate," *Journal of Politics in Latin America* 5, no. 1 (2013), 127–150.

4. Raymond A. Smith, "Our Odd Upper House: The U.S. Senate's Peculiarities Don't End with the Filibuster," *HuffPost*, Nov. 26, 2013, https://www.huffpost.com/entry/our-odd-upper-house-the-u_b_4326115.

5. A two-thirds majority is needed for the Senate to approve treaties negotiated by the president.

6. Madison had actually written Randolph, his fellow Virginian, the previous month, commenting, "The first step to be taken (at the Philadelphia Convention) is I think a change in the principle of representation." See Jack Rakove, "The Great Compromise: Ideas, Interests, and the Politics of Constitution Making," *The William and Mary Quarterly* 44, no. 3 (1987), 426.

7. Rakove, "The Great Compromise," 428.

8. Rakove, "The Great Compromise," 434.

9. See Joseph Morton, *Shapers of the Great Debate at the Constitutional Convention of 1787: A Biographical Dictionary (Shapers of the Great American Debates)* (Westport: Greenwood, 2005), 30.

10. Sherman had actually first proposed the compromise in June, when it was de-feated, six states to five. With the delegates at an impasse in July, the compromise received renewed attention.

11. Senators were chosen by state legislatures until 1917, when the Seventeenth Amendment allowed for their direct election by popular vote.

12. See James Madison, Edward J. Larson, and Michael P. Winship, *The Constitutional Convention: A Narrative History from the Notes of James Madison* (New York: Modern Library, 2011), 75.

13. While it is logical to assume that New York would have voted against the compromise because it was one of the largest states by population, two of the state's three delegates—John Lansing, Jr. and Robert Yates—had actually opposed the Virginia Plan. See Paul Carlsen and Jac Heckelman, "The (Questionable) Importance of New York at the Constitutional Convention," *Journal of Early American History* 7 (2017), 237–261.

14. New Jersey, Connecticut, North Carolina, Delaware, and Maryland supported the compromise, while Virginia, Pennsylvania, Georgia, and South Carolina opposed it.

15. Robert Dahl, *How Democratic is the American Constitution? (2nd ed.)* (New Haven: Yale University Press, 2003), 15.

16. All population figures I provide from the 1790 census include slaves.

17. See Gerald F. Seib, "The Varied—and Global—Threats Confronting Democracy," *The Wall Street Journal*, Nov. 21, 2017, https://www.wsj.com/articles/the-variedand-globalthreats-confronting-democracy-1511193763.

18. Osita Nwanevu, "The Real Threat to American Democracy Isn't Russia. It's the Right," *Slate*, July 17, 2018, https://slate.com/news-and-politics/2018/07/the-real-threat-to-american-democracy-is-the-right.html.

19. Cary M. Atlas, Thomas W. Gilligan, Robert J. Hendershott, and Mark A. Zupan, "Slicing the federal government net spending pie: Who wins, who loses, and why," *American Economic Review* 85, no. 3 (1995), 624–629.

20. Robert K. Fleck, "Population, land, economic conditions, and the allocation of new deal spending," *Explorations in Economic History* 38 (2003), 296–304; Gary A. Hoover and Paul Pecorino, "The political

determinants of federal expenditure at the state level," *Public Choice* 123, no. 1 (2005), 95–113; Valentino Larcinese, "Information Acquisition, Ideology and Turnout: Theory and Evidence from Britain," LSE STICERD Research Paper No. PEPP18, https://ssrn.com/abstract=1158340.

21. Frances E. and Bruce I. Oppenheimer, *Sizing up the Senate* (Chicago: University of Chicago Press, 1999).

22. Barry R. Weingast, "Political Stability and Civil War: Institutions, Commitment, and American Democracy," in *Analytic Narratives*, eds. Robert Bates, Avner Greif, Margaret Levi, Jean-Laurent Rosenthal, and Barry R. Weingast (Princeton: Princeton University Press, 1998), 166.

23. Dahl, *How Democratic is the American Constitution?*

24. Matthew E.K. Hall, "The Semiconstrained Court: Public Opinion, the Separation of Powers, and the U.S. Supreme Court's Fear of Nonimplementation," *American Journal of Political Science* 58, no. 2 (2013), 352–366.

25. Dahl, *How Democratic is the American Constitution?* 51.

26. Benjamin Eidelson, "The Majoritarian Filibuster," *Yale Law Journal* 122, no. 4 (2013), 980–1023.

27. *Reynolds v. Sims*, 377 U.S. 533 (1964).

28. Raymond A. Smith, "Our Odd Upper House: The U.S. Senate's Peculiarities Don't End with the Filibuster," *HuffPost*, Nov. 26, 2013, https://www.huffpost.com/entry/our-odd-upper-house-the-u_b_4326115.

29. *Griswold v. Connecticut*, 381 U.S. 479 (1965).

30. *Roe v. Wade*, 410 U.S. 113 (1973).

31. Akhil Reed Amar, *America's Constitution: A Biography* (New York: Random House, 2006), 293.

32. Richard Albert, "Amending Constitutional Amendment Rules," *International Journal of Constitutional Law* 13, no. 3 (2015), 8–9.

33. Eric W. Orts, "The Path to Give California 12 Senators, and Vermont Just One," *The Atlantic*, Jan. 2, 2019, https://www.theatlantic.com/ideas/archive/2019/01/heres-how-fix-senate/579172/.

34. Ian Millhiser, "DC is closer to becoming a state now than it has ever been,"

Vox, June 26, 2020, https://www.vox.com/2020/6/22/21293168/dc-statehood-vote-filibuster-supreme-court-joe-biden.

35. One statehood resolution, for Nebraska, was vetoed by President Andrew Johnson in 1866. It was passed by both houses of Congress over his veto (with a two-thirds vote), making Nebraska a state.

36. Frederick D. Williams, *The Northwest Ordinance: Essays on Its Formulation, Provisions, and Legacy* (Lansing: Michigan State University Press, 1989).

37. Lowell H. Harrison, *Kentucky's Road to Statehood* (Lexington: University Press of Kentucky, 1992).

38. John Finger, "Southwest Territory," *Tennessee Frontiers* (Bloomington: Indiana University Press, 2001), 125–151.

39. William Estill Heath, "The Yazoo Land Fraud," *The Georgia Historical Quarterly* 16, no. 4 (1932), 290–291.

40. See Merrill Fabry, "Now You Know: Why are There Two Dakotas?" *Time*, July 14, 2016, https://time.com/4377423/dakota-north-south-history-two/.

41. Robert W. Merry, *A Country of Vast Designs: James K. Polk, The Mexican War, and the Conquest of the American Continent* (New York: Simon & Schuster, 2009).

42. Per the terms in the Treaty of Guadalupe-Hidalgo, the U.S. also agreed to pay Mexico $15 million and assume $3.25 million in Mexican debts to the U.S.

43. "Pack the Union: A Proposal to Admit New States for the Purpose of Amending the Constitution to Ensure Equal Representation," *Harvard Law Review* 133, no. 3 (2020), https://harvardlawreview.org/2020/01/pack-the-union-a-proposal-to-admit-new-states-for-the-purpose-of-amending-the-constitution-to-ensure-equal-representation/.

44. Simon Barnicle, "The 53-State Solution," *The Atlantic*, Feb. 11, 2020, https://www.theatlantic.com/ideas/archive/2020/02/case-new-states/606148/.

45. "Sewards' Folly," Library of Congress, https://www.loc.gov/item/today-in-history/march-30/.

46. The Learning Network, "Jan. 17, 1893 | Hawaiian Monarchy Overthrown by America-Backed Businessmen," *New York Times*, Jan. 17, 2012, https://learning.blogs.nytimes.com/2012/01/17/jan-17-1893-hawaiian-monarchy-overthrown-by-america-backed-businessmen/.

47. Burt Neuborne, "Divide States to Democratize the Senate: A constitutionally sound fix to a vexing political problem," *The Wall Street Journal*, Nov. 19, 2018, https://www.wsj.com/articles/divide-states-to-democratize-the-senate-1542672828.

Chapter 2

1. Ben Schreckinger, "Trump attacks McCain: 'I like people who weren't captured,'" *Politico*, July 18, 2015, https://www.politico.com/story/2015/07/trump-attacks-mccain-i-like-people-who-werent-captured-120317.
2. Philip Rucker, "Trump says Fox's Megyn Kelly had 'blood coming out of her wherever,'" *Washington Post*, Aug. 8, 2015, https://www.washingtonpost.com/news/post-politics/wp/2015/08/07/trump-says-foxs-megyn-kelly-had-blood-coming-out-of-her-wherever/.
3. Matt Ford, "Why Is Donald Trump So Angry at Judge Gonzalo Curiel?" *The Atlantic*, June 3, 2016, https://www.theatlantic.com/politics/archive/2016/06/donald-trump-gonzalo-curiel/485636/.
4. The presence of seven faithless electors—to be discussed later in this chapter—changed the ultimate tally to 304–227.
5. Glenn Thrush and Nolan D. McCaskill, "Obama suggests Clinton didn't work as hard as he did," *Politico*, Nov. 14, 2016, https://www.politico.com/story/2016/11/obama-clinton-campaign-work-231370.
6. See Shlomo Slonim, "The Electoral College at Philadelphia: The Evolution of an Ad Hoc Congress for the Selection of a President," *The Journal of American History* 73, no. 1 (1986), 36.
7. See Mark David Hall and Kermit L. Hall (eds.), *Collected Works of James Wilson, vol. 1* (Online Library of Liberty, 2007), https://oll.libertyfund.org/title/hall-collected-works-of-james-wilson-vol-1.
8. Hall and Hall (eds.), *Collected Works of James Wilson, vol. 1.*
9. Robert M. Alexander, *Representation and the Electoral College* (Oxford: Oxford University Press, 2019).
10. Wilfred U. Codrington, "The Elec-toral College's Racist Origins," Brennan Center for Justice, Apr. 1, 2020, https://www.brennancenter.org/our-work/analysis-opinion/electoral-colleges-racist-origins.
11. "Debates in the Federal Convention of 1787: September 4," The Avalon Project, Yale Law School, https://avalon.law.yale.edu/18th_century/debates_904.asp.
12. Jack Rakove, "The Accidental Electors," *New York Times*, Dec. 19, 2000, https://www.nytimes.com/2000/12/19/opinion/the-accidental-electors.html.
13. Alexander, *Representation and the Electoral College*, 2019.
14. Alexander, *Representation and the Electoral College*, 2019. The author adds that South Carolina did not allow for direct election of electors until 1860.
15. Michael Waldman, *The Fight to Vote* (New York: Simon & Schuster, 2016).
16. Waldman, *The Fight to Vote*, 43.
17. John Ratcliffe, "The Right to Vote and the Rise of Democracy, 1787–1828," *Journal of the Early Republic* 33, no. 2 (2013), 219–254.
18. New Jersey actually permitted women to vote until 1807, when the right was repealed.
19. Only in Maine, Massachusetts, Vermont, Rhode Island, and New Hampshire could Black Americans vote "on the same footing" as whites prior to the Civil War. See Bennett Liebman, "The Quest for Black Voting Rights in New York State," Aug. 28, 2018, https://ssrn.com/abstract=3240214.
20. California had 55 electors in the 2020 election. It lost one elector following the 2020 census.
21. Maine and Nebraska also use a version of a winner-take-all system, but one which allows the states to split their electoral vote distribution. In each state, candidates are awarded one electoral vote for each House district that they win. Then, the state's final two electoral votes are awarded to the winner of the statewide vote.
22. *Bush v. Gore*, 531 U.S. 98 (2000).
23. In some ways, the term *faithless elector* is redundant, as the Framers always assumed that electors would use their own independent judgment.
24. *Chiafalo v. Washington*, 591 U.S. ___ (2020).
25. During this brief era, parties gen-

erally tried to ensure that at least one elector did not vote for the candidate intended to be vice president. In 1800, Democratic-Republicans failed to coordinate effectively, leading to a tie.

26. Grace Segers, "House approves bill that would admit Washington, D.C., as 51st state," *CBS News*, Apr. 22, 2021, https://www.cbsnews.com/news/dc-statehood-bill-pases-house/.

27. The Twelfth Amendment (1804) changed the original rules slightly, as previously the House could consider the top five finishers. In the event that only two candidates win electoral votes—as is usually the case—these would be the only candidates for whom the House could consider.

28. Rob Cook, "Ranking of States with The Highest Agricultural Receipts," *Beef2Live*. Sept. 14, 2020, https://beef2live.com/story-states-produce-food-value-0-107252.

29. Alexander, *Representation and the Electoral College*, 64.

30. Alexander, *Representation and the Electoral College*, 65.

31. Changes to the Constitution, as well as evolving interpretations of the document, have reduced state autonomy in notable ways. After the Civil War, most of the Bill of Rights was gradually incorporated to the states, meaning that state governments could no longer violate the rights expressed in the Constitution's first ten amendments. The 14th Amendment's Equal Protection Clause has denied states the ability to segregate schools, restrict same-sex marriages, or practice nearly all forms of gender inequality. The Constitution's Interstate Commerce Clause has been interpreted broadly since the 1930s, allowing the national government to supersede states when adopting rules regarding commerce. The Civil Rights Act of 1964 overrides state prerogatives regarding private discrimination laws, while the Voting Rights Act of 1965 allows the federal government to police state and local election administration to ensure that officials do not discriminate on the basis of race or ethnicity.

32. "Past Attempts at Reform," Fair Vote, https://www.fairvote.org/past_attempts_at_reform.

33. Lydia Saad, "Americans Would Swap Electoral College for Popular Vote," Gallup, Oct. 24, 2011. https://news.gallup.com/poll/150245/americans-swap-electoral-college-popular-vote.aspx.

34. Andrew Daniller, "A majority of Americans continue to favor replacing Electoral College with a nationwide popular vote," Pew Research Center, Mar. 13, 2020. https://www.pewresearch.org/fact-tank/2020/03/13/a-majority-of-americans-continue-to-favor-replacing-electoral-college-with-a-nationwide-popular-vote/.

35. Geoffrey Skelley, "Abolishing The Electoral College Used to Be a Bipartisan Position. Not Anymore," *FiveThirty Eight*, Apr. 2, 2019, https://fivethirtyeight.com/features/abolishing-the-electoral-college-used-to-be-bipartisan-position-not-anymore/.

36. The Oklahoma Senate passed the NPVIC in 2014, but it died in committee in the Oklahoma House. The opposite occurred in Arkansas in both 2007 and 2009, where the House approved the bill, but it died in the Senate.

37. See Michelle Rindels, "Sisolak vetoes bill that would pledge Nevada's support to winner of national popular vote, reject Electoral College," *The Nevada Independent*, May 30, 2019, https://thenevadaindependent.com/article/sisolak-vetoes-bill-that-would-pledge-nevadas-support-to-winner-of-national-popular-vote-reject-electoral-college.

38. *U.S. Steel v. Multistate Tax Commission*, 434 U.S. 452 (1978).

39. *U.S. Term Limits, Inc. v. Thornton*, 514 U.S. 779 (1995).

40. Andrew Gelman and Pierre-Antoine Kremp, "The Electoral College magnifies the power of White voters," *Vox*, Dec. 17, 2016, https://www.vox.com/the-big-idea/2016/11/22/13713148/electoral-college-democracy-race-White-voters.

41. *Reynolds v. Sims*, 377 U.S. 533 (1964).

Chapter 3

1. "Americans are United Against Partisan Gerrymandering," Brennan Center for Justice, Mar. 15, 2019, https://www.brennancenter.org/our-work/research-reports/americans-are-united-against-partisan-gerrymandering.

2. "Census Bureau Releases Estimates of Undercount and Overcount in the 2010 Census," United States Census Bureau, May 22, 2012, https://www.census.gov/newsroom/releases/archives/2010_census/cb12-95.html.

3. Michael Macagnone, "Census trying to fix history of undercounting minorities," *Roll Call*, June 18, 2020, https://www.rollcall.com/2020/06/18/census-trying-to-fix-history-of-undercounting-minorities/.

4. Michael Waldman, *The Fight to Vote* (New York: Simon & Schuster, 2016), 129.

5. Waldman, *The Fight to Vote*, 130.

6. There is one exception to this general fact. After Alaska and Hawaii were granted statehood in 1959, each received one House seat. This temporarily gave the House 437 seats. After the 1960 census, the House was reapportioned to again have a total of 435 seats.

7. An at-large district is a district that represents an entire population (e.g., a state), rather than simply a portion of it. Because some states have only one House seat, their districts are at-large seats.

8. Stephen Calabrese, "Multimember District Congressional Elections," *Legislative Studies Quarterly* 25 (2000), 611–43.

9. Tory Mast, "The History of Single Member Districts for Congress," FairVote, 1995, http://archive.fairvote.org/?page=526.

10. At that time, the Supreme Court had not yet certified that Article I, Section 4 confers this authority onto Congress.

11. *Deschler's Precedents, vol. 2* (U.S. Government Publishing Office), Ch. 7–9, https://www.govinfo.gov/content/pkg/GPO-HPREC-DESCHLERS-V2/html/GPO-HPREC-DESCHLERS-V2-2-2-3.htm.

12. Anthony J. McGann et al., *Gerrymandering in America: The House of Representatives, the Supreme Court, and the Future of Popular Sovereignty* (Cambridge: Cambridge University Press, 2016).

13. Richard V. Carpenter, "Wesberry v. Sanders: A Case of Oversimplification," *Villanova Law Review* 9, no. 3 (1964).

14. McGann, *Gerrymandering in America*, 26.

15. See Sally Dworak-Fisher, "Drawing the Line on Incumbency Protection," *Michigan Journal of Race and Law* 2 (1996).

16. *Baker v. Carr*, 369 U.S. 186 (1962).

17. *Wesberry v. Sanders*, 376 U.S. 1 (1964).

18. Douglas Smith, "When Not All Votes Were Equal," *The Atlantic*, July 26, 2015, https://www.theatlantic.com/politics/archive/2015/07/one-person-one-vote-a-history/399476/.

19. *Reynolds v. Sims*, 377 U.S. 533 (1964).

20. Smith, "When Not All Votes Were Equal."

21. McGann et al., *Gerrymandering in America*, 224.

22. Richard G. Niemi and Alan I. Abramowitz, "Partisan Redistricting and the 1992 Congressional Elections," *Journal of Politics* 56, no. 3 (1994), 811–17.

23. McGann et al., *Gerrymandering in America*, 161.

24. *Vieth v. Jubelirer*, 541 U.S. 267 (2004).

25. McGann et al., *Gerrymandering in America*, 50.

26. Vann R. Newkirk II, "How Redistricting Became a Technological Arms Race," *The Atlantic*, Oct. 28, 2017, https://www.theatlantic.com/politics/archive/2017/10/gerrymandering-technology-redmap-2020/543888/.

27. *Rucho v. Common Cause*, 588 U.S. ___ (2019).

28. Bernard Grofman and Lisa Handley, "The Impact of the Voting Rights Act on Black Representation in Southern State Legislatures," *Legislative Studies Quarterly* 16, no. 1 (1991), 112.

29. *Thornburg v. Gingles*, 478 U.S. 30 (1986).

30. Michael Li, "Does the Anti-Gerrymandering Campaign Threaten Minority Voting Rights?" Brennan Center for Justice, Oct. 10, 2017, https://www.brennancenter.org/our-work/analysis-opinion/does-anti-gerrymandering-campaign-threaten-minority-voting-rights.

31. *Shaw v. Reno*, 509 U.S. 630 (1993).

32. "Redistricting and the Supreme Court: The Most Significant Cases," National Conference on State Legislatures, Apr. 25, 2019, https://www.ncsl.org/research/redistricting/redistricting-and-the-supreme-court-the-most-significant-cases.aspx.

33. Robert Barnes and Jenna Portnoy, "Supreme Court leaves in place Va. redistricting decision, rejects GOP lawmakers' challenge," *Washington Post*, May 23,

2016, https://www.washingtonpost.com/politics/courts_law/supreme-court-leaves-in-place-va-redistricting-decision-rejects-gop-lawmakers-challenge/2016/05/23/1940110e-20f2-11e6-aa84-42391ba52c91_story.html.

34. Patricia Okonta, "Race-based Political Exclusion and Social Subjugation: Racial Gerrymandering as a Badge of Slavery," *Columbia Human Rights Law Review* 49 (2018), 270.

35. Micah Altman and Michael P. McDonald, "Paradoxes of Political Reform: Congressional Redistricting in Florida," in *Jigsaw Puzzle Politics in the Sunshine State* (Gainesville: University Press of Florida, 2014).

36. Iowie Chen and Jonathan Rodden, "Unintentional Gerrymandering: Political Geography and Electoral Bias in Legislatures," *Quarterly Journal of Political Science* 8 (2013), 239–269.

37. McGann et al., *Gerrymandering in America*, 124.

38. "Redistricting Criteria," National Conference on State Legislatures, Apr. 23, 2019, https://www.ncsl.org/research/redistricting/redistricting-criteria.aspx.

39. Justin Levitt, "The Latest." *All About Redistricting*, 2021, https://redistricting.lls.edu/.

40. Levitt, "The Latest."

41. "Redistricting Criteria."

42. While the Supreme Court ruled in 2019 that the Trump administration could not include a citizenship question on census forms, discussion of the issue may have deterred some non-citizens from participating in the process. See *Department of Commerce v. New York*, 588 U.S. ___ (2019).

43. Jeffrey Mervis, "Census Bureau needs outside help to save the 2020 census from political meddling, experts say," *Science*, Oct. 16, 2020, https://www.sciencemag.org/news/2020/10/census-bureau-needs-outside-help-save-2020-census-political-meddling-experts-say.

44. David Litt, "Congress Needs to Be Way, Way Bigger," *The Atlantic*, May 5, 2020, https://www.theatlantic.com/ideas/archive/2020/05/congress-needs-be-way-way-bigger/611068/.

45. Lee Drutman, "To Fix Congress, Make It Bigger. Much Bigger," *Washington Monthly*, November/December 2018, https://washingtonmonthly.com/magazine/november-december-2018/to-fix-congress-make-it-bigger-much-bigger/.

46. Karen Long Jusko, *Who Speaks for the Poor? Electoral Geography, Party Entry, and Representation* (Cambridge: Cambridge University Press, 2017).

47. In *LULAC v. Perry*, Justice Kennedy expressed concern that applying this standard would require justices to consider counterfactual election results. For example, suppose Republicans won 45 percent of the House vote in North Carolina in 2020, but won eight of 13 seats. It is impossible to know how many seats Republicans *would have won* if they had won 55 percent of the statewide popular vote because we would not know from where these additional votes would have come. Kennedy's concerns are valid. However, we *can* observe where a party gains support when it gains vote share in a state over time. By doing so, political scientists have observed that gains tend to be very symmetrical. In other words, when a party becomes more popular, its support in communities usually grows proportionate to its previous support throughout the state. For example, if Republicans usually win 60 percent of the House vote in Buncombe County, North Carolina when the party wins 45 percent of the statewide vote, we can assume that a ten percent improvement statewide implies a roughly 10 percent improvement in Buncombe County. If we assume that party shifts are generally symmetrical, a strong estimation for partisan bias in gerrymandering can be developed. While this metric is not perfect, if it was applied in a manner that allowed for a reasonable margin of error, it could accurately detect the worst cases of political gerrymandering.

Chapter 4

1. The portion donated by Virginia—Alexandria—was returned to the state in 1846. Today, only portions originally stemming from Maryland comprise the District of Columbia.

2. James Madison, "Federalist No.43," in *The Federalist Papers*, ed. Clinton Rossiter (New York: New American Library, 1961).

3. See Marisol Bello and Andrea Stone, "D.C. Residents Say They're Closer to a Vote in Congress," *ABC News*, Sept. 19, 2008, https://abcnews.go.com/Politics/5050/story?id=5837164&page=1.

4. Joseph L. Rauh, Jr., "D.C. Voting Rights: What Went Wrong?" *Washington Post*, Aug. 25, 1985, https://www.washingtonpost.com/archive/opinions/1985/08/25/dc-voting-rights-what-went-wrongthe-amendment-died-last-week-now-says-a-longtime-advocate-statehood-is-the-only-game-in-town/29a08136-93eb-4951-a854-6162bad4222e/.

5. As of 2021, the District of Columbia Voting Rights Amendment remains the last amendment that Congress approved and sent to the states for ratification.

6. German Lopez, "6 questions about Washington, DC, statehood you were too disenfranchised to ask," *Vox*, Nov. 8, 2016, https://www.vox.com/2014/11/12/7173895/dc-statehood-new-columbia.

7. "Americans United Opposes D.C. Voucher Plan," *Church and State Magazine*, April 2017, https://www.au.org/church-state/april-2017-church-state/au-bulletin/americans-united-opposes-dc-voucher-plan.

8. Grace Segers, "House approves bill that would admit Washington, D.C., as 51st state," *CBS News*, Apr. 22, 2021, https://www.cbsnews.com/news/dc-statehood-bill-pases-house/.

9. Had Utah's population been just 856 people higher in the 2000 census, it would have received a fourth seat in the House.

10. Sarah Ferris and Heather Caygle, "House passes bill to provide D.C. statehood," *Politico*, June 26, 2020, https://www.politico.com/news/2020/06/26/washington-dc-statehood-bill-passes-341591.

11. Colby Itkowitz and Jenna Portnoy, "Sen. Tom Cotton praises Wyoming as 'working-class state' in arguing against D.C. statehood," *Washington Post*, June 25, 2020, https://www.washingtonpost.com/politics/gop-senator-says-dc-residents-dont-measure-up-to-wyomings-working-middle-class/2020/06/25/39e66312-b721-11ea-a510-55bf26485c93_story.html.

12. 51 for 51 is an organization that advocates for the addition of D.C. as the fifty-first state. See Ian Millhiser, "DC is closer to becoming a state now than it has ever been," *Vox*, June 26, 2020, https://www.vox.com/2020/6/22/21293168/dc-statehood-vote-filibuster-supreme-court-joe-biden.

13. R. Hewitt Pate, "D.C. Statehood: Not Without a Constitutional Amendment," The Heritage Foundation, Aug. 27, 1993, https://www.heritage.org/political-process/report/dc-statehood-not-without-constitutional-amendment.

14. Kyle Dropp and Brendan Nyhan, "Nearly Half of Americans Don't Know Puerto Ricans Are Fellow Citizens," *New York Times*, Sept. 26, 2017, https://www.nytimes.com/2017/09/26/upshot/nearly-half-of-americans-dont-know-people-in-puerto-ricoans-are-fellow-citizens.html.

15. Doug Mack, *The Not-Quite States of America: Dispatches from the Territories and Other Far-Flung Outposts of the USA* (New York: W. W. Norton & Company, 2017).

16. Christopher Woolf, "How a violent history created the U.S. Virgin Islands as we know them," *Post-Gazette*, Sept. 15, 2017, https://www.post-gazette.com/news/nation/2017/09/14/How-a-violent-history-created-the-U.S.-Virgin-Islands-as-we-know-them/stories/201709140271.

17. Mack, *The Not-Quite States of America*.

18. *Downes v. Bidwell*, 182 U.S. 244 (1901).

19. *Hawaii v. Mankichi*, 190 U.S. 197 (1903).

20. *Dorr v. United States*, 195 U.S. 138 (1904).

21. See Alan Tauber, "The Empire Forgotten: The Application of the Bill of Rights to U.S. Territories," *Case Western Reserve Law Review* 57, no. 1 (2006), 169.

22. Mack, *The Not-Quite States of America*.

23. Marybeth Herald, "Does the Constitution Follow the Flag into United States Territories or Can It Be Separately Purchased and Sold," *Hastings Constitutional Law Quarterly* 22, no. 3 (1995).

24. Amy Picchi, "Puerto Rico residents on Social Security won't get stimulus checks until June," *Moneywatch*, May 15, 2020, https://www.cbsnews.com/news/stimulus-check-puerto-rico-residents-on-social-security-wont-get-checks-until-june/.

25. Rosanna Torres, "Shortchanging the territories in Medicaid funding," *The Hill*, May 23, 2019, https://thehill.com/blogs/congress-blog/healthcare/445235-shortchanging-the-territories-in-medicaid-funding.

26. Laura Sullivan, "FEMA Report Acknowledges Failures in Puerto Rico Disaster Response," *NPR*, July 13, 2018, https://www.npr.org/2018/07/13/628861808/fema-report-acknowledges-failures-in-puerto-rico-disaster-response.

27. Susanne Ramírez de Arellano, "Trump only wants to aid Puerto Rico's recovery from Hurricane Maria when it's an election year," *NBC News*, Sept. 21, 2020, https://www.nbcnews.com/think/opinion/trump-only-wants-aid-puerto-rico-s-recovery-hurricane-maria-ncna1240658.

28. Nicole Acevedo, "New bipartisan bill calls for Puerto Rico statehood," *NBC News*, June 27, 2018, https://www.nbcnews.com/news/latino/new-bipartisan-bill-calls-puerto-rico-statehood-n887116.

29. See Carl Hulse, "Advocates of Puerto Rico Statehood Plan to Demand Representation," *New York Times*, Jan. 9, 2018, https://www.nytimes.com/2018/01/09/us/politics/advocates-of-puerto-rico-statehood-plan-to-demand-representation.html.

30. Phil Ciciora, "Puerto Rico: Bankruptcy is not an option (yet)," *Illinois News Bureau*, Apr. 18, 2016, https://news.illinois.edu/view/6367/350656.

31. Mack, *The Not-Quite States of America*.

32. Steve Limtiaco, "No 'native inhabitant' vote after U.S. Supreme Court denies Guam's plebiscite appeal," *Pacific Daily News*, May 4, 2020, https://www.sctimes.com/story/news/2020/05/05/no-native-inhabitant-vote-supreme-court-denies-plebiscite-appeal/3080391001/.

Chapter 5

1. Gorsuch served on the U.S. Court of Appeals for the Tenth Circuit.

2. Recall (from Chapter 1) that when Democrats controlled the Senate in 2013, they had similarly changed the cloture rules to allow lower federal court and executive nominations to proceed with simple majorities.

3. Barrett served on the U.S. Court of Appeals for the Seventh Circuit.

4. *Janus v. American Federation of State, County, and Municipal Employees*, 585 U.S. ___ (2018).

5. *Burwell v. Hobby Lobby Stores, Inc.*, 573 U.S. 682 (2014).

6. *Trump v. Hawaii*, 585 U.S. ___ (2018).

7. *Trump v. Sierra Club et al.*, 594 U.S. ___ (2019).

8. Adam Liptak, "Affordable Care Act Survives Latest Supreme Court Challenge," *New York Times*, June 17, 2021, https://www.nytimes.com/2021/06/17/us/obamacare-supreme-court.html.

9. *Obergefell v. Hodges*, 576 U.S. 644 (2015).

10. *Department of Homeland Security v. Regents of the University of California*, 591 U.S. ___ (2020).

11. *Citizens United v. FEC*, 558 U.S. 310 (2010).

12. *Shelby County v. Holder*, 570 U.S. 529 (2013).

13. *Rucho v. Common Cause*, 588 U.S. ___ (2019).

14. Saikrishna B. Prakash and John C. Yoo, "The Origins of Judicial Review," *The University of Chicago Law Review* 70, no. 3 (2003), 946.

15. Prakash and Yoo, "The Origins of Judicial Review," 942.

16. *Hylton v. United States*, 3 U.S. 171 (1796).

17. See "Jefferson on the Supreme Court," *New York Times*, June 23, 1861.

18. Alexander Hamilton, "Federalist No. 78," in *The Federalist Papers*, ed. Clinton Rossiter (New York: New American Library, 1961).

19. *Ex parte Merryman*, 17 F. Cas. 144 (1861).

20. Michael Waldman, *The Fight to Vote* (New York: Simon & Schuster, 2016).

21. Alexander Hamilton, "Federalist No. 78."

22. See Richard J. Ellis and Michael Nelson (eds.), *Debating Reform; Conflicting Perspectives on How to Fix the American Political System (3rd edition)* (Washington: CQ Press, 2016).

23. Glenn Kessler, "Schumer's claim that 'blue slips' were a 'longstanding requirement' for judicial nominees," *Washington Post*, Apr. 5, 2019, https://www.washingtonpost.com/politics/2019/

04/05/schumers-claim-that-blue-slips-were-longstanding-requirement-judicial-nominees/.

24. Alicia Bannon, "The Impact of Judicial Vacancies on Federal Trial Courts," Brennan Center for Justice, July 21, 2014, https://www.brennancenter.org/our-work/research-reports/impact-judicial-vacancies-federal-trial-courts.

25. Marisa Fernandez, "House Democrats propose 18-year term limits for Supreme Court justices," *Axios*, Sept. 25, 2020, https://www.axios.com/supreme-court-term-limits-bill-18-years-7e461f48-3dfc-482e-8f5b-7c7411c1bb31.html.

26. E. J. Dionne Jr., "Bush's Judges," *Washington Post*, Nov. 1, 2002, https://www.washingtonpost.com/archive/opinions/2002/11/01/bushs-judges/59634274-a02c-48ae-8522-c1276b6a6d40/.

Chapter 6

1. Alec C. Ewald, *The Way We Vote: The Local Dimension of American Suffrage* (Nashville: Vanderbilt University Press, 2009).

2. Edmund S. Morgan, *Inventing the People: The Rise of Popular Sovereignty in England and America* (New York: Norton & Company, 1988).

3. Ewald, *The Way We Vote*.

4. Ed Crews, "Voting in Early America," *Colonial Williamsburg*, Spring 2007, https://www.history.org/foundation/journal/spring07/elections.cfm.

5. Bennett Liebman, "The Quest for Black Voting Rights in New York State," Aug. 28, 2018, https://papers.ssrn.com/sol3/papers.cfm?abstract_id=3240214.

6. Michael Waldman, *The Fight to Vote* (New York: Simon & Schuster, 2016), 44.

7. Waldman, *The Fight to Vote*, 44.

8. Waldman, *The Fight to Vote*, 44.

9. Steven Mintz, "Winning the Vote: A History of Voting Rights," Gilder Lehrman Institute of American History, Oct. 4, 2018, http://inside.sfuhs.org/dept/history/U.S._History_reader/Chapter2/Winning%20the%20VoteA%20History%20of%20Voting%20Rights%20Gilder%20Lehrman%20Institute%20of%20American%20History.pdf.

10. Ta-Nehisi Coates, "The Civil War Wasn't About Slavery," *The Atlantic*, Apr. 27, 2009, https://www.theatlantic.com/entertainment/archive/2009/04/the-civil-war-wasnt-about-slavery/16712/.

11. See Justin Ewers, "Abraham Lincoln's Great Awakening: From Moderate to Abolitionist," *U.S. News & World Report*, Feb. 9, 2009, https://www.usnews.com/news/history/articles/2009/02/09/abraham-lincolns-great-awakening-from-moderate-to-abolitionist.

12. Morgan J. Kousser, *Colorblind Injustice* (Chapel Hill: UNC Press, 1999).

13. *United States v. Reese*, 92 U.S. 214 (1876).

14. *Guinn v. United States*, 238 U.S. 347 (1915).

15. *Lane v. Wilson*, 307 U.S. 268 (1939).

16. *Smith v. Allwright*, 321 U.S. 649 (1944).

17. Sam Fulwood, III, "A Voting Rights Story," Center for American Progress, July 22, 2016, https://www.americanprogress.org/issues/race/reports/2016/07/22/141713/a-voting-rights-story/.

18. *Shelby County v. Holder*, 570 U.S. 529 (2013).

19. See "This Week in 19th Amendment History: Shifts and Splits in the Suffrage Movement," *Arlington Public Library*, May 14, 2020, https://library.arlingtonva.us/2020/05/14/this-week-in-Nineteenth-amendment-history-shifts-and-splits-in-the-suffrage-movement/.

20. Ann D. Gordon, "The Trial of Susan B. Anthony," Prepared for inclusion in *Federal Trials and Great Debates in United States History*, 2005, https://www.fjc.gov/sites/default/files/trials/susanbanthony.pdf.

21. *Minor v. Happersett*, 88 U.S. 162 (1875).

22. "Woman Suffrage Centennial," United States Senate, https://www.senate.gov/artandhistory/history/People/Women/Nineteenth_Amendment_Vertical_Timeline.htm.

23. Waldman, *The Fight to Vote*.

24. This might be putting it mildly. Paul was jailed during a hunger strike and had a five-foot-long tube inserted into her stomach by British officials. See Waldman, *The Fight to Vote*, 115.

25. See "Marching for the Vote: Remembering the Woman Suffrage Parade of 1913," Library of Congress, https://guides.loc.gov/american-women-essays/marching-for-the-vote.

26. Waldman, *The Fight to Vote.*

27. "Map: States grant women the right to vote," National Constitution Center, https://constitutioncenter.org/timeline/html/cw08_12159.html.

28. See Waldman, *The Fight to Vote,* 124.

29. Thomas H. Neale, "The Eighteen-Year-Old Vote: The Twenty-Sixth Amendment and Subsequent Voting Rates of Newly Enfranchised Age Groups," Congressional Research Service, 1983, http://digital.library.unt.edu/ark:/67531/metacrs8805/.

30. Neale, "The Eighteen-Year-Old Vote."

31. *Oregon v. Mitchell,* 400 U.S. 112 (1970).

32. Neale, "The Eighteen-Year-Old Vote."

33. See Michael P. McDonald, "2018 November General Election Early Voting," United States Elections Project, 2018, http://www.electproject.org/early_2018; Michael P. McDonald, "2020 General Election Early Vote Statistics," United States Elections Project, 2020, https://electproject.github.io/Early-Vote-2020G/index.html.

34. Drew DeSilver, "In past elections, U.S. trailed most developed countries in voter turnout," Pew Research Center, Nov. 3, 2020, https://www.pewresearch.org/fact-tank/2020/11/03/in-past-elections-u-s-trailed-most-developed-countries-in-voter-turnout/.

35. It has also been suggested that November 1 was unappealing to Catholics because it is All Saints Day, a holy day of obligation. Given the minimal political power of Catholics in 1840s America, however, it seems unlikely that this was a significant consideration.

36. In those days, Election Day often featured lavish celebrations that spanned an entire day.

37. Paul Gronke, Eva Galanes-Rosenbaum, and Peter Miller, "Convenience Voting," *Annual Review of Political Science* 11 (2008), 437–455.

38. Bill Anderson, "Arapahoe Dems Run Uphill," *The Denver Post,* Oct. 26, 1994.

39. Elliott Fullmer, *Tuesday's Gone* (Lanham: Lexington Books, 2021).

40. North Dakota is an exception, as the state abolished voter registration in 1951.

41. Waldman, *The Fight to Vote.*

42. See Charles Thomas Johnson, "The National German-American Alliance, 1901–1918: Cultural Politics and Ethnicity in Peace and War," ScholarWorks at Western Michigan University, https://scholarworks.wmich.edu/cgi/viewcontent.cgi?article=2655&context=dissertations.

43. See Kate Kenski, Bruce W. Hardy, and Kathleen Hall Jamieson, *The Obama Victory: How Media, Money, and Message Shaped the 2008 Election* (Oxford: Oxford University Press, 2010), 304.

44. "They Want to Make Voting Harder?" *New York Times,* June 5, 2011, http://www.nytimes.com/2011/06/06/opinion/06mon1.html.

45. Cynthia Tucker, "Hardball with Chris Matthews," *MSNBC.com,* Nov. 3, 2011, http://www.msnbc.msn.com/id/45163637/ns/msnbc_tv-hardball_with_chris_matthews/t/hardball-chris-matthews-thursday-november-rd/#.TE0lBfLzE0.

46. See Fullmer, *Tuesday's Gone.*

47. Michael C. Herron and Daniel A. Smith, "Race, Party, and the Consequences of Restricting Early Voting in Florida in the 2012 General Election," *Political Research Quarterly* 67, no. 3 (2014), 646–665.

48. See Wendy R. Weiser and Lawrence Norden, "Voting Law Changes in 2012," Brennan Center for Justice, 2012, https://www.brennancenter.org/sites/default/files/2019-08/Report_Voting_Law_Changes_2012.pdf.

49. Amber McReynolds and Charles Stewart III, "Let's put the vote-by-mail 'fraud' myth to rest," *The Hill,* Apr. 28, 2020, https://thehill.com/opinion/campaign/494189-lets-put-the-vote-by-mail-fraud-myth-to-rest.

50. Keesha Gaskins and Sundeep Iyer, "The Challenge of Obtaining Voter Identification," Brennan Center for Justice, July 18, 2012, https://www.brennancenter.org/our-work/research-reports/challenge-obtaining-voter-identification.

51. Gaskins and Iyer, "The Challenge of Obtaining Voter Identification."

52. See MacKenzie Weinger, "Pa. pol: Voter ID helps GOP win state," *Politico,* June 25, 2012, https://www.politico.com/story/2012/06/pa-pol-voter-id-helps-gop-win-state-077811.

53. Arturo Garcia, "NC GOP official

fired after bragging voter ID law would 'kick the Democrats' butt,'" *Raw Story*, Oct. 24, 2013, https://www.rawstory.com/2013/10/nc-gop-official-fired-after-bragging-voter-id-law-would-kick-the-democrats-butt/.

54. See German Lopez, "A Republican lawmaker may have inadvertently confirmed Democrats' suspicions of voter ID," *Vox*, Apr. 6, 2016, https://www.vox.com/2016/4/6/11377078/voter-id-republicans-grothman.

55. Daniel R. Biggers and Michael J. Hanmer, "Understanding the Adoption of Voter Identification Laws in the American States," *American Politics Research* 45, no. 4 (2017), 560–588.

56. John Kuk, Zoltan Hajnal, and Nazita Lajevardi, "A disproportionate burden: strict voter identification laws and minority turnout," *Politics, Groups, and Identities* (2020). DOI: 10.1080/21565503.2020.1773280.

57. Barry Burden, David Canon, Kenneth Mayer, and Donald Moynihan, "Election Laws, Mobilization, and Turnout: The Unanticipated Consequences of Election Reform," *American Journal of Political Science* 58, no. 1 (2014), 95–109.

58. Jessica Campisi, "Southern states have closed hundreds of polling places since Supreme Court decision: civil rights group," *The Hill*, Sept. 10, 2019, https://thehill.com/blogs/blog-briefing-room/news/460644-southern-states-have-closed-hundred-of-polling-places-since-.

59. Hannah Klain, Kevin Morris, Rebecca Ayala, and Max Feldman, "Waiting to Vote," Brennan Center for Justice, June 3, 2020, https://www.brennancenter.org/our-work/research-reports/waiting-vote.

60. "State Voting Bills Tracker 2021," Brennan Center for Justice, May 28, 2021, https://www.brennancenter.org/our-work/research-reports/state-voting-bills-tracker-2021.

61. See Fullmer, *Tuesday's Gone*.

62. "Federal judge blocks North Carolina's voter ID law, citing its discriminatory intent," *The Guardian*, Jan. 1, 2020, https://www.theguardian.com/us-news/2020/jan/01/north-carolina-voter-id-law-blocked-discriminatory.

63. David Graham, "Ohio's 'Golden Week' of Early Voting Is Dead, Again,"

The Atlantic, Aug. 23, 2016, https://www.theatlantic.com/politics/archive/2016/08/ohio-voting-decision/497066/.

64. Sam Levine, "Wisconsin Voting Rights Groups Promise Lawsuit Over Early Voting Cuts," *HuffPost*, Dec. 14, 2018, https://www.huffpost.com/entry/wisconsin-early-voting_n_5c141be8e4b049efa7524568.

65. Patrick Marley, "Appeals court limits Wisconsin early voting to 2 weeks before election, stops voters from receiving ballots via email, fax," *Milwaukee Journal Sentinel*, June 29, 2020, https://www.jsonline.com/story/news/politics/2020/06/29/wisconsin-early-voting-limited-appeals-court-tightens-election-law/3283006001/.

66. *Husted v. A. Philip Randolph Institute*, 584 U.S. ___ (2018).

67. Kevin Morris et al., "Purges: A Growing Threat to the Right to Vote," Brennan Center for Justice, July 20, 2018, https://www.brennancenter.org/our-work/research-reports/purges-growing-threat-right-vote.

68. "Same Day Voter Registration," National Conference of State Legislatures, May 7, 2021, https://www.ncsl.org/research/elections-and-campaigns/same-day-registration.aspx.

69. "Automatic Voter Registration," National Conference of State Legislatures, Feb. 8, 2021, https://www.ncsl.org/research/elections-and-campaigns/automatic-voter-registration.aspx.

70. Jake Grumbach and Charlotte Hill, "Automatic Voter Registration Boosts Turnout Among Young and Low Income People," *Data for Progress*, July 11, 2019, https://www.dataforprogress.org/blog/2019/7/11/automatic-voter-registration-boosts-turnout-among-young-and-low-income-people.

71. Jean Chung, "Felony Disenfranchisement: A Primer," The Sentencing Project, June 27, 2019, https://www.sentencingproject.org/publications/felony-disenfranchisement-a-primer/.

72. The nine states who proactively mailed vote-by-mail applications to all voters were Delaware, Illinois, Iowa, Ohio, Maryland, Massachusetts, Michigan, Rhode Island, and Wisconsin. See Quinn Scanlan, "Here's how states have changed the rules around voting amid the coro-

navirus pandemic," *ABC News*, Sept. 22, 2020, https://abcnews.go.com/Politics/states-changed-rules-voting-amid-coronavirus-pandemic/story?id=72309089.

73. According to Scanlan, the eight states who already had drop boxes before 2020 were Arizona, California, Colorado, Hawaii, Montana, New Mexico, Oregon, and Washington.

74. Beth LeBlanc, "2.1M Michigan voters have already cast their ballots," *The Detroit News*, Oct. 27, 2020, https://www.detroitnews.com/story/news/politics/2020/10/27/2-1-m-michigan-voters-have-already-cast-their-ballots/3745743001/.

75. Mark Sherman, "High court won't extend Wisconsin's absentee ballot deadline," *Associated Press*, Oct. 26, 2020, https://apnews.com/article/election-2020-virus-outbreak-wisconsin-elections-us-supreme-court-dcf1e115d0804e203ef2cf9887cfabff.

76. Stephen Montemayor, "Judge won't halt challenge to Minnesota extended ballot deadline," *Star Tribune*, Nov. 6, 2020, https://www.startribune.com/judge-won-t-halt-challenge-to-minnesota-extended-ballot-deadline/572984572/.

77. Andrew Prokop, "Pennsylvania's naked ballot problem, explained," *Vox*, Sept. 28, 2020, https://www.vox.com/21452393/naked-ballots-pennsylvania-secrecy-envelope.

78. Michaela Winberg, "Good job, Philly: Only 1% of city mail ballots were 'naked,'" *Billy Penn*, Nov. 11, 2020, https://billypenn.com/2020/11/11/philly-naked-ballots-pennsylvania-mail-votes-november-election/.

79. David A. Graham, "Signed, Sealed, Delivered—then Discarded," *The Atlantic*, Oct. 21, 2020, https://www.theatlantic.com/ideas/archive/2020/10/signature-matching-is-the-phrenology-of-elections/616790/.

80. Graham, "Signed, Sealed, Delivered—then Discarded."

81. Meryl Kornfield and Felicia Sonmez, "Texas governor's limit on drop-off sites for mail-in ballots criticized as voter suppression," *Washington Post*, Oct. 1, 2020, https://www.washingtonpost.com/politics/2020/10/01/texas-voting-abbott/.

82. Eric Lutz, "Absurdly Long Lines to Vote in Georgia are a Preview of What's to Come," *Vanity Fair*, Oct. 13, 2020, https://www.vanityfair.com/news/2020/10/georgia-early-voting-long-lines.

83. Lee Drutman and Charlotte Hill, "America Needs a Federal Elections Agency," *New America*, Nov. 4, 2020, https://www.newamerica.org/political-reform/reports/america-needs-federal-elections-agency/.

84. David Weigel, "The Trailer: Democrats won the White House and lost a myth about turnout," *Washington Post*, Nov. 8, 2020, https://www.washingtonpost.com/politics/2020/11/08/trailer-democrats-won-white-house-lost-myth-about-turnout/.

85. See Weigel, "The Trailer."

86. "Text—S.4263–116th Congress (2019–2020): John Lewis Voting Rights Advancement Act," Congress.gov, July 22, 2020, https://www.congress.gov/bill/116th-congress/senate-bill/4263/text.

87. Ian Millhiser, "Joe Manchin's surprisingly bold proposal to fix America's voting rights problem," *Vox*, May 13, 2021, https://www.vox.com/22434054/joe-manchin-voting-rights-act-for-the-people-john-lewis-preclearance-filibuster-senate.

88. "Text—H.R.1–117th Congress (2021–2022): For the People Act of 2021," Congress.gov, Mar. 11, 2021, https://www.congress.gov/bill/117th-congress/house-bill/1/text.

89. Stephen Fowler, "Why Do Nonwhite Georgia Voters Have to Wait in Line for Hours? Too Few Polling Places," *NPR*, Oct. 17, 2020, https://www.npr.org/2020/10/17/924527679/why-do-nonwhite-georgia-voters-have-to-wait-in-line-for-hours-too-few-polling-pl.

90. See Drutman and Hill, "America Needs a Federal Elections Agency."

91. Garrett Epps, "What Does the Constitution Actually Say About Voting Rights," *The Atlantic*, Aug. 19, 2013, https://www.theatlantic.com/national/archive/2013/08/what-does-the-constitution-actually-say-about-voting-rights/278782/.

Chapter 7

1. Paul Bedard, "George Washington Plied Voters with Booze," *U.S. News & World Report*, Nov. 8, 2011, https://www.usnews.com/news/

blogs/washington-whispers/2011/11/08/george-washington-plied-voters-with-booze.

2. Jack Beatty, "A Sisyphean History of Campaign Finance Reform," *The Atlantic*, July 2007, https://webcache.googleusercontent.com/search?q=cache:IlW_yPH8044J:https://www.theatlantic.com/magazine/archive/2007/07/a-sisyphean-history-of-campaign-finance-reform/306066/+&cd=4&hl=en&ct=clnk&gl=us.

3. Campaign dollars also support strategic advisors, lawyers, communications teams, travel logistics, field staff, web developers, accountants, and more.

4. APSA stands for American Political Science Association.

5. Amy Melissa McKay, "Buying Amendments? Lobbyists' Campaign Contributions and Microlegislation in the Creation of the Affordable Care Act," *Legislative Studies Quarterly* 45, no. 2 (2020), 327–60.

6. Gail Russell Chaddock, "Health-care reform: Obama cut private deals with likely foes," *Christian Science Monitor*, Nov. 6, 2009, https://www.csmonitor.com/USA/Politics/2009/1106/healthcare-reform-obama-cut-private-deals-with-likely-foes.

7. See "How Campaign Donations Influence the Congressional Economic Agenda," Russell Sage Foundation, Mar. 23, 2018, https://www.russellsage.org/how-campaign-donations-influence-congressional-economic-agenda.

8. Joshua L. Kalla and David E. Broockman, "Campaign Contributions Facilitate Access to Congressional Officials: A Randomized Field Experiment," *American Journal of Political Science* 60, no. 3 (2016), 545–558.

9. See Renae Merle, "Mulvaney discloses 'hierarchy' for meeting lobbyists, saying some would be seen only if they paid," *Washington Post*, Apr. 25, 2018, https://www.washingtonpost.com/news/business/wp/2018/04/25/mick-mulvaney-faces-backlash-after-telling-bankers-if-you-were-a-lobbyist-who-never-gave-us-money-i-didnt-talk-to-you/.

10. Maggie Koerth, "Everyone Knows Money Influences Politics … Except Scientists," *FiveThirtyEight*, June 4, 2019, https://fivethirtyeight.com/features/everyone-knows-money-influences-politics-except-scientists/.

11. Elaine Meckler, "Whatever happened to America?" *The Union*, Dec. 29, 2015, https://www.theunion.com/news/twi/elaine-meckler-whatever-happened-to-america/.

12. John Dunbar, "A Modern History of Campaign Finance: From Watergate to 'Citizens United,'" The Center for Public Integrity, Jan. 22, 2018, https://publicintegrity.org/politics/a-modern-history-of-campaign-finance-from-watergate-to-citizens-united/.

13. *Buckley v. Valeo*, 424 U.S. 1 (1976).

14. The limits now increase for inflation every federal election cycle (every two years). For the 2021–22 cycle, individuals may give a federal candidate (i.e., a House, Senate, or presidential candidate) up to $2,900. This amount may be given once during the party nomination process and once during the general election period. Individual donors may give national parties up to $36,500 each year, though this is a bit misleading for a few reasons. First, donors may give up to $36,500 to the national party organization, *as well as* both the parties' House and Senate campaign committees. Second, donors can also donate $10,000 to various state parties, who can easily transfer the money to the national party. In sum, a single donor can contribute close to a half-million dollars to a political party each year. Notably, PAC limits do not increase with inflation. An individual may still only give a PAC up to a $5,000 each year. See "FEC announces 2021–2022 campaign cycle contribution limits," Federal Election Commission, Feb. 2, 2021, https://www.fec.gov/updates/fec-announces-2021-2022-campaign-cycle-contribution-limits/.

15. *Federal Election Commission v. Wisconsin Right to Life, Inc.*, 551 U.S. 449 (2007).

16. *Citizens United v. Federal Election Commission*, 558 U.S. 310 (2010).

17. "Total Outside Spending by Election Cycle, Excluding Party Committees," Center for Responsive Politics, 2020, https://www.opensecrets.org/outsidespending/cycle_tots.php.

18. Michelle Ye Hee Lee, "Eleven donors have plowed $1 billion into super PACs since they were created," *Washington Post*,

Oct. 26, 2018, https://www.washington post.com/politics/eleven-donors-plowed-1-billion-into-super-pacs-since-2010/2018/10/26/31a07510-d70a-11e8-aeb7-ddcad4a0a54e_story.html.

19. Idrees Kahloon, "Does Money Matter?" *Harvard Magazine*, July–August 2016, https://www.harvardmagazine.com/2016/07/does-money-matter.

20. Bradley Jones, "Most Americans want to limit campaign spending, say big donors have greater political influence," Pew Research Center, May 8, 2018, https://www.pewresearch.org/fact-tank/2018/05/08/most-americans-want-to-limit-campaign-spending-say-big-donors-have-greater-political-influence/.

21. "Most expensive midterm ever: Cost of 2018 election surpasses $5.7 billion," Center for Responsive Politics, Feb. 6, 2019, https://www.opensecrets.org/news/2019/02/cost-of-2018-election-5pnt7bil/.

22. "2020 Outside Spending, by Group," Center for Responsive Politics, 2020, https://www.opensecrets.org/outside spending/summ.php?cycle=2020&type=p&disp=O.

23. "Text—H.R.1–117th Congress (2021–2022): For the People Act of 2021," Congress.gov, Mar. 11, 2021, https://www.congress.gov/bill/117th-congress/house-bill/1/text.

24. *Harper v. Virginia State Board of Elections*, 383 U.S. 663 (1966).

25. *Harper v. Virginia State Board of Elections* (1966).

Chapter 8

1. Alan I. Abramowitz and Steven W. Webster, "Negative Partisanship: Why Americans Dislike Parties but Behave Like Rabid Partisans," *Advances in Political Psychology* 39, no. 1 (2018).

2. Lilliana Mason, *Uncivil Agreement: How Politics Became Our Identity* (Chicago: University of Chicago Press, 2018).

3. *Engel v. Vitale*, 370 U.S. 421 (1962).

4. *Brown v. Board of Education of Topeka*, 347 U.S. 483 (1954).

5. *Swann v. Charlotte-Mecklenburg Board of Education*, 402 U.S. 1 (1971).

6. "Patrick Joseph Buchanan, 'Culture War Speech Address to the Republican National Convention (17 August 1992),'"

Voices of Democracy—the U.S. Oratory Project, https://voicesofdemocracy.umd.edu/buchanan-culture-war-speech-speech-text/.

7. Monica Hesse, "Rush Limbaugh had a lot to say about feminism. Women learned how to not care," *Washington Post*, Feb. 19, 2021, https://www.washingtonpost.com/lifestyle/style/rush-limbaugh-feminism-feminazis/2021/02/19/3a00f852-7202-11eb-85fa-e0ccb3660358_story.html.

8. See Andrew Seifter, "Limbaugh on the NBA: "Call it the TBA, the Thug Basketball Association ... They're going in to watch the Crips and the Bloods," *Media Matters for America*, Dec. 10, 2004, https://www.mediamatters.org/rush-limbaugh/limbaugh-nba-call-it-tba-thug-basketball-association-theyre-going-watch-crips-and.

9. Christi Parsons, "Limbaugh draws fire on Obama parody," *The Seattle Times*, May 6, 2007, https://www.seattletimes.com/nation-world/limbaugh-draws-fire-on-obama-parody/.

10. Steven Kull, Clay Ramsay, and Evan Lewis, "Misperceptions, the Media, and the Iraq War," *Political Science Quarterly* 118, no. 4 (Winter 2003/2004), 569–598.

11. Jon Krosnick and Bo MacInnis, "Frequent Viewers of Fox News Are Less Likely to Accept Scientists' Views of Global Warming," Stanford Woods Institute for the Environment, Nov. 30, 2010, https://woods.stanford.edu/publications/frequent-viewers-fox-news-are-less-likely-accept-scientists-views-global-warming.

12. Margaret Sullivan, "The data is in: Fox News may have kept millions from taking the coronavirus threat seriously," *Washington Post*, June 28, 2020, https://www.washingtonpost.com/lifestyle/media/the-data-is-in-fox-news-may-have-kept-millions-from-taking-the-coronavirus-threat-seriously/2020/06/26/60d88aa2-b7c3-11ea-a8da-693df3d7674a_story.html.

13. Michael B. Kelley, "Study: Watching Only Fox News Makes You Less Informed Than Watching No News at All," *Business Insider*, May 22, 2012, https://www.businessinsider.com/study-watching-fox-news-makes-you-less-informed-than-watching-no-news-at-all-2012-5.

14. A.W. Geiger, "Key findings about the online news landscape in America,"

Pew Research Center, Sept. 11, 2019, https://www.pewresearch.org/fact-tank/2019/09/11/key-findings-about-the-online-news-landscape-in-america/.

15. See Janna Anderson and Lee Rainie, "Concerns about democracy in the digital age," Pew Research Center, Feb. 21, 2020, https://www.pewresearch.org/internet/2020/02/21/concerns-about-democracy-in-the-digital-age/.

16. Kristen Hare, "The coronavirus has closed more than 70 local newsrooms across America. And counting," *Poynter*, July 7, 2020, https://www.poynter.org/locally/2021/the-coronavirus-has-closed-more-than-60-local-newsrooms-across-america-and-counting/.

17. Elizabeth Grieco, "Fast facts about the newspaper industry's financial struggles as McClatchy files for bankruptcy," Pew Research Center, Feb. 14, 2020, https://www.pewresearch.org/fact-tank/2020/02/14/fast-facts-about-the-newspaper-industrys-financial-struggles/.

18. See Anderson and Rainie, "Concerns about democracy in the digital age."

19. Ferris Jabr, "Why Your Brain Needs More Downtime," *Scientific American*, Oct. 15, 2013, https://www.scientificamerican.com/article/mental-downtime/.

20. Furthermore, hackers affiliated with the Russian military intelligence service (GRU) gained access to email accounts at the Democratic National Committee (DNC), the Democratic Congressional Campaign Committee (DCCC), and the Clinton campaign. The stolen files were then released to WikiLeaks, who slowly released them in an effort to damage Clinton's candidacy. See T.S. Allen and Stephen Rodriguez, "To Protect Democracy, Protect the Internet," *Foreign Policy*, July 14, 2020, https://foreignpolicy.com/2020/07/14/united-states-election-interference-illegal-social-media/.

21. Greg Myre and Shannon Bond, "'Russia Doesn't Have to Make Fake News': Biggest Election Threat Is Closer To Home," *NPR*, Sept. 29, 2020, https://www.npr.org/2020/09/29/917725209/russia-doesnt-have-to-make-fake-news-biggest-election-threat-is-closer-to-home.

22. Laurence Arnold, "QAnon, the Conspiracy Theory Creeping into U.S. Politics," *Washington Post*, Aug. 25, 2020, https://www.washingtonpost.com/business/energy/qanon-the-conspiracy-theory-creeping-into-us-politics/2020/08/24/0638de5c-e62c-11ea-bf44-0d31c85838a5_story.html.

23. Emma Bowman, "Why QAnon Survives After Trump," *NPR*, Feb. 4, 2021, https://www.npr.org/2021/02/04/963861418/why-qanon-survives-after-trump?utm_source=facebook.com&utm_medium=social&utm_campaign=npr&utm_term=nprnews&fbclid=IwAR3q-ICphR5BInKvzGiKYr61BxULHg_IHdSXZ84JmAo1nEJuewLgGhBxsGU.

24. Peter Dizikes, "Study: On Twitter, false news travels faster than true stories," *MIT News Office*, Mar. 8, 2018, https://news.mit.edu/2018/study-twitter-false-news-travels-faster-true-stories-0308.

25. Amy Mitchell et al., "Americans Who Mainly Get Their News on Social Media Are Less Engaged, Less Knowledgeable," Pew Research Center, July 30, 2020, https://www.journalism.org/2020/07/30/americans-who-mainly-get-their-news-on-social-media-are-less-engaged-less-knowledgeable/.

26. See Anderson and Rainie, "Concerns about democracy in the digital age."

27. See Anderson and Rainie, "Concerns about democracy in the digital age."

28. See Anderson and Rainie, "Concerns about democracy in the digital age."

29. See Anderson and Rainie, "Concerns about democracy in the digital age."

30. See Anderson and Rainie, "Concerns about democracy in the digital age."

31. *Red Lion Broadcasting Co. v. Federal Communications Commission*, 395 U.S. 367 (1969).

32. Rebecca Kern, "Renewed Liability Shield Bill Aims to Hold Tech Accountable," *Bloomberg Law*, Mar. 17, 2021, https://news.bloomberglaw.com/tech-and-telecom-law/senators-renew-liability-shield-attack-to-hold-tech-accountable.

33. Chuck Todd et al., "Add social media to the list of things souring Americans on politics," *NBC News*, Apr. 5, 2019, https://www.nbcnews.com/politics/meet-the-press/add-social-media-list-things-souring-americans-politics-n991276.

34. Emily A. Vogels, "56% of Americans support more regulation of major technology companies," Pew Research Center, July 20, 2021, https://www.pewresearch.

org/fact-tank/2021/07/20/56-of-americans-support-more-regulation-of-major-technology-companies/.

35. Sarah Shapiro and Catherine Brown, "The State of Civics Education," Center for American Progress, Feb. 21, 2018, https://www.americanprogress.org/issues/education-k-12/reports/2018/02/21/446857/state-civics-education/.

36. See Valerie Strauss, "Many Americans know nothing about their government. Here's a bold way schools can fix that," *Washington Post*, Sept. 27, 2016, https://www.washingtonpost.com/news/answer-sheet/wp/2016/09/27/many-americans-know-nothing-about-their-government-heres-a-bold-way-schools-can-fix-that/.

37. Shapiro and Brown, "The State of Civics Education."

Conclusion

1. It is possible that the total number of votes cast was a bit higher than this figure, but only these popular votes can be confirmed. See "U.S. President—National Vote," *Our Campaigns*, 2008, https://www.ourcampaigns.com/RaceDetail.html?RaceID=59540.

2. See Robert Cohen, "Was the Constitution Pro-Slavery? The Changing View of Frederick Douglass," *Social Education* 72, no. 5 (2008), 248.

3. *Reynolds v. Sims*, 377 U.S. 533 (1964).

4. Eric W. Orts, "The Path to Give California 12 Senators, and Vermont Just One," *The Atlantic*, Jan. 2, 2019, https://www.theatlantic.com/ideas/archive/2019/01/heres-how-fix-senate/579172/.

5. Matt Stevens and Isabella Grullón Paz, "Democratic National Convention's Roll Call Showcases Voices from Across America," *New York Times*, Aug. 19, 2020, https://www.nytimes.com/2020/08/19/us/politics/dnc-roll-call.html.

6. See "Politics," Oxford Reference, https://www.oxfordreference.com/view/10.1093/acref/9780191826719.001.0001/q-oro-ed4-00008442.

7. Simon Barnicle, "The 53-State Solution," *The Atlantic*, Feb. 11, 2020, https://www.theatlantic.com/ideas/archive/2020/02/case-new-states/606148/.

8. See Merrill Fabry, "Now You Know: Why are There Two Dakotas?" *Time*, July 14, 2016, https://time.com/4377423/dakota-north-south-history-two/.

9. Miles Rapoport and Cecily Hines, "A New Playing Field for Democracy Reform," *The American Prospect*, Dec. 24, 2018, https://prospect.org/power/new-playing-field-democracy-reform/.

References

Abramowitz, Alan I., and Steven W. Webster. "Negative Partisanship: Why Americans Dislike Parties but Behave Like Rabid Partisans." *Advances in Political Psychology* 39, no. 1 (2018).

Acevedo, Nicole. "New bipartisan bill calls for Puerto Rico statehood." *NBC News,* June 27, 2018. https://www.nbcnews.com/news/latino/new-bipartisan-bill-calls-puerto-rico-statehood-n887116.

Albert, Richard. "Amending Constitutional Amendment Rules." *International Journal of Constitutional Law* 13, no. 3 (2015): 655–685.

Alexander, Robert M. *Representation and the Electoral College.* Oxford: Oxford University Press, 2019.

Allen, T.S., and Stephen Rodriguez. "To Protect Democracy, Protect the Internet." *Foreign Policy,* July 14, 2020. https://foreignpolicy.com/2020/07/14/united-states-election-interference-illegal-social-media/.

Altman, Micah, and Michael P. McDonald. "Paradoxes of Political Reform: Congressional Redistricting in Florida." In *Jigsaw Puzzle Politics in the Sunshine State.* Gainesville: University Press of Florida, 2014.

Amar, Akhil Reed. *America's Constitution: A Biography.* New York: Random House, 2006.

"American War and Military Operations Casualties: Lists and Statistics." Congressional Research Service, July 29, 2020. https://fas.org/sgp/crs/natsec/RL32492.pdf.

"Americans are United Against Partisan Gerrymandering." Brennan Center for Justice, Mar. 15, 2019. https://www.brennancenter.org/our-work/research-reports/americans-are-united-against-partisan-gerrymandering.

"Americans United Opposes D.C. Voucher Plan." *Church and State Magazine,* April 2017. https://www.au.org/church-state/april-2017-church-state/au-bulletin/americans-united-opposes-dc-voucher-plan.

Anderson, Bill. "Arapahoe Dems Run Uphill." *The Denver Post,* Oct. 26, 1994.

Anderson, Janna, and Lee Rainie. "Concerns about democracy in the digital age." Pew Research Center, Feb. 21, 2020. https://www.pewresearch.org/internet/2020/02/21/concerns-about-democracy-in-the-digital-age/.

Arnesen, Sveinung, and Yvette Peters. *Comparative Political Studies* 51, no. 7 (2018): 868–899.

Arnold, Laurence. "QAnon, the Conspiracy Theory Creeping into U.S. Politics." *Washington Post,* Aug. 25, 2020. https://www.washingtonpost.com/business/energy/qanon-the-conspiracy-theory-creeping-into-us-politics/2020/08/24/0638de5c-e62c-11ea-bf44-0d31c85838a5_story.html.

Atlas, Cary M., Thomas W. Gilligan, Robert J. Hendershott, and Mark A. Zupan, "Slicing the federal government net spending pie: Who wins, who loses, and why." *American Economic Review* 85, no. 3 (1995): 624–629.

"Automatic Voter Registration." National Conference of State Legislatures, Feb. 8, 2021. https://www.ncsl.org/research/elections-and-campaigns/automatic-voter-registration.aspx.

Bannon, Alicia. "The Impact of Judicial Vacancies on Federal Trial Courts."

Brennan Center for Justice, July 21, 2014. https://www.brennancenter.org/our-work/research-reports/impact-judicial-vacancies-federal-trial-courts.

Barnes, Robert, and Jenna Portnoy. "Supreme Court leaves in place Va. redistricting decision, rejects GOP lawmakers' challenge." *Washington Post,* May 23, 2016. https://www.washingtonpost.com/politics/courts_law/supreme-court-leaves-in-place-va-redistricting-decision-rejects-gop-lawmakers-challenge/2016/05/23/1940110e-20f2-11e6-aa84-42391ba52c91_story.html.

Barnicle, Simon. "The 53-State Solution." *The Atlantic,* Feb. 11, 2020. https://www.theatlantic.com/ideas/archive/2020/02/case-new-states/606148/.

Beatty, Jack. "A Sisyphean History of Campaign Finance Reform." *The Atlantic,* July 2007. https://webcache.googleusercontent.com/search?q=cache:11W_yPH8044J:https://www.theatlantic.com/magazine/archive/2007/07/a-sisyphean-history-of-campaign-finance-reform/306066/+&cd=4&hl=en&ct=clnk&gl=us.

Bedard, Paul. "George Washington Plied Voters with Booze." *U.S. News & World Report,* Nov. 8, 2011. https://www.usnews.com/news/blogs/washington-whispers/2011/11/08/george-washington-plied-voters-with-booze.

Bello, Marisol, and Andrea Stone. "D.C. Residents Say They're Closer to a Vote in Congress." *ABC News,* Sept. 19, 2008. https://abcnews.go.com/Politics/5050/story?id=5837164&page=1.

Biggers, Daniel R., and Michael J. Hanmer. "Understanding the Adoption of Voter Identification Laws in the American States." *American Politics Research* 45, no. 4 (2017): 560–588.

Bowman, Emma. "Why QAnon Survives After Trump." *NPR,* Feb. 4, 2021. https://www.npr.org/2021/02/04/963861418/why-qanon-survives-after-trump.

Brosnan, Sarah F., and Frans B. M. de Waal. "Monkeys reject unequal pay." *Nature* 425 (2003): 297–299.

Burden, Barry, David Canon, Kenneth Mayer, and Donald Moynihan. "Election Laws, Mobilization, and Turnout: The Unanticipated Consequences of Election Reform." *American Journal of Political Science* 58, no. 1 (2014): 95–109.

Burke, Edmund. "Speeches on Arrival at Bristol and at the Conclusion of the Poll." *The Works of the Right Honorable Edmund Burke.* Boston: Little Brown, 1889.

Calabrese, Stephen. "Multimember District Congressional Elections." *Legislative Studies Quarterly* 25, no. 4 (2020): 611–43.

Campisi, Jessica. "Southern states have closed hundreds of polling places since Supreme Court decision: civil rights group." *The Hill,* Sept. 10, 2019. https://thehill.com/blogs/blog-briefing-room/news/460644-southern-states-have-closed-hundred-of-polling-places-since.

Carlsen, Paul, and Jac Heckelman. "The (Questionable) Importance of New York at the Constitutional Convention." *Journal of Early American History* 7 (2017): 237–261.

Carpenter, Richard V. "Wesberry v. Sanders: A Case of Oversimplification." *Villanova Law Review* 9, no. 3 (1964).

"Census Bureau Releases Estimates of Undercount and Overcount in the 2010 Census." United States Census Bureau, May 22, 2012. https://www.census.gov/newsroom/releases/archives/2010_census/cb12-95.html.

Chaddock, Gail Russell. "Healthcare reform: Obama cut private deals with likely foes." *Christian Science Monitor,* Nov. 6, 2009. https://www.csmonitor.com/USA/Politics/2009/1106/health care-reform-obama-cut-private-deals-with-likely-foes.

Chen, Iowie, and Jonathan Rodden. "Unintentional Gerrymandering: Political Geography and Electoral Bias in Legislatures." *Quarterly Journal of Political Science* 8, no. 3 (2013): 239–269.

Chung, Jean. "Felony Disenfranchisement: A Primer." The Sentencing Project, June 27, 2019. https://www.sentencingproject.org/publications/felony-disenfranchisement-a-primer/.

Ciciora, Phil. "Puerto Rico: Bankruptcy is not an option (yet)." *Illinois News Bureau,* Apr. 18, 2016. https://news.illinois.edu/view/6367/350656.

Coates, Ta-Nehisi. "The Civil War Wasn't About Slavery." *The Atlantic,* Apr. 27, 2009. https://www.theatlantic.com/entertainment/archive/2009/04/the-civil-war-wasnt-about-slavery/16712/.

Codrington, Wilfred U. "The Electoral College's Racist Origins." Brennan Center for Justice, Apr. 1, 2020. https://www.brennancenter.org/our-work/analysis-opinion/electoral-colleges-racist-origins.

Cohen, Robert. "Was the Constitution Pro-Slavery? The Changing View of Frederick Douglass." *Social Education* 72, no. 5 (2008): 246–250.

Cook, Rob. "Ranking of States with The Highest Agricultural Receipts." *Beef2 Live,* Sept. 14, 2020. https://beef2live.com/story-states-produce-food-value-0-107252.

Crews, Ed. "Voting in Early America." *Colonial Williamsburg,* Spring 2007. https://www.history.org/foundation/journal/spring07/elections.cfm.

Dahl, Robert A. *How Democratic is the American Constitution?* New Haven: Yale University Press, 2003.

Dahl, Robert A. *On Political Equality.* New Haven: Yale University Press, 2006.

Dahlberg, Stefan, Jonas Linde, and Stefan Holmberg. "Democratic discontent in old and new democracies: Assessing the importance of democratic input and governmental output." *Political Studies* 63, S1 (2015): 18–37.

Daniller, Andrew. "A majority of Americans continue to favor replacing Electoral College with a nationwide popular vote." Pew Research Center, Mar. 13, 2020. https://www.pewresearch.org/fact-tank/2020/03/13/a-majority-of-americans-continue-to-favor-replacing-electoral-college-with-a-nationwide-popular-vote/.

"Debates in the Federal Convention of 1787: September 4." The Avalon Project. Yale Law School. https://avalon.law.yale.edu/18th_century/debates_904.asp.

Deschler's Precedents, Vol. 2. U.S. Government Publishing Office. https://www.govinfo.gov/content/pkg/GPO-HPREC-DESCHLERS-V2/html/GPO-HPREC-DESCHLERS-V2-2-2-3.htm.

DeSilver, Drew. "In past elections, U.S. trailed most developed countries in voter turnout." Pew Research Center, Nov. 3, 2020. https://www.pewresearch.org/fact-tank/2020/11/03/in-past-elections-u-s-trailed-most-developed-countries-in-voter-turnout/.

Dionne, E.J., Jr. "Bush's Judges." *Washington Post,* Nov. 1, 2002. https://www.washingtonpost.com/archive/opinions/2002/11/01/bushs-judges/59634274-a02c-48ae-8522-c1276b6a6d40/.

Dizikes, Peter. "Study: On Twitter, false news travels faster than true stories." *MIT News Office,* Mar. 8, 2018. https://news.mit.edu/2018/study-twitter-false-news-travels-faster-true-stories-0308.

Dropp, Kyle, and Brendan Nyhan. "Nearly Half of Americans Don't Know Puerto Ricans Are Fellow Citizens." *New York Times,* Sept. 26, 2017. https://www.nytimes.com/2017/09/26/upshot/nearly-half-of-americans-dont-know-people-in-puerto-ricoans-are-fellow-citizens.html.

Drutman, Lee. "To Fix Congress, Make It Bigger. Much Bigger." *Washington Monthly,* November/December 2018. https://washingtonmonthly.com/magazine/november-december-2018/to-fix-congress-make-it-bigger-much-bigger/.

Drutman, Lee, and Charlotte Hill. "America Needs a Federal Elections Agency." New America, Nov. 4, 2020. https://www.newamerica.org/political-reform/reports/america-needs-federal-elections-agency/.

Dunbar, John. "A Modern History of Campaign Finance: From Watergate to 'Citizens United.'" Center for Public Integrity, Jan. 22, 2018. https://publicintegrity.org/politics/a-modern-history-of-campaign-finance-from-watergate-to-citizens-united/.

Dworak-Fisher, Sally. "Drawing the Line on Incumbency Protection." *Michigan Journal of Race and Law* 2 (1996).

Edwards, George C. *Why the Electoral College Is Bad for America: Second Edition.* New Haven: Yale University Press, 2011.

Eidelson, Benjamin. "The Majoritarian Filibuster." *Yale Law Journal* 122, no. 4 (2013): 980–1023.

Elections Project, 2018. http://www.electproject.org/early_2018.

Epps, Garrett. "What Does the Constitution Actually Say About Voting Rights." *The Atlantic,* Aug. 19, 2013. https://www.theatlantic.com/national/archive/2013/08/what-does-the-constitution-actually-say-about-voting-rights/278782/.

Estlund, David. *Democratic Authority: A Philosophical Framework*. Princeton: Princeton University Press, 2009.

Ewald, Alec. C. *The Way We Vote: The Local Dimension of American Suffrage*. Nashville: Vanderbilt University Press, 2009.

Ewers, Justin. "Abraham Lincoln's Great Awakening: From Moderate to Abolitionist." *U.S. News & World Report*, Feb. 9, 2009. https://www.usnews.com/news/history/articles/2009/02/09/abraham-lincolns-great-awakening-from-moderate-to-abolitionist.

Fabry, Merrill. "Now You Know: Why are There Two Dakotas?" *Time*, July 14, 2016. https://time.com/4377423/dakota-north-south-history-two/.

"FEC announces 2021–2022 campaign cycle contribution limits." Federal Election Commission, Feb. 2, 2021. https://www.fec.gov/updates/fec-announces-2021-2022-campaign-cycle-contribution-limits/.

"Federal judge blocks North Carolina's voter ID law, citing its discriminatory intent." *The Guardian*, Jan. 1, 2020. https://www.theguardian.com/us-news/2020/jan/01/north-carolina-voter-id-law-blocked-discriminatory.

Fernandez, Marisa. "House Democrats propose 18-year term limits for Supreme Court justices." *Axios*, Sept. 25, 2020. https://www.axios.com/supreme-court-term-limits-bill-18-years-7e461f48-3dfc-482e-8f5b-7c7411c1bb31.html.

Ferris, Sarah, and Heather Caygle. "House passes bill to provide D.C. statehood." *Politico*, June 26, 2020. https://www.politico.com/news/2020/06/26/washington-dc-statehood-bill-passes-341591.

Finger, John. "Southwest Territory." *Tennessee Frontiers*. Bloomington: Indiana University Press, 2001.

Fleck, Robert K. "Population, land, economic conditions, and the allocation of new deal spending." *Explorations in Economic History* 38 (2003): 296–304.

Ford, Matt. "Why Is Donald Trump So Angry at Judge Gonzalo Curiel?" *The Atlantic*, June 3, 2016. https://www.theatlantic.com/politics/archive/2016/06/donald-trump-gonzalo-curiel/485636/.

Fowler, Stephen. "Why Do Nonwhite Georgia Voters Have to Wait in Line for Hours? Too Few Polling Places." *NPR*, Oct. 17, 2020. https://www.npr.org/2020/10/17/924527679/why-do-nonwhite-georgia-voters-have-to-wait-in-line-for-hours-too-few-polling-pl.

Fullmer, Elliott. *Tuesday's Gone: America's Early Voting Revolution*. Lanham: Lexington Books, 2021.

Fulwood, Sam. "A Voting Rights Story." Center for American Progress, July 22, 2016. https://www.americanprogress.org/issues/race/reports/2016/07/22/141713/a-voting-rights-story/.

Garcia, Arturo. "NC GOP official fired after bragging voter ID law would 'kick the Democrats' butt.'" *Raw Story*, Oct. 24, 2013. https://www.rawstory.com/2013/10/nc-gop-official-fired-after-bragging-voter-id-law-would-kick-the-democrats-butt/.

Gaskins, Keesha, and Sundeep Iyer. "The Challenge of Obtaining Voter Identification," Brennan Center for Justice, July 18, 2012. https://www.brennancenter.org/our-work/research-reports/challenge-obtaining-voter-identification.

Geiger, A.W. "Key findings about the online news landscape in America." Pew Research Center, Sept. 11, 2019. https://www.pewresearch.org/fact-tank/2019/09/11/key-findings-about-the-online-news-landscape-in-america/.

Gelman, Andrew, and Pierre-Antoine Kremp. "The Electoral College magnifies the power of White voters." *Vox*, Dec. 17, 2016. https://www.vox.com/the-big-idea/2016/11/22/13713148/electoral-college-democracy-race-White-voters.

Gibbons, Fiachra. "Bruce Springsteen: 'What was done to my country was un–American.'" *The Guardian*, Feb. 17, 2012. https://www.theguardian.com/music/2012/feb/17/bruce-springsteen-wrecking-ball.

Gordon, Ann D. "The Trial of Susan B. Anthony." Prepared for inclusion in *Federal Trials and Great Debates in United States History*, 2005. https://www.fjc.gov/sites/default/files/trials/susanbanthony.pdf.

Graham, David. "Ohio's 'Golden Week' of Early Voting Is Dead, Again." *The Atlantic*, Aug. 23, 2016. https://www.theatlantic.com/politics/archive/2016/08/ohio-voting-decision/497066/.

Graham, David A. "Signed, Sealed, Delivered—then Discarded." *The Atlantic,* Oct. 21, 2020. https://www.theatlantic.com/ideas/archive/2020/10/signature-matching-is-the-phrenology-of-elections/616790/.

Grieco, Elizabeth. "Fast facts about the newspaper industry's financial struggles as McClatchy files for bankruptcy." Pew Research Center, Feb. 14, 2020. https://www.pewresearch.org/fact-tank/2020/02/14/fast-facts-about-the-newspaper-industrys-financial-struggles/.

Grofman, Bernard, and Lisa Handley. "The Impact of the Voting Rights Act on Black Representation in Southern State Legislatures." *Legislative Studies Quarterly* 16, no. 1 (1991): 111–128.

Gronke, Paul, Eva Galanes-Rosenbaum, and Peter Miller. "Convenience Voting." *Annual Review of Political Science* 11 (2008): 437–455.

Grumbach, Jake, and Charlotte Hill. "Automatic Voter Registration Boosts Turnout Among Young and Low Income People." *Data for Progress,* July 11, 2019. https://www.dataforprogress.org/blog/2019/7/11/automatic-voter-registration-boosts-turnout-among-young-and-low-income-people.

Hall, Mark David, and Kermit L. Hall (eds.). "Collected Works of James Wilson, vol. 1." *Online Library of Liberty,* 2007. https://oll.libertyfund.org/titles/wilson-collected-works-of-james-wilson-vol-1.

Hall, Matthew E.K. "The Semiconstrained Court: Public Opinion, the Separation of Powers, and the U.S. Supreme Court's Fear of Nonimplementation." *American Journal of Political Science* 58, no. 2 (2013): 352–366.

Hamilton, Alexander. "Federalist No. 78." In *The Federalist Papers,* edited by Clinton Rossiter. New York: New American Library, 1961.

Hare, Kristen Hare. "The coronavirus has closed more than 70 local newsrooms across America. And counting." *Poynter,* July 7, 2020. https://www.poynter.org/locally/2021/the-coronavirus-has-closed-more-than-60-local-newsrooms-across-america-and-counting/.

Harrison, Lowell H. *Kentucky's Road to Statehood.* Lexington: University Press of Kentucky, 1992.

Heath, William Estill. "The Yazoo Land Fraud." *The Georgia Historical Quarterly* 16, no. 4 (1932): 274–291.

Herald, Marybeth. "Does the Constitution Follow the Flag into United States Territories or Can It Be Separately Purchased and Sold." *Hastings Constitutional Law Quarterly* 22, no. 3 (1995).

Herron, Michael C., and Daniel A. Smith. "Race, Party, and the Consequences of Restricting Early Voting in Florida in the 2012 General Election." *Political Research Quarterly* 67, no. 3 (2014): 646–665.

Hesse, Monica. "Rush Limbaugh had a lot to say about feminism. Women learned how to not care." *Washington Post,* Feb. 19, 2021. https://www.washingtonpost.com/lifestyle/style/rush-limbaugh-feminism-feminazis/2021/02/19/3a00f852-7202-11eb-85fa-e0ccb3660358_story.html.

Hibbing, John R., and Elizabeth Theiss-Morse. *Stealth Democracy: Americans' Beliefs about How Government Should Work.* Cambridge: Cambridge University Press, 2002.

Hiroi, Taeko, and Pedro Neiva. "Malapportionment and Geographical Bases of Electoral Support in the Brazilian Senate." *Journal of Politics in Latin America* 5, no. 1 (2013): 127–150.

Hoover, Gary A., and Paul Pecorino. "The political determinants of federal expenditure at the state level." *Public Choice* 123, no. 1 (2005): 95–113. http://www.nytimes.com/2011/06/06/opinion/06mon1.html.

"How Campaign Donations Influence the Congressional Economic Agenda." Russell Sage Foundation, Mar. 23, 2018. https://www.russellsage.org/how-campaign-donations-influence-congressional-economic-agenda.

Hulse, Carl. "Advocates of Puerto Rico Statehood Plan to Demand Representation." *New York Times,* Jan. 9, 2018. https://www.nytimes.com/2018/01/09/us/politics/advocates-of-puerto-rico-statehood-plan-to-demand-representation.html.

Itkowitz, Colby, and Jenna Portnoy. "Sen. Tom Cotton praises Wyoming as 'working-class state' in arguing against D.C. statehood." *Washington Post,* June 25, 2020. https://www.washingtonpost.

com/politics/gop-senator-says-dc-residents-dont-measure-up-to-wyomings-working-middle-class/2020/06/25/39e66312-b721-11ea-a510-55bf26485c93_story.html.

Jabr, Ferris. "Why Your Brain Needs More Downtime." *Scientific American*, Oct. 15, 2013. https://www.scientific american.com/article/mental-downtime/.

"Jan. 17, 1893 | Hawaiian Monarchy Overthrown by America-Backed Businessmen." *New York Times*, Jan. 17, 2012. https://learning.blogs.nytimes.com/2012/01/17/jan-17-1893-hawaiian-monarchy-overthrown-by-america-backed-businessmen/.

"Jefferson on the Supreme Court." *New York Times*, June 23, 1861.

Johnson, Charles Thomas. "The National German-American Alliance, 1901–1918: Cultural Politics and Ethnicity in Peace and War." ScholarWorks at Western Michigan University. https://scholarworks.wmich.edu/cgi/view content.cgi?article=2655&context=dissertations.

Jones, Bradley. "Most Americans want to limit campaign spending, say big donors have greater political influence." Pew Research Center, May 8, 2018. https://www.pewresearch.org/fact-tank/2018/05/08/most-americans-want-to-limit-campaign-spending-say-big-donors-have-greater-political-influence/.

Kahloon, Idrees. "Does Money Matter?" *Harvard Magazine*, July-August 2016. https://www.harvardmagazine.com/2016/07/does-money-matter.

Kalla, Joshua L., and David E. Broockman. "Campaign Contributions Facilitate Access to Congressional Officials: A Randomized Field Experiment." *American Journal of Political Science* 60, no. 3 (2016): 545–558.

Karol, David. "Resolved, the terms of Supreme Court justices should be limited to eighteen years." In *Debating Reform; Conflicting Perspectives on How to Fix the American Political System (3rd edition)*, edited by Richard J. Ellis and Michael Nelson. Washington: CQ Press, 2016.

Kelley, Michael B. "Study: Watching Only Fox News Makes You Less Informed

Than Watching No News at All." *Business Insider*, May 22, 2012. https://www.businessinsider.com/study-watching-fox-news-makes-you-less-informed-than-watching-no-news-at-all-2012-5.

Kenski, Kate, Bruce W. Hardy, and Kathleen Hall Jamieson. *The Obama Victory: How Media, Money, and Message Shaped the 2008 Election*. Oxford: Oxford University Press, 2010.

Kern, Rebecca. "Renewed Liability Shield Bill Aims to Hold Tech Accountable." *Bloomberg Law*, Mar. 17, 2021. https://news.bloomberglaw.com/tech-and-telecom-law/senators-renew-liability-shield-attack-to-hold-tech-accountable.

Kessler, Glenn. "Schumer's claim that 'blue slips' were a 'longstanding requirement' for judicial nominees." *Washington Post*, Apr. 5, 2019. https://www.washingtonpost.com/politics/2019/04/05/schumers-claim-that-blue-slips-were-longstanding-requirement-judicial-nominees/.

Klain, Hannah, Kevin Morris, Rebecca Ayala, and Max Feldman. "Waiting to Vote." Brennan Center for Justice, June 3, 2020. https://www.brennancenter.org/our-work/research-reports/waiting-vote.

Koerth, Maggie. "Everyone Knows Money Influences Politics … Except Scientists." *FiveThirtyEight*, June 4, 2019. https://fivethirtyeight.com/features/everyone-knows-money-influences-politics-except-scientists/.

Kornfield, Meryl, and Felicia Sonmez. "Texas governor's limit on drop-off sites for mail-in ballots criticized as voter suppression." *Washington Post*, Oct. 1, 2020. https://www.washingtonpost.com/politics/2020/10/01/texas-voting-abbott/.

Kousser, Morgan J. *Colorblind Injustice*. Chapel Hill: UNC Press, 1999.

Krosnick, Jon, and Bo MacInnis. "Frequent Viewers of Fox News Are Less Likely to Accept Scientists' Views of Global Warming." Stanford Woods Institute for the Environment, Nov. 30, 2010. https://woods.stanford.edu/publications/frequent-viewers-fox-news-are-less-likely-accept-scientists-views-global-warming.

Kuk, John, Zoltan Hajnal, and Nazita Lajevardi. "A disproportionate burden: strict voter identification laws and minority turnout." *Politics, Groups, and Identities*, 2020. DOI: 10.1080/21565503.2020. 1773280.

Kull, Steven, Clay Ramsay, and Evan Lewis. "Misperceptions, the Media, and the Iraq War." *Political Science Quarterly* 118, no. 4 (2003): 569–598.

Larcinese, Valentino. "Information Acquisition, Ideology and Turnout: Theory and Evidence from Britain." LSE STICERD Research Paper No. PEPP18. https://ssrn.com/abstract=1158340.

LeBlanc, Beth. "2.1M Michigan voters have already cast their ballots." *The Detroit News*, Oct. 27, 2020. https://www.detroitnews.com/story/news/politics/2020/10/27/2-1-m-michigan-voters-have-already-cast-their-ballots/3745743001/.

Lee, Frances, and Bruce I. Oppenheimer. *Sizing up the Senate*. Chicago: University of Chicago Press, 1999.

Levine, Sam. "Wisconsin Voting Rights Groups Promise Lawsuit Over Early Voting Cuts." *HuffPost*, Dec. 14, 2018. https://www.huffpost.com/entry/wisconsin-early-voting_n_5c141be8e4b049efa7524568.

Levitt, Justin. "The Latest." All About Redistricting, 2020. https://redistricting.lls.edu/.

Li, Michael. "Does the Anti-Gerrymandering Campaign Threaten Minority Voting Rights?" Brennan Center for Justice, Oct. 10, 2017. https://www.brennancenter.org/our-work/analysis-opinion/does-anti-gerrymandering-campaign-threaten-minority-voting-rights.

Liebman, Bennett. "The Quest for Black Voting Rights in New York State." Aug. 28, 2018. https://ssrn.com/abstract=3240214.

Limtiaco, Steve. "No 'native inhabitant' vote after U.S. Supreme Court denies Guam's plebiscite appeal." *Pacific Daily News*, May 4, 2020. https://www.sctimes.com/story/news/2020/05/05/no-native-inhabitant-vote-supreme-court-denies-plebiscite-appeal/3080391001/.

Liptak, Adam. "Affordable Care Act Survives Latest Supreme Court Challenge." *New York Times*, June 17, 2021. https://www.nytimes.com/2021/06/17/us/obamacare-supreme-court.html.

Litt, David. "Congress Needs to Be Way, Way Bigger." *The Atlantic*, May 5, 2020. https://www.theatlantic.com/ideas/archive/2020/05/congress-needs-be-way-way-bigger/611068/.

Long Jusko, Karen. *Who Speaks for the Poor? Electoral Geography, Party Entry, and Representation*. Cambridge: Cambridge University Press, 2017.

Lopez, German. "A Republican lawmaker may have inadvertently confirmed Democrats' suspicions of voter ID." *Vox*, Apr. 6, 2016. https://www.vox.com/2016/4/6/11377078/voter-id-republicans-grothman.

Lopez, German. "6 questions about Washington, D.C., statehood you were too disenfranchised to ask." *Vox*, Nov. 8, 2016. https://www.vox.com/2014/11/12/7173895/dc-statehood-new-columbia.

Lutz, Eric. "Absurdly Long Lines to Vote in Georgia are a Preview of What's to Come." *Vanity Fair*, Oct. 13, 2020. https://www.vanityfair.com/news/2020/10/georgia-early-voting-long-lines.

Macagnone, Michael. "Census trying to fix history of undercounting minorities." *Roll Call*, June 18, 2020. https://www.rollcall.com/2020/06/18/census-trying-to-fix-history-of-undercounting-minorities/.

Mack, Doug. *The Not-Quite States of America: Dispatches from the Territories and Other Far-Flung Outposts of the USA*. New York: W. W. Norton & Company, 2017.

Madison, James. "Federalist No. 43." In *The Federalist Papers*, edited by Clinton Rossiter. New York: New American Library, 1961.

Madison, James, Edward J. Larson, and Michael P. Winship. *The Constitutional Convention: A Narrative History from the Notes of James Madison*. New York: Modern Library, 2011.

"Map: States grant women the right to vote." National Constitution Center. https://constitutioncenter.org/timeline/html/cw08_12159.html.

"Marching for the Vote: Remembering the Woman Suffrage Parade of 1913." Library of Congress. https://guides.loc.gov/american-women-essays/marching-for-the-vote.

Marley, Patrick. "Appeals court limits Wisconsin early voting to 2 weeks before election, stops voters from receiving ballots via email, fax." *Milwaukee Journal Sentinel,* June 29, 2020. https://www.jsonline.com/story/news/politics/2020/06/29/wisconsin-early-voting-limited-appeals-court-tightens-election-law/3283006001/.

Martin, Gregory J., and Ali Yurukoglu. "Bias in Cable News: Persuasion and Polarization." *American Economic Review* 107, no. 9 (2017): 2565–99.

Mason, Lilliana. *Uncivil Agreement: How Politics Became Our Identity.* Chicago: University of Chicago Press, 2018.

Mast, Tory. "The History of Single Member Districts for Congress." FairVote, 1995. http://archive.fairvote.org/?page=526.

McDonald, Michael P. "2018 General Election Early Vote Statistics." United States Elections Project, 2018. http://www.electproject.org/early_2018.

McDonald, Michael P. "2020 General Election Early Vote Statistics." United States Elections Project, 2020. https://electproject.github.io/Early-Vote-2020G/index.html.

McGann, Anthony J., Charles Anthony Smith, Michael Latner, and Alex Keena. *Gerrymandering in America: The House of Representatives, the Supreme Court, and the Future of Popular Sovereignty.* Cambridge: Cambridge University Press, 2016.

McKay, Amy Melissa. "Buying Amendments? Lobbyists' Campaign Contributions and Microlegislation in the Creation of the Affordable Care Act." *Legislative Studies Quarterly* 45, no. 2 (2020): 327–60.

McNeil, Tommie. "Virginia's 3rd District Still Dealing with Redistricting Issues." *wvtf.org,* May 22, 2014. https://www.wvtf.org/post/virginias-3rd-district-still-dealing-redistricting-issues#stream/0.

McReynolds, Amber, and Charles Stewart III. "Let's put the vote-by-mail 'fraud' myth to rest." *The Hill,* Apr. 28, 2020. https://thehill.com/opinion/campaign/494189-lets-put-the-vote-by-mail-fraud-myth-to-rest.

Meckler, Elaine. "Whatever happened to America?" *The Union,* Dec. 29, 2015. https://www.theunion.com/news/twi/elaine-meckler-whatever-happened-to-america/.

Merle, Renae. "Mulvaney discloses 'hierarchy' for meeting lobbyists, saying some would be seen only if they paid." *Washington Post,* Apr. 25, 2018. https://www.washingtonpost.com/news/business/wp/2018/04/25/mick-mulvaney-faces-backlash-after-telling-bankers-if-you-were-a-lobbyist-who-never-gave-us-money-i-didnt-talk-to-you/.

Merry, Robert W. *A Country of Vast Designs: James K. Polk, The Mexican War, and the Conquest of the American Continent.* New York: Simon & Schuster, 2009.

Mervis, Jeffrey. "Census Bureau needs outside help to save the 2020 census from political meddling, experts say." *Science,* Oct. 16, 2020. https://www.sciencemag.org/news/2020/10/census-bureau-needs-outside-help-save-2020-census-political-meddling-experts-say.

Millhiser, Ian. "DC is closer to becoming a state now than it has ever been." *Vox,* June 26, 2020. https://www.vox.com/2020/6/22/21293168/dc-statehood-vote-filibuster-supreme-court-joe-biden.

Millhiser, Ian. "Joe Manchin's surprisingly bold proposal to fix America's voting rights problem." *Vox,* May 13, 2021. https://www.vox.com/22434054/joe-manchin-voting-rights-act-for-the-people-john-lewis-preclearance-filibuster-senate.

Mintz, Steven. "Winning the Vote: A History of Voting Rights." Gilder Lehrman Institute of American History, Oct. 4, 2018. http://inside.sfuhs.org/dept/history/US_History_reader/Chapter2/Winning%20the%20VoteA%20History%20of%20Voting%20Rights%20Gilder%20Lehrman%20Institute%20of%20American%20History.pdf.

Mitchell, Amy, and Mark Jurkowitz, J. Baxter Oliphant, and Elisa Shearer. "Americans Who Mainly Get Their News on Social Media Are Less Engaged, Less Knowledgeable." Pew Research Center, July 30, 2020. https://www.journalism.org/2020/07/30/americans-who-mainly-get-their-news-on-social-media-are-less-engaged-less-knowledgeable/.

Montemayor, Stephen. "Judge won't halt challenge to Minnesota extended ballot deadline." *Star Tribune,* Nov. 6, 2020.

https://www.startribune.com/judge-won-t-halt-challenge-to-minnesota-extended-ballot-deadline/572984572/.

Morgan, Edmund S. *Inventing the People: The Rise of Popular Sovereignty in England and America.* New York: Norton & Company, 1988.

Morris, Kevin, Myrna Perez, Jonathan Brater, and Christopher Deluzio. "Purges: A Growing Threat to the Right to Vote." Brennan Center for Justice, July 20, 2018. https://www.brennancenter.org/our-work/research-reports/purges-growing-threat-right-vote.

Morton, Joseph. *Shapers of the Great Debate at the Constitutional Convention of 1787: A Biographical Dictionary (Shapers of the Great American Debates).* Westport: Greenwood, 2005.

"Most expensive midterm ever: Cost of 2018 election surpasses $5.7 billion." Center for Responsive Politics, Feb. 6, 2019. https://www.opensecrets.org/news/2019/02/cost-of-2018-election-5pnt7bil/.

Myre, Greg, and Shannon Bond. "'Russia Doesn't Have to Make Fake News: Biggest Election Threat is Closer to Home." *NPR,* Sept. 29, 2020. https://www.npr.org/2020/09/29/917725209/russia-doesn-t-have-to-make-fake-news-biggest-election-threat-is-closer-to-home.

Neale, Thomas H. "The Eighteen-Year-Old Vote: The Twenty-Sixth Amendment and Subsequent Voting Rates of Newly Enfranchised Age Groups." Congressional Research Service, 1983. http://digital.library.unt.edu/ark:/67531/metacrs8805/.

Neuborne, Burt. "Divide States to Democratize the Senate: A constitutionally sound fix to a vexing political problem." *Wall Street Journal,* Nov. 19, 2018. https://www.wsj.com/articles/divide-states-to-democratize-the-senate-1542672828.

Newkirk, Vann R., II. "How Redistricting Became a Technological Arms Race." *The Atlantic,* Oct. 28, 2017. https://www.theatlantic.com/politics/archive/2017/10/gerrymandering-technology-redmap-2020/543888/.

Niemi, Richard G., and Alan I. Abramowitz. "Partisan Redistricting and the 1992 Congressional Elections." *Journal of Politics* 56, no. 3 (1994): 811–17.

Nwanevu, Osita. "The Real Threat to American Democracy Isn't Russia. It's the Right." *Slate,* July 17, 2018. https://slate.com/news-and-politics/2018/07/the-real-threat-to-american-democracy-is-the-right.html.

Okonta, Patricia. "Race-based Political Exclusion and Social Subjugation: Racial Gerrymandering as a Badge of Slavery." *Columbia Human Rights Law Review* 49, Winter (2018): 255–296.

Orts, Eric W. "The Path to Give California 12 Senators, and Vermont Just One." *The Atlantic,* Jan. 2, 2019. https://www.theatlantic.com/ideas/archive/2019/01/heres-how-fix-senate/579172/.

"Pack the Union: A Proposal to Admit New States for the Purpose of Amending the Constitution to Ensure Equal Representation." 133 *Harvard Law Review* 1049 (2020). https://harvardlawreview.org/2020/01/pack-the-union-a-proposal-to-admit-new-states-for-the-purpose-of-amending-the-constitution-to-ensure-equal-representation/.

Parsons, Christi. "Limbaugh draws fire on Obama parody." *The Seattle Times,* May 6, 2007. https://www.seattletimes.com/nation-world/limbaugh-draws-fire-on-obama-parody/.

"Past Attempts at Reform." FairVote. https://www.fairvote.org/past_attempts_at_reform.

Pate, R. Hewitt. "D.C. Statehood: Not Without a Constitutional Amendment." The Heritage Foundation, Aug. 27, 1993. https://www.heritage.org/political-process/report/dc-statehood-not-without-constitutional-amendment.

"Patrick Joseph Buchanan, 'Culture War Speech Address to the Republican National Convention (17 August 1992).'" Voices of Democracy—the U.S. Oratory Project. https://voicesofdemocracy.umd.edu/buchanan-culture-war-speech-speech-text/.

Picchi, Amy. "Puerto Rico residents on Social Security won't get stimulus checks until June." *Moneywatch,* May 15, 2020. https://www.cbsnews.com/news/stimulus-check-puerto-rico-residents-on-social-security-wont-get-checks-until-june/.

Pitkin, Hanna. *The Concept of Representation.* Los Angeles: University of California Press, 1967.

Prakash, Saikrishna B., and John C. Yoo. "The Origins of Judicial Review." *The University of Chicago Law Review* 70, no. 3 (2003): 886–982.

Prokop, Andrew. "Pennsylvania's naked ballot problem, explained." *Vox,* Sept. 28, 2020. https://www.vox.com/2145 2393/naked-ballots-pennsylvania-secrecy-envelope.

Rakove, Jack. "The Accidental Electors." *New York Times,* Dec. 19, 2020. https://www.nytimes.com/2000/12/19/opinion/the-accidental-electors.html.

Rakove, Jack. "The Great Compromise: Ideas, Interests, and the Politics of Constitution Making." *The William and Mary Quarterly* 44, no. 3 (1987): 424–457.

Ramírez de Arellano, Susanne. "Trump only wants to aid Puerto Rico's recovery from Hurricane Maria when it's an election year." *NBC News,* Sept. 21, 2020. https://www.nbcnews.com/think/opinion/trump-only-wants-aid-puerto-rico-s-recovery-hurricane-maria-ncna1 240658.

Rapoport, Miles, and Cecily Hines. "A New Playing Field for Democracy Reform." *The American Prospect,* Dec. 24, 2018. https://prospect.org/power/new-playing-field-democracy-reform/.

Ratcliffe, John. "The Right to Vote and the Rise of Democracy, 1787–1828." *Journal of the Early Republic* 33, no. 2 (2013): 219–254.

Rauh, Joseph L., Jr. "D.C. Voting Rights: What Went Wrong?" *Washington Post,* Aug. 25, 1985. https://www.washington post.com/archive/opinions/1985/08/25/dc-voting-rights-what-went-wrongthe-amendment-died-last-week-now-says-a-longtime-advocate-statehood-is-the-only-game-in-town/29a08136-93eb-4951-a854-6162bad4222e/.

Rawls, John. *A Theory of Justice.* Cambridge: The Belknap Press of Harvard University Press, 1971.

"Redistricting and the Supreme Court: The Most Significant Cases." National Conference on State Legislatures, Apr. 25, 2019. https://www.ncsl.org/research/redistricting/redistricting-and-the-supreme-court-the-most-significant-cases.aspx.

"Redistricting Criteria." National Conference on State Legislatures, Apr. 23, 2019. https://www.ncsl.org/research/redistricting/redistricting-criteria.aspx.

Rindels, Michelle. "Sisolak vetoes bill that would pledge Nevada's support to win-ner of national popular vote, reject Electoral College." *The Nevada Independent,* May 30, 2019. https://thenevada independent.com/article/sisolak-vetoes-bill-that-would-pledge-nevadas-support-to-winner-of-national-popular-vote-reject-electoral-college.

Rothstein, Bo. "Creating Political Legitimacy: Electoral Democracy Versus Quality of Government." *American Behavioral Scientist* 53, no. 3 (2009): 311–330.

Rucker, Philip. "Trump says Fox's Megyn Kelly had 'blood coming out of her wherever.'" *Washington Post,* Aug. 8, 2015. https://www.washingtonpost.com/news/post-politics/wp/2015/08/07/trump-says-foxs-megyn-kelly-had-blood-coming-out-of-her-wherever/.

Saad, Lydia. "Americans Would Swap Electoral College for Popular Vote." Gallup. Oct. 2, 2011. https://news.gallup.com/poll/150245/americans-swap-electoral-college-popular-vote.aspx.

"Same Day Voter Registration." National Conference of State Legislatures, May 7, 2021. https://www.ncsl.org/research/elections-and-campaigns/same-day-registration.aspx.

Scanlan, Quinn. "Here's how states have changed the rules around voting amid the coronavirus pandemic." *ABC News,* Sept. 22, 2020. https://abcnews.go.com/Politics/states-changed-rules-voting-amid-coronavirus-pandemic/story?id=72309089.

Schreckinger, Ben. "Trump attacks McCain: 'I like people who weren't captured.'" *Politico,* July 18, 2015. https://www.politico.com/story/2015/07/trump-attacks-mccain-i-like-people-who-werent-captured-120317.

Segers, Grace. "House approves bill that would admit Washington, D.C., as 51st state." *CBS News,* Apr. 22, 2021. https://www.cbsnews.com/news/dc-statehood-bill-pases-house/.

Seib, Gerald F. "The Varied—and Global—Threats Confronting Democracy." *Wall Street Journal,* Nov. 21, 2017. https://www.wsj.com/articles/the-variedand-globalthreats-confronting-democracy-1511193763.

Seifter, Andrew. "Limbaugh on the NBA: Call it the TBA, the Thug Basketball Association ... They're going in to watch the Crips and the Bloods." Media Matters for America, Dec. 10, 2004. https://www.mediamatters.org/rush-limbaugh/limbaugh-nba-call-it-tba-thug-basketball-association-theyre-going-watch-crips-and.

"Seward's Folly." Library of Congress. https://www.loc.gov/item/today-in-history/march-30/.

Shapiro, Sarah, and Catherine Brown. "The State of Civics Education." Center for American Progress, Feb. 21, 2018. https://www.americanprogress.org/issues/education-k-12/reports/2018/02/21/446812/state-civics-education/.

Sherman, Mark. "High court won't extend Wisconsin's absentee ballot deadline." *Associated Press,* Oct. 26, 2020. https://apnews.com/article/election-2020-virus-outbreak-wisconsin-elections-us-supreme-court-dcf1e115d0804e203ef2cf9887cfabff.

Skelley, Geoffrey. "Abolishing The Electoral College Used to Be a Bipartisan Position. Not Anymore." *FiveThirty Eight,* Apr. 2, 2019. https://fivethirtyeight.com/features/abolishing-the-electoral-college-used-to-be-bipartisan-position-not-anymore/.

Slonim, Shlomo. "The Electoral College at Philadelphia: The Evolution of an Ad Hoc Congress for the Selection of a President." *The Journal of American History* 73, no. 1 (1986): 35–58.

Smith, Douglas. "When Not All Votes Were Equal." *The Atlantic,* July 26, 2015. https://www.theatlantic.com/politics/archive/2015/07/one-person-one-vote-a-history/399476/.

Smith, Raymond A. "Our Odd Upper House: The U.S. Senate's Peculiarities Don't End with the Filibuster." *HuffPost,* Nov. 26, 2013. https://www.huffpost.com/entry/our-odd-upper-house-the-u_b_4326115.

"State Voting Bills Tracker 2021." Brennan Center for Justice, May 28, 2021. https://www.brennancenter.org/our-work/research-reports/state-voting-bills-tracker-2021.

Stevens, Matt, and Isabella Grullón Paz. "Democratic National Convention's Roll Call Showcases Voices from Across America." *New York Times,* Aug. 19, 2020. https://www.nytimes.com/2020/08/19/us/politics/dnc-roll-call.html.

Strauss, Valerie. "Many Americans know nothing about their government. Here's a bold way schools can fix that." *Washington Post,* Sept. 27, 2016. https://www.washingtonpost.com/news/answer-sheet/wp/2016/09/27/many-americans-know-nothing-about-their-government-heres-a-bold-way-schools-can-fix-that/.

Sullivan, Laura. "FEMA Report Acknowledges Failures in Puerto Rico Disaster Response." *NPR,* July 13, 2018. https://www.npr.org/2018/07/13/628861808/fema-report-acknowledges-failures-in-puerto-rico-disaster-response.

Sullivan, Margaret. "The data is in: Fox News may have kept millions from taking the coronavirus threat seriously." *Washington Post,* June 28, 2020. https://www.washingtonpost.com/lifestyle/media/the-data-is-in-fox-news-may-have-kept-millions-from-taking-the-coronavirus-threat-seriously/2020/06/26/60d88aa2-b7c3-11ea-a8da-693df3d7674a_story.html.

Tauber, Alan. "The Empire Forgotten: The Application of the Bill of Rights to U.S. Territories." *Case Western Reserve Law Review* 57, no. 1 (2006): 146–78.

"They Want to Make Voting Harder?" *New York Times,* June 5, 2011.

"This Week in 19th Amendment History: Shifts and Splits in the Suffrage Movement." Arlington Public Library, May 14, 2020. https://library.arlingtonva.us/2020/05/14/this-week-in-19th-amendment-history-shifts-and-splits-in-the-suffrage-movement/.

Thrush, Glenn, and Nolan D. McCaskill. "Obama suggests Clinton didn't work as hard as he did." *Politico,* Nov. 14, 2016. https://www.politico.com/story/2016/11/obama-clinton-campaign-work-231370.

Todd, Chuck, Mark Murray, and Ben Kamisar. "Add social media to the list of things souring Americans on politics." *NBC News,* Apr. 5, 2019. https://www.nbcnews.com/politics/meet-the-press/add-social-media-list-things-souring-americans-politics-n991276.

Torres, Rosanna. "Shortchanging the territories in Medicaid funding." *The Hill,*

May 23, 2019. https://thehill.com/blogs/congress-blog/healthcare/445235-shortchanging-the-territories-in-medicaid-funding.

"Total Outside Spending by Election Cycle, Excluding Party Committees." Center for Responsive Politics, 2020. https://www.opensecrets.org/outsidespending/cycle_tots.php.

Tucker, Cynthia. "Hardball with Chris Matthews." MSNBC.com, Nov. 3, 2011. http://www.msnbc.msn.com/id/45163637/ns/msnbc_tv-hardball_with_chris_matthews/t/hardball-chris-matthews-thursday-november-rd/#.T-E0lBfLzE0.

"2020 Outside Spending, by Group." Center for Responsive Politics, 2020. https://www.opensecrets.org/outside spending/summ.php?cycle=2020&type=p&disp=O.

"US President—National Vote." Our Campaigns, 2008. https://www.our campaigns.com/RaceDetail.html?RaceID=59540.

Vogels, Emily A. "56% of Americans support more regulation of major technology companies." Pew Research Center, July 20, 2021. https://www.pewresearch.org/fact-tank/2021/07/20/56-of-americans-support-more-regulation-of-major-technology-companies/.

Waldman, Michael. The Fight to Vote. New York: Simon & Schuster, 2016.

Weigel, David. "The Trailer: Democrats won the White House and lost a myth about turnout." Washington Post, Nov. 8, 2020. https://www.washingtonpost.com/politics/2020/11/08/trailer-democrats-won-white-house-lost-myth-about-turnout/.

Weingast, Barry R. "Political Stability and Civil War: Institutions, Commitment, and American Democracy." In Analytic Narratives, edited by Robert Bates, Avner Greif, Margaret Levi, Jean-Laurent Rosenthal, and Barry R. Weingast. Princeton: Princeton University Press, 1998.

Weinger, MacKenzie. "Pa. pol: Voter ID helps GOP win state." Politico, June 25, 2012. https://www.politico.com/story/2012/06/pa-pol-voter-id-helps-gop-win-state-077811.

Weiser, Wendy R., and Lawrence Norden. "Voting Law Changes in 2012." Brennan Center for Justice, 2012. https://www.brennancenter.org/sites/default/files/2019-08/Report_Voting_Law_Changes_2012.pdf.

Williams, Frederick D. The Northwest Ordinance: Essays on Its Formulation, Provisions, and Legacy. Lansing: Michigan State University Press, 1989.

Winberg, Michaela. "Good job, Philly: Only 1% of city mail ballots were 'naked.'" Billy Penn, Nov. 11, 2020. https://billypenn.com/2020/11/11/philly-naked-ballots-pennsylvania-mail-votes-november-election/.

"Woman Suffrage Centennial." United States Senate. https://www.senate.gov/artandhistory/history/People/Women/Nineteenth_Amendment_Vertical_Timeline.htm.

Woolf, Christopher. "How a violent history created the U.S. Virgin Islands as we know them." Post-Gazette, Sept. 15, 2017. https://www.post-gazette.com/news/nation/2017/09/14/How-a-violent-history-created-the-US-Virgin-Islands-as-we-know-them/stories/201709140271.

Ye Hee Lee, Michelle. "Eleven donors have plowed $1 billion into super PACs since they were created." Washington Post, Oct. 26, 2018. https://www.washingtonpost.com/politics/eleven-donors-plowed-1-billion-into-super-pacs-since-2010/2018/10/26/31a07510-d70a-11e8-aeb7-ddcad4a0a54e_story.html.

Index

abolition movement 131–132, 136, 193
absentee voting 143, 148, 154–155
Access Hollywood 41
accountability of elected leaders 7
Adams, John 17, 47, 98
Adams, John Quincy 51, 57, 130
Adelson, Sheldon 169
Affordable Care Act of 2010 28, 82, 108, 117, 164
Air America Radio 178
Alamo 37
Albert, Richard 32
Alexander, Robert M. 56, 62
Alito, Samuel 207*n*1
All Voting Is Local (organization) 155
Altman, Micah 87
Amar, Akhil 32
amendments *see* constitutional amendments
American Equal Rights Association (AERA) 136
American Political Science Association (APSA) 164
American Prospect 181, 205
American Rescue Plan Act of 2021 28
American Samoa 106, 108, 109, 112; *see also* U.S. territories
American Statistical Association 89, 90–91
American Woman Suffrage Association (AWSA) 136
Americans *see* citizens
Annenberg Public Policy Center study 188
Anthony, Susan B. 136, 137
Apportionment Amendment 91
Article IV of U.S. Constitution 34
Article V of U.S. Constitution 29, 32, 33
Articles of Confederation 17, 18, 35, 201
at-large districts *see* districts (voting)
Atlanta-Journal Constitution 145
Atlantic (magazine) 155, 161, 181
automatic voter registration (AVR) 152

Baker, Charles 77
Baker v. Carr 77, 78, 82, 84, 121
ballot: arrival dates in 2020 presidential election 153–154; drop boxes 155; issues in 2000 presidential election 53–54; rejections 155
Barrett, Amy Coney 3–4, 117, 123, 125, 215*n*3
Battle Cry of Freedom (McPherson) 131
Beck, Glenn 178
Bedford, Gunning, Jr. 17
Beyer, Don 124
bias (towards one political party) 80–84, 86–87
Biden, Joe: appointment of Supreme Court Justices 122–123; on influence of campaign finance 165; 2020 presidential election 56, 57, 114, 149
Biggers, Daniel 148
Bill of Rights 26, 61–62, 91
Bipartisan Campaign Finance Reform Act (BCRA) 167–168
bipartisan definition 12
Birdsell, David 21
Black, Hugo 77
Black Lives Matter movement 12, 115
Bloomberg, Michael 169
border wall 117
Brennan Center for Justice: members 38–39, 73, 130; role in building awareness of voter inequality 205; study on impact of federal court vacancies 124; study on voter access to polling locations 147–148; study on voter purges 151
Broockman, David 165
Brown v. Board of Education 175
Bryan, William Jennings 162
Buchanan, Pat 54, 176
Buckley v. Valeo 167
budget reconciliation process 28
Burden, Barry 149
bureaucracy, inertia of 27

237